Towns & Villages of Britain:
CUMBRIA

Terry Marsh
Series Editor

Copyright © Terry Marsh, 1999

Published by Sigma Leisure – an imprint of
Sigma Press, 1 South Oak Lane, Wilmslow, Cheshire SK9 6AR, England.

British Library Cataloguing in Publication Data
A CIP record for this book is available from the British Library.

ISBN: 1-85058-615-2

Series Editor: Terry Marsh

Typesetting and Design by: Sigma Press, Wilmslow, Cheshire.

Cover Design: MFP Design & Print

Cover photographs: main picture – Braithwaite & Bassenthwaite Lake;
smaller pictures, from top: Kirkandrews-on-Esk church; Caldbeck church and packhorse bridge; Kendal medieval market.

Photographs: by the author, except where otherwise acknowledged

Map: Morag Perrott

Printed by: MFP Design & Print

Foreword

Cumbria's huge attraction to legions of visitors each year is its incomparable country-side, centred mainly on the 880 square miles of the Lake District National Park. But the explorer of the widespread county outside the park is rewarded with many surprises, not the least being the superbly rich and varied landscape, from the plains of the long coastline, around the central mountains, to the lush valleys of Eden and the wild moors to the east and north. But to call the landscape 'natural', as if it had been so since before human settlement, would be misconceived. Primeval earth movements and the Ice Ages shaped its natural features, but the intriguing varied textures, colours and patterns have been imposed by human history from the Bronze Age.

The history can be read in the human settlements which found their natural places in this superb countryside. They show evidence of good times and lean times, their dependence on agriculture and mining, and how they protected themselves in a border and coastal area which has seen more than its share of conflicts, from Hadrian to John Paul Jones.

Terry Marsh has produced a remarkably comprehensive guide to the towns and villages of Cumbria, from the smallest hamlets, which look as if they have grown out of the landscape, to the larger towns and the city that grew from commerce. Enough here to whet the appetite of any explorer, even those, like myself, who might think that they've been everywhere.

John Wyatt
Former Chief Ranger
Lake District National Park

Acknowledgements

I have received masses of help, goodwill and good wishes during the preparation of this book, from a number of sources. Many, in supplying information, have simply been doing their job, though I am no less grateful to them for that. Others are volunteers, and gave specialist advice. I would like to mention a few, notably Caroline Audemar of the National Trust for much help with information about National Trust properties in Cumbria; John Botterill, Kirkby Lonsdale for information about the Victorian Fair; David Boulton, Hobsons Farm, Dent for information about the Dent 'Sidesmen'; Alan Clements of Egremont for information about the Egremont Crab Fair; Mrs D Graham, Whitehaven Civic Hall for details of 'The Biggest Liar in the World' competition; John Owen of Heversham for information about Kendal Medieval Market and the legend of Dickie Doodle; South Lakeland District Council for information about the Furness and Cartmel Peninsulas; The Ceramics and Glass Department of the Victoria and Albert Museum for information about 'The Luck of Edenhall', and, of course, the Cumbria Tourist Board.

Contents

CUMBRIA

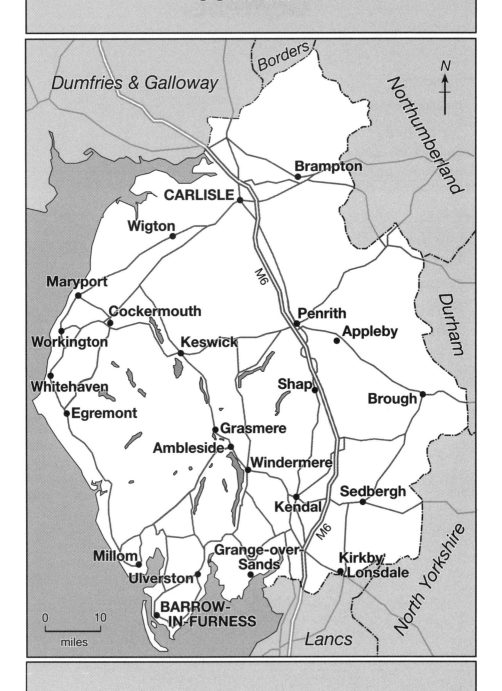

Introduction

Introduction to the series

The 'Town and Villages of Britain' is a series of titles detailing a county-by-county approach to the many delights and fascinations of our country's cities, towns, villages and hamlets. There is much of interest and value throughout our towns and villages, but not all of it is widely documented, and some of it, particularly local customs, folklore and traditions, is in danger of being lost forever. By bringing all this information together, county-by-county, it becomes possible to build a unique and substantially comprehensive library of knowledge.

All the books in the series are compiled to the same specification and in gazetteer format, and include information about the way or the reason a town or village evolved. In addition, there are references to anything associated with the preservation of the past, such as museums, heritage centres, historic or prehistoric sites, battle sites, places of worship and other locally or architecturally important buildings. Landscape features are also detailed, including important natural history sites, geological sites, water features, etc. as is information about important local people, and details of events or traditions, such as well-dressings and rush-bearing ceremonies. There are also notes about any significant present-day informal amenity/recreational features, like country parks, open access land, Areas of Outstanding Natural Beauty, nature reserves, and Sites of Special Scientific Interest. Finally, information is given on any significant Roman or prehistory context, and any anecdotal or endemic folklore references associated with the town or village which might illustrate a particular way of life or social development. The books are therefore eminently suitable for anyone interested in their own locality or in local history; students of history, folklore and related subjects; professional journalists wanting up-to-date and comprehensive information; public relations and similar businesses; photographers and artists, and, of course, the tourists and visitors to the counties.

Explanatory Notes

It has been suggested that to qualify as a village, a 'community' must possess a school, a pub, a post office and a church. Such a requirement, however, excludes a large number of places in Cumbria that are of immense interest, many having important historical associations, and which have played a vital part in the development of the county and its people. So, for the purposes of the books in this series, the criteria for inclusion have been kept deliberately simple: there must be something of interest about the place; or it must have associations with events and people of countywide or wider significance.

Often, the 'something of interest' will simply be the village church (its history, contents or architecture), or its green or river bridge, all common features of the former counties of Cumberland, Westmorland and, in part, Lancashire. In addition, the village may be important to the heritage of Cumbria because it maintains the traditions, ways and beliefs of Cumbrian culture, or has played a key role in the social, economic or political history of the county or the country as a whole.

Only occasionally, however, is the village pub of especial interest in this context, and often the development of large supermarkets within easy travelling distance of the villages has, sadly, signalled the demise of the traditional village shop. Local schools have often been swallowed up by larger schools, and far too many post offices are proving difficult to sustain as viable concerns. So, while that 'classic' definition of a village has much to commend it, in reality it is today too restrictive.

Quite what makes a town is another, arguable, matter. But the precise definition is here not too important; it's the place and its people, not its status, that matters. As a very broad distinction, that no-one should take seriously, a 'hamlet' (a few of which appear in these books) is a distinct community, while a 'village' could be said to be a hamlet with a church, and a 'town' is a village with a market.

In many cases, the historical development of the community, whether a tiny village, a town or a city, is fascinating in itself, and so it is that each entry gradually builds up a picture of Cumbria that is unique. That is what this book endeavours to portray, in a logical and easily accessible way, as well as being a source of reference.

Inevitably, there will be places that have been omitted that others might argue should have been included. But the value each community has to bring to a work of this nature has been carefully weighed; invariably, borderline cases have been given the benefit of the doubt and included.

It is equally clear that, taken to its logical conclusion, this book would be ten times larger, and there has had to be a considerable degree of selective editing to make it of manageable size. One day, perhaps, there could be one book that says everything there is to say about Cumbria. But could we afford to buy it? Could we carry it? Would we want it, when part of the beauty of what does exist is the range of voices and shades of opinion so many different authors can bring?

Organisation

Following the general Introduction, the book becomes a gazetteer, listing the towns and villages of Cumbria in alphabetical order.

After each town or village name there appears, in square brackets [ ], the name of the relevant district council.

Next appears a two-letter, four-figure grid reference, which will pinpoint the settlement to within half a mile (one kilometre). This is followed by an approximate distance from some other, usually larger, settlement, together with an equally approximate direction indicator.

Those features or people 'of interest' directly associated with the settlement are highlighted in bold text, while an index lists other features or people only incidentally associated.

Where information is given about events, such as agricultural shows, or facilities, like museums, details of dates and hours of opening are available from either the Cumbria Tourist Board, Ashleigh, Holly Road, Windermere, Cumbria, LA23 2AQ (Tel: 015394 44444: Fax: 015394 44041), who publish an annual bulletin, or from any of the Tourist Information Centres listed below.

County Information Centres

Ambleside, The Old Courthouse, Church Street, Ambleside LA22 0BT (Tel: 015394 32582: Fax: 015394 34901)

Bowness*, Bowness Bay, Bowness-on-Windermere (Tel: 015394 42895: Fax: 015394 88005)

Broughton-in-Furness*, Town Hall, The Square, Broughton-in-Furness (Tel: 01229 716115)

Coniston, Main car park, Coniston (Tel: 015394 41533: Fax: 015394 41802)

Egremont*, 12 Main Street, Egremont, CA22 2DW (Tel: 01946 820693)

Grange-over-Sands, Victoria Hall, Main Street, Grange-over-Sands LA11 6PT (Tel: 015395 34026)

Grasmere, Red Bank Road, Grasmere (Tel: 015394 35245: Fax: 015394 35057)

Hawkshead*, Main car park, Hawkshead (Tel: 015394 36525: 015394 36349)

Kendal, Town Hall, Highgate, Kendal LA9 4DL (Tel: 01539 725758: Fax: 01539 734457)

Killington Lake*, Road Chef Service Area, M6 (Southbound), Nr Kendal (Tel: 015396 20138)

Kirkby Lonsdale, 24 Main Street, Kirkby Lonsdale LA6 2AE (Tel/Fax: 015242 71437)

Kirkby Stephen, Market Square, Kirkby Stephen, CA17 4QN (Tel: 017683 71199)

Seatoller, Borrowdale, Keswick CA12 5XN (Tel: 017687 77294)

Sedbergh*, Yorkshire Dales National Park Centre, Main Street, Sedbergh (Tel: 015396 20125)

Ulverston, Coronation Hall, County Square, Ulverston LA12 7LZ (Tel: 01229 587120: Fax: 01229 582610)

Waterhead*, The Car Park, Waterhead, Ambleside LA23 1AD (Tel: 015394 32729: Fax: 015394 31728)

Windermere, Victoria Street, Windermere, LA23 1AD (Tel: 015394 46499: Fax: 015394 47439)

* = Summer only

District Councils

The relevant district councils are:

Allerdale, Allerdale House, New Bridge Road, Workington, Cumbria (Tel: 01900 604351)

Barrow-in-Furness, Town Hall, Barrow-in-Furness, Cumbria LA14 2LD (Tel: 01229 825500)

Carlisle, The Civic Centre, Carlisle, Cumbria CA3 8QG (Tel: 01228 523411)

Copeland, The Council Offices, Catherine Street, Whitehaven Cumbria CA28 7NY (Tel: 01946 852585)

Eden, Town Hall, Penrith, Cumbria CA11 7QF (Tel: 01768 864671)

South Lakeland, South Lakeland House, Lowther Street, Kendal, Cumbria LA9 4UQ (Tel: 01539 733333)

Cumbria

There can be few places in Britain with as diverse a landscape as Cumbria, a place of mountains and lakes, dales and rivers that have combined to inspire many to seek out and capture the true essence of this remarkable county. There can be few regions that set the pulse racing quite so enthusiastically as that wistful landscape of blue-purple fells and eye-bright tarns that, for most folk, lies to the west of the M6 motorway, but which in reality flanks it, also rolling eastwards to embrace the great hills of the Northern Pennines.

Few visitors can fail to be moved by the play of light and shade on the fells, the sounds of nature that fill the air, the timeless air of tranquillity that persists in spite of the immense pressures of tourism that the beauties of the county generate. Those who look to the west of the motorway are thinking 'Lake District'; those who recognise the wider scene are looking at 'Cumbria'. It is a county only loosely held together by a name, for this is an amalgamation of many different and fascinating cultures, where Westmerians meet Cumbrians meet Lancastrians. At the northern end, many people of Carlisle have at least a foot in Scotland, and probably quite a few relatives, too. To the south, the population of Furness once formed part of the County Palatine of Lancaster, a region known as Lancashire-over-the-Sands. While to the east, the ancient county of Westmorland lives on only in the hearts and minds of its people and their traditions.

Yet it is the synergy of these ancient cultural differences that makes Cumbria today; that, and a stunning landscape to which, as Wordsworth described, people flocked 'in all the spirit of adventurers, not a little oppressed by their own hardihood, and furnished forth with all the necessary emotional equipment'.

Yet, despite the often overpowering display of Nature at its best, Cumbria is a county much-fashioned by man, from the days of our prehistoric ancestors to the present day.

Indeed, it is the people who made the towns and villages, the people who developed Cumbria's unique and distinctive culture, and the people of this extraordinary county that bring a different dimension to a region that is already outstanding.

This book lists almost 400 towns, villages and hamlets in Cumbria, and, as well as being concerned with the towns and villages as they are today, looks at the things that were, the things we are in danger of losing, the things that might have been, from the importance and development of the settlements to the outstanding buildings and people of past times, including many that have influenced the prosperity of the region.

Folklore and local customs, legends and the web of fantasy, here cross threads with accounts of the lives of the legendary John Peel, the beautiful Maid of Buttermere, the Lake Poets, the first explorers, and the men and women of power and influence.

Early History

Until man became literate there is little of his life and ways about which we can be certain, and that gleaned only from the few material artefacts that have survived, such as traces of the hunter-fisher economy, flints, knives and arrowheads. Old Stone Age man was already resident further south in Britain, but Cumbria, still buried beneath a mantle of ice, had to wait for Neolithic, or New Stone Age, man, who appeared about 5500BC, to make his presence felt as he rose to the challenge of the forests.

Towards the end of the Neolithic period new settlers, the Beaker people, mainly herdsmen and hunters, arrived from the North European Plain around 2000BC. They were followed by the Celts, the 'Cymry', a term meaning 'the compatriots', and used by early writers to describe the Celtic people both of Wales and the kingdom of Strathclyde, of which early Cumbria was a part. It was these people, arriving 2-300BC, who gave the name to the region, and introduced the Iron Age to Cumbria.

The Roman Period

By the time the Romans came, around AD70, the Cumbrian people were well established. They were farmers and fisherman, able to build strong fortresses, and with a religion centred on reincarnation. The Romans called them 'Brigantes', and they were both shrewd and strong enough to outlast the Roman occupation, and to oppose it when their laws seemed too oppressive.

The evidence of Roman times, however, remains to this day. Hadrian's Wall is by far the best-known example, but dotted across the landscape are a number of forts and road networks, as at Hardknott and across High Street, and these have formed a framework on which the present-day towns and villages of Cumbria have grown.

Stainmore and the Lune valley were obvious approaches from which the Romans could begin their occupation of Cumbria, but it is clear from the way they built their forts around the edges that they found the inner core, the heart of the Lake

District, difficult to operate in. In accordance with their well-established practice, they built many of their forts along river valleys and at estuaries, both of which meant they could manage and control lines of communication and supply. So it is that traces of Roman sites can be found at Burgh-by-Sands, Bowness-on-Solway, Beckfoot, Maryport, Moresby and Ravenglass.

There is a tendency, however, to think of Roman occupation as a period of oppression. In reality it led to a prolonged period of peace and prosperity that blossomed not only from the supervision and encouragement that the Roman presence afforded, but from the trade routes that their roads opened up.

And it is here in Roman times that the first clear pattern of today's towns and villages of Cumbria can be seen to be evolving. Almost without exception (the principal exception being Hardknott), the site of every Roman fort has had later settlements built around or over it. Many of the forts, even in Roman times, had towns (*vici*) built beside them, populated by people who had travelled with the army, and by enterprising and industrious locals who saw the economic opportunities the Roman way of life represented.

As a rule, *vici* would develop along the roads leading away from the forts, and would expand, and in some instances collapse, as need determined. But while the *vici* would undoubtedly have provided a stable base for many of the local people, a large number would have remained in the countryside, developing their skills as farmers. It is not fanciful to suppose that these would be increased in number by soldiers who had reached the age of retirement.

The need for timber for building took one step further the deforestation of the region, and as the forests were cleared, so other building materials, rock and rubble, would be used, and found to be more resilient to the elements.

Increasingly, as the Romans started to leave Britain, the local population began to rely on their own resources. They may well have built new settlements away from the Roman sites as building materials became exhausted, or as the need for increased self-provision sent them in search of better land on which to build or farm, and places better suited to defence against rival factions among the tribes that remained.

The Dark Ages

In Cumbria, where the vague period known as the Dark Ages produced large changes to parts of the landscape, the period was, if anything, darker than elsewhere in England, and it is especially difficult to know with certainty how the county evolved between the 5th and 12th centuries, and there are many conflicting accounts.

During the 5th century, Cumbria evolved into a British kingdom called Rheged, which probably embraced land on both sides of the Solway. By the end of the 6th century, Rheged, which had for a time been a major political force in the north, had faded from the scene, and by the turn of the century what remained of it had been incorporated into the expanding kingdom of Northumbria, possibly by marriage rather than conquest.

By the early 10th century, however, the Northumbrian kingdom fell before the onslaught of the Danish, leaving a vacuum that was to be filled by the kingdom of Strathclyde. In spite of this, Cumbria seems to have continued under its own line of kings until 1018. In that year, the last Cumbrian king, Owen the Bald, allied himself with Malcolm II of Scotland, and was later killed in battle against the English. As a result, Malcolm was free to annex Cumbria into Scotland, and so it remained until 1032.

During this period came the settlement of the Scandinavians, mainly Norse. It was their influence that gave Cumbria many of its place-names: tarn is derived from *tjorn*, dale from *dahl*, and fell from *fjall*. While the suffix '-thwaite', which means 'a clearing', crops up in many places – Stonethwaite, Rosthwaite, Bassenthwaite, Braithwaite, and so on.

The Normans

At the end of the 11th century, the Norman barons came north in search of wealth and prosperity, some of them brought north as colonists by William Rufus, who had a castle built at Carlisle. Their influence on the landscape was considerable. They had a strong liking for hunting, and developed many of the hunting forests that once covered the region, and whose names you still find across the modern map – Skiddaw, Inglewood and Copeland. But their most important legacy was the monasteries. During the 12th century, many monasteries were founded – Wetheral (1106), St Bees (1120), Furness (1123), Holme Cultram (1150) and Shap (1200). The monasteries became immense landowners, expanding high into the mountain areas and cultivating ground that had previously remained barren.

With the development of the monasteries, however, came much-improved documentary records that give a much clearer picture of life in Cumbria from then on.

Farms, and the cottages and hamlets that evolved around them, were instrumental in determining the settlement pattern of Cumbria, and the key to this lies in the system of feudalism that existed. The pattern evolved around great baronial estates, and though much of the land was designated as 'forest' or 'chase' – in both cases meaning a place for hunting – the lords of the estates tolerated the development of peasant communities, and so created embryonic villages.

In the centuries that followed there was a period of sustained population growth, and almost every county in England had farms and small hamlets carved from the rugged and wild landscapes that surrounded the baronial estates.

The Border

By 1300, the Cumbrian valleys were extensively populated, but the state of evolving peace was to be shattered by the waves of destruction that flowed during the time of the Border Troubles, and by the incidence of the Black Death (1348-9). For 150 years, the development of Cumbrian villages was held in check: what was built, was destroyed; what was grown, was taken. This state of affairs lasted until the Union of the Crowns in 1603 (and beyond), but much earlier than that a tide of change swept across Cumbria with the growth of the woollen cloth industry, notably in Kendal. Once again population levels increased, and provoked a demand for land which soon could only be satisfied by expanding beyond existing holdings.

Wealth came not only from the produce the farming fraternity grew for themselves and the lords, but from taking surplus or short-life goods to markets held in the ancient market towns of Cumbria, many of which were granted charters in the 13th and 14th centuries.

The period between 1550 and 1700 saw flourishing the 'statesmen' farmers. This term, rather romanticised by Wordsworth, was applied to small, family farmers whose tenure in effect gave them

security equivalent to freehold. It was by their efforts that the dales of Cumbria were carved into small 'estates'; and these in turn were a key factor in shaping the human landscape. Wherever there was an area of viable ploughland or hay meadow in the valley bottom, so a communal form of farming evolved. These 'townfields' were areas of arable land and meadow serving a group of farms, and so forming a small village or hamlet. Examples of this form of development are to be found at Coniston, Grasmere, Buttermere, and Braithwaite near Keswick where towards the end of the 16th century there had already evolved a small village of sixteen farmsteads in an open landscape. Elsewhere, lesser groups of farms developed into the small hamlets that still exist today. But whether large or small, the pattern was much the same: each farmstead held a small patch of ploughland and meadow, along with common rights over the fellside pastures that flanked the dales. This common interest in a specific, confined area provided a focus, a nucleus from which, or around which, larger communities developed.

But it was not a constant process. During the next 150 years, many Lakeland communities decreased in size as farms were amalgamated into fewer, larger holdings. Much of this was done piecemeal as farmers agreed to consolidate their holdings, often on an informal and unrecorded basis. But the result was a gradual drawing together of communities; some expanded, others contracted.

Minerals

And in the same way that settlements evolved around the viable agricultural land, so they sprang up, in some cases almost overnight, once the exploitation of Cumbria's mineral wealth took off.

What was Coniston without its copper, or Whitehaven without its coal and the means to export it seaward, or Shap without its granite, or Borrowdale without the lead for the pencil industry that developed in Keswick? Across the whole face of Cumbria communities evolved to serve the needs of industry – copper, lead, graphite, tungsten, iron ore, coal, granite and limestone. In some cases further industries developed to serve or benefit from the earlier ones – iron smelting bloomeries needed charcoal, as did the charcoal-fuelled blast furnaces; mills of all kinds took advantage of the abundant water supply to power the production of bobbins, gunpowder, textiles and paper.

All that remained was to link all these places together. Reliance on Roman roads, packhorse routes, monastic ways and the traditional mountain passes was no longer good enough. The network of roads that evolved in the 18th and 19th centuries was instrumental in securing the economic, social and political development of the county. With the coming of the turnpikes the die was cast, and the of stage set for the final development of the towns and villages as they appear today.

Architecture

Finally, Cumbria is a county with an outstanding legacy of architectural riches, from pre-Roman stone circles to modern, some would say less endearing, structures. Inevitably, given the expansion of religion throughout the county, the greatest number of non-domestic buildings are churches. These range from splendid examples of Norman and pre-Norman buildings to numerous Victorian churches, some of which emulate earlier periods, while others, it must be said, rather lack imagination.

Castles, historic houses great and small, farmhouses, cottages, village halls, bridges, viaducts and even copies of lighthouses are among the treasures of Cumbria. Just to visit everything mentioned in this book will take months; to understand its full significance, will need years. If this book persuades you to make a start, it will have served its purpose.

The Towns and Villages

ABBEYTOWN [Allerdale]

NY1750: 4 miles (6km) SE of Silloth

Lying amid a spread of ancient farms and their patchwork fields of green and red, the small village of Abbeytown is appropriately named. Not only does it owe its settlement development to the 12th-century Holme Cultram Abbey, but to the fact that when the abbey fell into ruin, many of its stones were appropriated for the buildings in the village. At its height, however, the abbey flourished, and was one of the principal suppliers of wool in the north of England. Its lands were granted by Alan fitz Waldave, a Norman, but its foundation charter was confirmed by Prince Henry, son of David I of Scotland. Even when the abbey was later given the protection of Henry II of England, it remained ecclesiastically under the rule of Melrose Abbey in Scotland.

Inevitably, the proximity of the village to the Scottish border meant that it carried more than its fair share of the attentions of Scottish raiders, as the borderlands continued to be disputed, and changed sides often.

Records show that Edward I (1272-1307), the 'Hammer of the Scots' stayed at Abbeytown in 1300, and again just before his death on Burgh Sands on the Solway. On this second visit he made the abbot, Robert de Keldsik, a member of his council.

After Edward's death, however, the Scots regained much of the ground they had lost, and Robert the Bruce (1274-1329), the future King Robert I of Scotland, devastated the abbey in 1319, even though his own father, Robert de Bruce, the Earl of Carrick (1253-1304), was buried in the grounds.

The fate of the abbey was sealed more than 200 years later, when, in 1536, at the time of Henry VIII's Dissolution of the Monasteries, the abbot, Thomas Carter, joined the ill-fated Pilgrimage of Grace (1536-7). This rebellion against the seizure by the king of church lands was the most serious 16th-century challenge to central government, and the king wreaked savage retribution.

The **church of St Mary** is the parish church, and a glorious building, but all that remains of the great Holme Cultram Abbey. The nave dates from the 12th century, while the walls, which take the place of the arcade openings, are from a period of reconstruction between 1727 and 1739. The western entrance is a magnificent Norman portal, framed by a porch with four orders of shafts on each side, and dating from 1507. One of the bells in the bellcot is from 1465.

Excavations have shown that the church had three more bays of nave and aisles, along with small chapels and a straight-ended chancel.

That St Mary's survives at all is a minor miracle, for when the abbey was destroyed under Henry VIII's decree, it was only the pleas of locals, who pointed out that no other building offered adequate protection against Border raids, that saved the church.

AGLIONBY [Carlisle]

NY4456: 3 miles (5km) E of Carlisle

Lying on low ground to the south of the River Eden, on the outskirts of Carlisle, the village of Aglionby derives its name from the family who held the manor from the time of the Norman conquest until

1785. The family provided numerous mayors of Carlisle from 1463 until the 18th century, with some members of the family becoming mayor more than once. One of them, Edward, who was murdered just before Christmas in 1599, is cited as having been 'often maior of Carlel, and ever ready to serve the Quene'. Another, Henry, who was mayor at the time of Bonnie Prince Charlie's Rebellion in 1745, however, never appears to have set foot in the city during these troubled times, leaving all the business of the administration to his deputy.

AIKTON [Allerdale]

NY2753: 3 miles (5km) N of Wigton

The place of oaks, Aikton is a small, widespread village surrounded by farmland on the coastal plain north of Wigton. Joan de Morville, daughter of Hugh de Morville, one of the men implicated in the murder of Thomas à Becket in 1170, used to live in the manor.

The **church of St Andrew**, a small, stone-built Early English church, stands among farm fields a short distance from the village. It has a narrow Norman chancel arch to which a south aisle was added in 1869.

AINSTABLE [Eden]

NY5246: 10 miles (16km) N of Penrith

Ainstable is a quiet village on rising ground to the east of the River Eden, and was originally a Viking settlement with the name Einstapli.

The village was the birthplace of **John Leake** (1729-1792), who wrote many books on childbirth and women's diseases, as well as founding the Westmin-

ster Lying-In Hospital. He was the first male midwife, and is among a number of Cumbrians who lie buried in Westminster Abbey.

The **church of St Michael** was rebuilt in 1872, and stands on a site that has been occupied by places of worship for over 900 years. The churchyard is entered through a lych-gate that also serves as a war memorial.

Lost among the trees of **Broomrigg Plantation** is a fascinating complex of stone circles and a ruinous cairn circle. They are thought to date from the Early Bronze Age, and finds from the site are now in the Tullie Museum in Carlisle.

ALDINGHAM [South Lakeland]

SD2870: 4½ miles (7km) S of Ulverston

Aldingham is a small coastal village with an outstanding view across Morecambe Bay. Legend has it that all the houses of the village were swept away in a tidal wave in 1553, though there is little real evidence to support this.

The name means 'the village of Alda's people', and as a settlement it existed in Saxon times. It is recorded in the Domesday Book and on an inscription in Durham Cathedral as among the places where the disciples of St Cuthbert rested with his body during their flight from the Danes, and in consequence the church carries the saint's dedication.

The **church of St Cuthbert**, parts of which, notably the chancel, are from the 12th century, has a crooked chancel arch. This is a typical feature in some old churches, said to represent the body of Christ with his head leaning to one side. Queen Victoria visited the church as she returned from a visit to Furness Abbey in 1848, and her Royal Arms feature above the chancel arch.

ALLITHWAITE
[South Lakeland]

SD3876: 1 mile (2km) SW of Grange-over-Sands

This is a small coastal, mainly residential village surrounded by the low fells of southern Lakeland. Its name means 'the clearing of Eilifr', a Norseman. The village once had both a brewery and a corn mill (now cottages), and quarrying used to be a major industry.

The **church of St Mary** is a Victorian structure, built in 1865 at the same time as the school and vicarage. The church windows commemorate the dead of two World Wars.

A little under 2 miles (3km) south of the village is **Humphrey Head**, a long finger of ground poking into Morecambe Bay. On its western flank is a holy well to which 18th- and 19th-century miners, in particular, came to partake of its allegedly curative waters which were thought to be a remedy for the industrial illnesses of their work. This slender promontory also has a cave in which prehistoric and Roman artefacts have been found, including pottery, rings, coins and spear heads. According to legend, it was at Humphrey Head that the last wolf in England was slain, by Sir Edgar Harrington who lived at Wraysholme Tower.

ALLONBY [Allerdale]

NY0842: 5 miles (8km) NE of Maryport

An 18th-century seaside resort, described in 1748 as having 'considerable concourse for bathing in the sea', that still retains much of its charm, Allonby also used to be an important herring fishing centre.

The first church was built in 1744, though the present **Christ Church** is an unattractive product of 1845. The earlier church, of course, was little more than a chapel, and it is recorded that after one service, the clerk gave notice that there would be a horse race at Allonby a few days later. This practice of announcing race meetings in church is a peculiarity of Cumberland and Westmorland churches, and continued until the mid-19th century.

The church contains a monument to **Captain Joseph Huddart** (1741-1816), a navigator, born at Allonby and buried at St Martin-in-the-Fields, London. He worked for the East India Company, charted much of the sea area around Sumatra and the Indian coast, and was instrumental in introducing safety improvement in ships.

ALSTON [Eden]

NY7146: 16 miles (26km) NE of Penrith

Lying just below the Pennine watershed, in the valley of the River South Tyne, Alston shares with Buxton in Derbyshire the claim to be the highest market town in Britain. The town, in spite of its remoteness, is a busy place, but still retains many of its cobbled streets and traditional shop fronts.

The area surrounding the town falls within the North Pennines Area of Outstanding Natural Beauty (AONB), but its visual attractions were of little concern to those, and there were many, who came to Alston to mine for lead and silver. In the 13th century, silver automatically belonged to the Crown, and the Norman kings were keen to ensure that any lead containing silver was designated as silver, and their property. Because of this the royal miners became something of a privileged breed, and Henry III (1216-1272) granted his miners 'liberties and free customs', and protected them by imposing a fine of £10 on anyone who disturbed them.

Inevitably there were many disputes over who owned the region. The king of the Scots claimed manorial rights, but that was an altogether different matter from the wealth that lay beneath the manor's grounds, and those who owned the mineral rights were not slow to exploit it. Lead from the Alston mines went into the Cistercian Abbey at Clairvaux in France, while over 500 cartloads of lead were ordered to be delivered to the Sheriff of Northumberland for transportation to Caen.

Lead mining, however, was not confined to this period. There is evidence that the Romans developed mines, and, more recently, at the beginning of the 18th century, the London Lead Mining Company, a Quaker organisation, was formed, and was to become the main employer in the area for more than 200 years.

The **church of St Augustine** was built in Victorian times to replace an earlier church of 1770, which itself stood on the site of a medieval church. St Augustine's, St Paul's Methodist chapel and the former Congregational church are all large and substantial buildings, an indication of the size of the population of Alston in years gone by.

John Wesley preached in Alston, though at the time he appears to have made little immediate impression on the people.

AMBLESIDE [South Lakeland]

NY3704: 4 miles (6km) NW of
Windermere

Ambleside is a popular tourist centre on the northern edge of Lake Windermere, and is passed through by anyone travelling from south Lakeland to Keswick. It is almost entirely composed of slate houses, cottages and hotels built in traditional Lakeland style; even new development in the centre of the town continues this characteristic, and the whole impression is one of a pleasing and attractive town that copes well with modern tourist attentions. Ambleside is really a large village, though it received a market charter in 1650. A small market is held on Wednesday each week in King Street.

An area of land to the south of the present village, today called Borrans Field, is the site of the **Roman fort** of Galava, established during the first century, and linking with their forts at Hard Knott and Ravenglass. The original fort would have been built of wood and earth, and was later replaced by a stone-built structure.

The town's great inn is the **Salutation**, clearly, in spite of modifications, an old

Bridge House

coaching inn. Whether it was at the Salutation, or some other hotel, that Thomas Gray 'on looking into the best bedchamber, dark and damp as a cellar, grew delicate', is not clear. But Ambleside has certainly improved, and brought many noted travellers and writers to its shelter – Keats, Joseph Budworth, John Stuart Mill, Tennyson (who was working on his *Morte d'Arthur*) and Edward Fitzgerald.

The **Bridge House**, standing on what was probably an old packhorse bridge spanning Stock Ghyll in the middle of Ambleside, is now used as a National Trust information centre. It was built in the 18th century, and is said to have housed a family with six children. Originally, it was built as a summer house, part of the demolished Ambleside Hall, and in its time has been used as a cobbler's shop and an antique shop.

The parish **church of St Mary the Virgin**, however, seems totally out of keeping with the rest of the town. It was built between 1850 and 1854 in the Early Gothic style, and, unlike most Lakeland churches, it has a spire, and makes use of large quantities of sandstone, known as 'freestone' because of the ease with which it can be worked, in its construction.

On a Saturday in July, the church holds a **rush-bearing ceremony**, an event depicted on a mural, painted in 1944, at the western end of the nave (see Grasmere).

Just on the edge of Ambleside is **Stockghyll Park** which has some fine waterfalls that, for hundreds of years, provided the force to power a wide range of mills – carding and fulling, linen, paper, corn and saw. Above the village, **Wansfell Pike** provides a lofty perch from which to gaze down on the length of Windermere, and is a popular, if steep, walk from the centre of the village.

The Armitt is Ambleside's own interactive exhibition of Lakeland life and times, exploring Lakeland history from the Bronze Age to present times. Upstairs is housed the Armitt Library, which contains numerous books and manuscripts contributed by many famous authors – Charlotte Mason, Harriet Martineau, Canon Rawnsley, Collingwood, Arthur Ransome, and Beatrix Potter.

South of Ambleside, along the main road to Windermere, stands **Brockhole**. Originally it was a large country house built by a Manchester businessman, Henry Gaddum. Later it was used as a convalescent home, and it now serves as the National Park's visitor centre, housing permanent displays and exhibitions.

ANTHORN [Allerdale]

NY2058: 15 miles (21km) W of Carlisle

Anthorn is a small, straggling village on the shores of Moricambe Bay, with a NATO radio station close by at Cardunock. The village, its name means 'the single thorn bush', gazes out across treacherous estuarial sands and mudflats. The oldest parts of the village date from the 13th century, and are mainly agricultural.

In 1964, a NATO station opened on the site of *HMS Nuthatch*, a Royal Naval Air Station that closed in 1957.

By the side of the road, just past one of the entrances to the radio station, and partly concealed among low gorse bushes, is an **ancient cross**, a small, very eroded lump of stone that is easily missed, and is singularly unimpressive. It may well have marked the boundary of some monastic influence.

Across the road from the cross stands a tower, known locally as **Mary's Tower**, and said to be the place where Mary,

Queen of Scots was held prisoner in 1568, on her way south into England. Another local story says that the tower was built as a studio for Mary Backhouse in the 1850s. Tunnels are said to run underground, linking the tower and the village, a plausible suggestion since these coasts were used by smugglers, for whom tunnels and secret storage places for themselves and their contraband would have been essential.

APPLEBY-IN-WESTMORLAND [Eden]

NY6820: 12 miles (19km) SE of Penrith

Appleby is a market town of great character on the River Eden, and was the county town of Westmorland. It is a town in two parts, divided by the river. The area around St Michael's church was called Old Appleby, while the centre, along Boroughgate, is New Appleby. Founded about 1110 by Ranulph de Meschines, it is essentially just one very wide, steeply sloping street, running from the church at the bottom to the castle. The church closes the view down the High Street, where the road takes a sharp turn before crossing the river; the result is to give the impression of a separate central part of the town, like a large town square.

Boroughgate is considered by many to be among the finest main streets in any English town. It is flanked by lime trees and attractive properties in red sandstone that give the centre of the town a mellow, warm appearance. The buildings date from many periods, ranging from Jacobean to Victorian, and including a number of fine Georgian properties. The town hall, or Moot Hall (a place where meetings are held), dates from the 16th century.

The town is famous for its lively **Horse Fair**, the largest gypsy gathering in Britain. The fair is over 300 years old and takes place in June, though the gypsies start to arrive much earlier than this. A couple of months later, in August, Appleby holds its annual **agricultural show**.

Lady Anne's Hospital, Appleby-in-Westmorland

The town is overlooked by **Appleby Castle** which dates from Norman times, though largely restored and rebuilt in the 17th century. The castle belonged to the Viponts before it became Clifford property in the late 13th century, only leaving that estate on the death of Lady Anne Clifford, when it went to her son-in-law, the Earl of Thanet. It is an imposing building, at the top of the town, on a steep bank above the River Eden, and surrounded by moats that mark an inner and at least two outer baileys.

The 12th-century keep still remains and is open to the public during summer months, while in its grounds is the Rare Breeds Survival Trust Centre, where rare breeds of domestic farm animals and birds are housed.

The **church of St Lawrence**, partly restored and rebuilt by Lady Anne Clifford, has a mainly Perpendicular exterior with some intriguing gargoyles, and examples of Early English and Decorated work inside, as well as a ceiling in panelled plaster in the Gothic Revival style.

The church also houses one of the oldest organs still in working order in Britain. It is said to have been moved from Carlisle Cathedral, and dates in part from 1542-7. The effigy of Margaret, Countess of Cumberland and mother of Lady Anne Clifford, fashioned in 1617, lies in the north-east chapel.

The churchyard is entered through a Gothic arcade in the lovely pink local stone, which also lends a beautiful colour to the elevations of the church.

The **church of St Michael** has a doorway of Saxon proportions and a Saxon hogback gravestone used as a lintel. The north tower was added in 1885-6.

The castle, the church and many other buildings in the region owe their existence or restoration to the redoubtable Lady Anne Clifford who lies buried in the churchyard. She was the daughter of George Clifford, 3rd Earl of Cumberland (1558-1605), a naval commander. She was born in Skipton in 1590, and was married twice, first to the Earl of Dorset, and then to the Earl of Pembroke and Montgomery. She was unhappy with and outlived them both. She inherited the Clifford estates in 1643, at the time of the Civil War, and moved north. She was to be a thorn in Cromwell's side, frequently defying his express orders and rebuilding and restoring her castles at Appleby, Bardon Tower, Brough, Brougham, Pendragon and Skipton. She lived in each in turn, and entertained generously.

At the Restoration, Lady Anne, then 70, celebrated the event by having two scaffolds erected in Appleby, where she, the mayor and alderman of the town drank the health of the king.

Lady Anne also founded **St Anne's Hospital** in Boroughgate, a delightful building constructed, between 1651 and 1653, around a tranquil courtyard. When she died in 1676, Lady Anne was buried in St Lawrence's churchyard in a black marble tomb.

A plaque in the town commemorates a headmaster of Appleby Grammar School, **Richard Yates**, who taught the two elder half-brothers of George Washington, first president of the United States of America. In 1743, George was to follow his two half-brothers to school in Appleby, but he was kept at home in America by the death of his father. The old grammar school, founded in 1574 by charter from Elizabeth I, has been demolished, but the present school includes the headmaster's porch from the old building and is dated 1671.

William Pitt the Younger (1759-1806), Britain's youngest prime minister, was elected Member of Parliament for Appleby in 1781.

APPLETHWAITE [Allerdale]

NY2625: 1½ miles (2km) N of Keswick

At the very foot of Skiddaw, Applethwaite is a small hamlet where Wordsworth's descendants built a small cottage on land given to the poet in 1803 by Sir George Beaumont. The hope was that it would enable Wordsworth to build a house and so live close by Coleridge, then at Greta Hall. Although Wordsworth never did so, the land gave him voting rights as a freeholder in the county of Cumberland, which meant he could play a part in local politics.

ARLECDON [Copeland]

NY0418: 4 miles (7km) N of Egremont

Arlecdon, on the outer fringe of Frizington, is, like many of the villages in this part of the old county of Cumberland, a former mining village.

The **church of St Michael**, standing in isolation north of the village, was originally built in 1829, but was much added to in 1904.

ARMATHWAITE [Eden]

NY5046: 9 miles (14km) SE of Carlisle

The delightful village of Armathwaite, the name means 'the clearing of the hermit', is secluded in a wooded hollow beside the River Eden, and its few houses gather near its bridge in a peaceful setting. It stands on the Settle - Carlisle railway line, and when the line was being built the prosperity of the village increased enormously as workers flooded in.

The **chapel of Christ and Mary**, rebuilt during the 17th century, was at one time in such a dilapidated state that it was used to shelter cattle. It contains stained glass windows made in 1926 by the William Morris workshops, continuing his skills and traditions long after he died in 1896.

Armathwaite Castle stands beside the river, and was the home of John Skelton, Poet Laureate to Henry VIII. It is a pele tower, but its front is early Georgian. Between the reigns of Edward II and Henry VIII, members of the Skelton family were Members of Parliament both for the county and the city of Carlisle.

ARNSIDE [South Lakeland]

SD4578: 6 miles (10km) N of Carnforth

Still popular today, Arnside, where the River Kent enters Morecambe Bay, was especially so in the 19th century when pleasure boats would arrive from Morecambe and Fleetwood, and barges plied the river, carrying coal and limestone. Then it was a busy little port in the county of Westmorland (and the county's only link with the sea), but one that succumbed as more accessible places robbed it of its trade. Before the 19th century, Arnside was only a small village, part of the parish of Beetham, and without its own graveyard, which meant that the dead had to be carried to Beetham for burial.

Now Arnside is a modest-sized, unspoilt holiday resort of limestone-built houses and cottages.

The estuary is a haven for coastal birds, and the surrounding countryside contains a wealth of flora and fauna, including deer, red squirrels, foxes and badgers, while anglers fish the fast-flowing estuarial waters for eels and flounders.

Arnside Knott stands above the village to the south, with distant views of

Arnside Tower

the Cumbrian fells. Access is by rights of way only, though it has been in National Trust ownership since it was given anonymously in 1946-7. The Knott is surrounded by wooded hills, heathland and salt marshes that have done much to secure for Arnside and its neighbouring village of Silverdale in Lancashire the designation of an Area of Outstanding Natural Beauty.

The village owes much to the coming of the railway during the 19th century. A splendid **viaduct**, originally built by the Furness Railway Company, connects Arnside with the north bank of the Kent, a service that today provides a vital and invaluable link between Lancashire and the towns and villages of Furness (which once belonged to Lancashire).

The ruined remains of **Arnside Tower** stand in a wide valley to the south of Arnside Knott. It is a large pele tower, thought to have been constructed in the 15th century as a defence against raiding Scots. Fire virtually destroyed the tower in 1602.

The **church of St James**, built by Miles Thompson of Kendal, is late Victorian, enlarged in 1884, 1905 and 1914.

ASKAM-IN-FURNESS [Barrow-in-Furness]

SD2177: 3 miles (5km) N of Dalton-in-Furness

Boasting spectacular views across the Duddon estuary, Askam-in-Furness is an old ironworks' and mining town that developed mainly during the 19th century. The industry is still commemorated in its street names, though most signs of the industry have long gone.

ASKHAM [Eden]

NY5123: 4 miles (6km) S of Penrith

Askham is an ancient and pleasing village on the eastern rim of Lakeland, adjoining the River Lowther and built around two greens. The village, which contains many whitewashed cottages dating from the 17th century, is over-looked by the towers of Lowther Castle. This pleasant ruin was built between 1806 and 1811 by Robert Smirke, who later built the British Museum, the east wing of Somerset House, the Carlton Club and the College of Physicians in Trafalgar Square.

Askham is one of the most attractive villages in the former county of Westmorland. In 1280, the manor was bought by Sir Thomas de Hellbeck, and passed by marriage to the Swynburn family in 1314. The Swynburns were responsible for building the first defensive structure where the present hall stands.

In 1375, the manor was transferred once more, this time to the Sandfords. After they settled in the village, Askham Hall, set back at the foot of the village, was the home of the Sandford family. It later became, and still is, the home of the earls of Lonsdale. The fifth Earl, Hugh Cecil Lonsdale (1857-1944) instituted the Lonsdale Belt for boxing and was the first president of the Automobile Association (see also Lowther).

Standing a short distance from the village, above the Lowther, the **church of St Peter** was built in 1832 on the site of an older church. It is also by Smirke, and is in a neo-Norman style. The south transept dates from the 16th century, and was long used as the burial chapel for the Sandfords of Askham Hall.

The area around Askham has been inhabited since the Late Stone Age, and there are prehistoric settlements, two roughly oval, embanked enclosures about 250m/yds apart, on nearby **Skirsgill Hill**. Each contains hut circles. More prehistoric sites exist at nearby **Moor Divock**. These were opened in the 19th century, and found to contain cremated remains.

ASKERTON [Carlisle]

NY5569: 5 miles (8km) N of Brampton

Askerton is one of four small hamlets in an area of delightful countryside in the north-east corner of the county and to the north of Hadrian's Wall.

Askerton has an impressive, small castle, first built as a fortified house in the 15th century, to which Lord Dacre added a tower at each end in the early part of the 16th century. Part of the castle is now used as a farmhouse.

ASPATRIA [Allerdale]

NY1441: 8 miles (13km) NE of Maryport

Aspatria – the name means 'the place of St Patrick's ash' – has been a settlement since the earliest times, people have lived here for more than 3000 years. The settlement lay along a busy Roman road, while in the Dark Ages, Celtic Christians who followed St Patrick, St Ninian and St Kentigern, raised their cross on Church Hill. Saxons built a great hall on Richmond Hill, which was later captured by Vikings from the Isle of Man, and, like so many other towns and villages in Cumberland, Aspatria received it share of attention from Scottish raiders.

In the centre of the town is an elaborate memorial fountain to **Sir Wilfred Lawson** (1829-1906), Member of Parliament for nearly forty years, first for Carlisle and then Cockermouth. He was a much-respected man, and a crusader of the Temperance Movement.

The **church of St Kentigern** stands on the site of a Norman church built between 1130 and 1150, and possibly on the site of an earlier church. When the church was being rebuilt in the 1840s, traces of Saxon masonry were found. The church contains a number of ancient relics including a Viking hogsback tombstone.

AYSIDE [South Lakeland]

SD3983: 2 miles (3km) SE of Newby Bridge

An attractive village with mainly stone cottages and colourful gardens, adjoining Ayside Beck. The village has more than once won the accolade of being the prettiest small village in the Lake District.

The name of the village derives from the beck that flows through it, and in which the monks at Cartmel Priory used to catch their fish.

BACKBARROW [South Lakeland]

SD3584: 1 mile (2km) SW of Newby Bridge

The last place in England to smelt iron ore with charcoal, Backbarrow's straggling cottages sit on the River Leven at the southern end of Windermere.

There are still weirs in the nearby River Leven, relics from the days when the monks of Cartmel Priory had a flour mill here. Much later, it is said, the owners of the mill used orphans from London and other cities as a workforce. Today, the mill is part of the Lakeland Village, a timeshare complex.

It was to Backbarrow that **Isaac Wilkinson**, father of John Wilkinson (1728-1808), the English ironmaster and inventor, moved in 1738, and developed the earliest iron furnaces, in what was then northern Lancashire.

BAMPTON [Eden]

NY5118: 3½ miles (6km) NW of Shap

Believed to have been visited by St Patrick, the compact village of Bampton lies on the edge of the Lowther Valley, from where its river flows north to meet the River Eamont at Penrith. The village and its neighbour, Bampton Grange, during the 19th century were typically self-sufficient, having their own communities of tradespeople, from blacksmiths and clog makers to tailors and grocers.

BAMPTON GRANGE [Eden]

NY5218: 3 miles (5km) NW of Shap

Close by the village of Bampton, Bampton Grange is an attractive group of cottages and house, set in farmland adjoining the River Lowther. Some of the houses have early 18th-century dates.

The **church of St Patrick** underpins the tradition that St Patrick visited this area, the church is one of only ten in England to be dedicated to the saint. The church was built in 1726-7, and its chancel restored in 1885, though a church has existed on this site for 800 years, and the village has produced an unusually large number of churchmen.

In the church is a portrait of the **Reverend John Boustead** (1754-1841), minister of Mardale church and master of Bampton Grammar School. He is said to have educated more students for the church than any other man in England.

The church also contains a portrait of the **Reverend Edmund Gibson** (1669-1748), who was born in Bampton parish, and later became Bishop of Lincoln and then London.

The village also produced another bishop, the **Reverend Hugh Curwen** (c1490-1568). He was successively chaplain to Henry VIII, Roman Catholic Archbishop of Dublin under Queen Mary, and a Protestant after Elizabeth I came to the throne.

BANKS [Carlisle]

NY5664: 3 miles (5km) NE of Brampton

Banks is a small village built on raised ground, occupied by Hadrian's Wall, above the River Irthing. There are a number of Roman wall turrets in the vicinity of the village.

BARBON [Eden]

SD6282: 3 miles (5km) N of Kirkby Lonsdale

Set against Thorn Moor, and lying in a narrow dale through which the road leads to Dent, Barbon is a quiet, scattered village. Barbon Beck runs on to meet the River Lune, and en route is spanned by an old packhorse bridge.

The **church of St Bartholomew**, built in the Perpendicular style by Paley and Austin in 1893, is believed to be on the site of a chapel dating from the 12th century. Much of the wood carving in the church is thought to have been done by local craftsmen, and there are a few examples of earlier work, notably from the 17th century.

The village was once served by a railway, the Ingleton to Lowgill branch line, which began in 1861, but was closed to passenger traffic just over 90 years later, and to goods traffic in 1964. Sadly, this is a tale that threads the tapestry of Barbon's history. A creamery which stood beside the station closed in 1965, and is now a housing estate. The village school closed in 1982, the former reading room is now a cottage, and the smithy has gone, along with a cobbler, carpenters, a police station and the vicarage.

Each year, in August, the village stages an **agricultural show** and **sheepdog trials**, an event that has been held for over fifty years.

BARDSEA [South Lakeland]

SD3074: 3 miles (5km) S of Ulverston

This tranquil village on the northern shore of Morecambe Bay began as a fishing hamlet, backed inland by small farms. Before the introduction of the railway and the improvement of road links, the only way to reach Bardsea, in what was a remote part of Lancashire, was by the treacherous over-sands route from Lancaster. Sea-going vessels, of course, simply coasted over this problem, calling at Bardsea to unload coal, and take on iron ore and corn. Today the only sea-going vessels are tractors and trailers that venture out onto the sands to catch fish and shrimps.

The village is dominated by the limestone **church of Holy Trinity** which was designed by George Webster of Keswick between 1843 and 1853. Work was started by Colonel Braddyll of Conishead Priory, but he failed to finish the job, and the incomplete church was put up for auction in London. It was bought by the man who became its first curate, the Reverend T Petty. It was consecrated in 1853.

There is little of particular note about the church, although it does have some attractively coloured windows, and, of course, it commands a beautiful position above the bay, and has fine views to the Lakeland fells to the north and the Pennines and Yorkshire Dales summits to the east. Inland the land rises to the modest elevation of **Birkrigg Common**, on which there is an ancient stone circle. Adjoining the tiny hamlet of Sunbrick is a Quaker burial ground where more than 200 'Friends' lie buried, including Margaret Fell, later Fox, of Swarthmoor Hall, the wife of George Fox, founder of the Quaker movement.

Just to the south of Bardsea a small stretch of the beautiful coastline has been designated a country park, and provides a splendid spot from which to gaze out across the bay. Further south Sea Wood drops to the shore, and once provided timber for shipbuilding.

Offshore, **Chapel Island**, a little over a mile (2km) to the north-west, was inhabited in the past by monks, who provided refuge for travellers crossing the sands.

Conishead Priory lies a mile (2km) to the north of Bardsea and was built, in Gothic Revival style on the site of a former leper colony. It was established by Augustinian canons in the 12th century, and after the Dissolution of the Monasteries in 1539, a private mansion was built here. This was demolished in 1821 by Colonel Braddyll, who constructed the present building, ornate and impressive, as a country seat. In the fashion of the time, the building was decorated with battlements and extensive decorations. Subsequently, it has been a rest home for miners, and now serves as a retreat for the Tibetan Buddhist Manjushri Institute.

BARROW-IN-FURNESS [Barrow-in-Furness]

SD2070: 18 miles (29km) NW of Lancaster

Barrow-in-Furness is largely a 19th-century industrial town, with long, narrow streets of terraced housing, which, as with many similar towns, grew up around its railway. This was introduced to carry locally produced iron ore, slate and limestone to a new deep-water port. Its prosperity grew with the development of the steel production and shipbuilding industries; indeed, the whole region of Furness, formerly part of Lancashire, owes most of its economic development to the exploitation of its natural resources by the monks of Furness Abbey.

Furness Abbey was a major monastic settlement when it was built in the 12th century and for centuries later, and it still remains today one of the most important monastic sites in the country. It is managed by English Heritage.

Building began in 1127 under the Savigny Order after Stephen, then Count of Boulogne, and later King of England, transferred the abbey from Tulketh, near Preston. Construction at first was slow, but probably accelerated when the Abbey was absorbed into the Cistercian Order in 1147. In time it became second in wealth only to Fountains Abbey in Yorkshire, in spite of what was a remote setting. After the Dissolution of the Monasteries, it became part of the estate of Thomas Cromwell and fell into disrepair.

Found straddling a Victorian graving dock, the **Dock Museum**, along North Road, is regarded as the flagship attraction in Barrow. The museum depicts the story of the town and its people.

BARTON [Eden]

NY4826: 3 miles (5km) SW of Penrith

The village of Barton is a compact farming community amid low, rolling hillsides adjoining the River Eamont, beyond the northern extreme of Ullswater.

Beautifully situated with rolling fells all around, the **church of St Michael** is part Norman, having been built around 1150. The south aisle was then added in 1250 and further alterations were made, notably between 1318 and 1536, when the church belonged to the Augustinian canons of Wartre Priory, near York. The north aisle was added at the turn of the century, and the whole church restored in 1904.

In the churchyard are buried the grandfather of William Wordsworth, Richard, two of his aunts and his grandson. Church Farm, standing nearby, is partly 16th century, with later additions in 1628.

BASSENTHWAITE [Allerdale]

NY2332: 6 miles (10km) NNW of Keswick

Bassenthwaite is a small village not far from Bassenthwaite Lake, in the shadow of the Skiddaw massif. There are remains here left by ancient Britons and the Romans, and it is clear from these that the area around Bassenthwaite was settled more or less permanently from the time of the Vikings.

Like many villages in the Lake District during the 19th century, Bassenthwaite was very much self-sufficient and had a wide range of tradespeople living and working there as well as corn mills, mines and a number of shops.

There are two churches here, though neither is actually in the village. The **church of St John**, built in 1878 as replacement for a chapel-of-ease dating from 1470, stands about half a mile (1km) south of the village on the A581, while the Norman **church of St Bega** is even further away, almost 2 miles (3km) south of Bassenthwaite, by the lake shore. St Bega's church is undoubtedly one of the most attractively located churches in Cumbria. It is thought to be late 13th century, but was, externally at least, restored in 1874. But there is one church in the village, a Methodist chapel, just off the green, which dates from 1865.

Bassenthwaite Lake is the most northerly of the Lake District 'lakes'. In fact, it is Lakeland's only 'lake', since all the others are 'meres', 'waters', 'tarns' and so on. Bedded on the smooth Skiddaw Slates, the village, the lake and its surrounding area lacks the craggy profiles of central Lakeland, but is no less beautiful or inspiring. The main source of water for the lake is the River Derwent, which has already flowed through Derwent Water. Between the two lakes the land is very flat, and water predominates in a network of drains and streams, leading to the logi-cal conclusion that before the deposition of glacial debris both lakes were one.

At the northern end of the lake stands **Armathwaite Hall**, a castellated, Victorian 'Tudor' mansion, built in 1881, and the former home of the Spedding and Vane families. South, beyond St Bega's church is **Mire House**, originally built in 1666, but bought by the Spedding family in late Georgian times. The house was renowned as a literary centre, and was attended by Southey, Tennyson and Wordsworth. It was during Tennyson's stay at Mire House that he was moved to write *Idylls of the King* in which he describes the passing of Arthur. Here it was that Sir Bedivere cast Excalibur, and here that the black barge bore away the dying king.

BAYCLIFF [South Lakeland]

SD2872: 3 miles (5km) S of Ulverston

Baycliff is a small, compact coastal village of limestone cottages, directly overlooking Morecambe Bay, and an ideal place for birdwatching. Until the 20th century, Baycliff was little more than a small hamlet, but it has since seen much residential development.

Quarrying and iron mining provided what prosperity there was for the village, and boats took the ore to the Wilkinson furnaces at Backbarrow. Stone from around the village was also in great demand, having a white and marble-like quality.

Seawood Farm, to the north of the village, was where the manor court was held, to hear grievances and mete out justice.

BEAUMONT [Carlisle]

NY3459: 4 miles (6km) NW of Carlisle

Hadrian's Wall runs through the tiny village of Beaumont, beside the River Eden on the outskirts of Carlisle. The name of the village, which means 'beautiful hill', describes its setting on rising ground above the river. On the highest point stands the **church of St Mary**, which dates from the late 12th century, and was built on the site of a Roman milecastle using stones from Hadrian's Wall. The church was restored in 1872. As might be expected of a church on high ground overlooking the low-lying Solway Plain, the views from Beaumont are especially fine, north into southern Scotland, south to the fells of Lakeland, and east to the northern Pennines.

During the time of the Border Troubles, which raged for over 300 years, Beaumont, as elsewhere in this frontier land, would have known much destruction and hardship. A hardship of a different kind, however, that of providing water for the villagers, was common. Many villagers relied on wells, including St Ann's Well by the river. Later a windmill was built to pump water from the river to a small reservoir tank near the church, but this provided a supply to a few houses only.

The **Carlisle Canal** was opened in 1823, and this meant that boats up to 100 tons could reach Carlisle from Port Carlisle. The canal, however, did not survive for long, and it was drained. But all was not lost for the canal bed was used for a railway line which linked Carlisle with Silloth, a venture that flourished until the line closed in 1964.

BECKERMET [Copeland]

NY0106: 2½ miles (4km) S of Egremont

Rather dominated by the towers and buildings of Sellafield Nuclear Power Station to the south, Beckermet is a sizeable coastal village in rolling grasslands south of Egremont. The village is really

two villages, each named after its church – Beckermet St Bridget and Beckermet St John.

The village lies at the confluence of two streams, Black Beck and Kirk Beck, and was named by the Vikings – Becker-met – 'the meeting of becks'.

The **church of St Bridget**, south-west of the village, is the older of the two churches in Beckermet. It is roughcast, and is little more than a nave with a bellcot and chancel. In the churchyard are two Saxon cross shafts, but they are not entirely legible, though one has a clear runic inscription. The church is only used for funerals, and has effectively been replaced by the church of the same name at Calder Bridge.

The **church of St John** was built in red sandstone in 1878-9, and replaces a church demolished in 1810, which must have been old, probably Norman.

On the outskirts of the village, to the north, are the mounds of the motte of **Caernarvon Castle**, standing in the middle of a bailey. East-south-east is the Ehenside Tarn Neolithic settlement, only discovered in the 19th century, when the tarn was drained. Around the tarn a number of hearths and other signs of occupation were discovered including a dug-out canoe and paddle, spears and throwing-sticks along with numerous stone axes that came from the axe factories in Greater Langdale.

BEETHAM [South Lakeland]

SD4979: 6 miles (10km) N of Carnforth

With the opening of the M6, a reign of peacefulness once more descended on this 'estate' village of grey limestone cottages and cobbled forecourts on the banks of the River Bela. During the Second World War Italian and German prisoners were held at nearby Bela River Camp. The prisoners stayed until 1948, to be followed over the next four years by displaced persons, mainly Poles and Ukrainians. In October 1951, the *Westmorland Gazette* announced that the Bela River Camp was to be retained as a reception centre for evacuees in the next war!

The large and imposing Georgian Ashton House stands at the western edge of the village, about 100m/yds south of the **church of St Michael**. The church has a tower dating from the late 12th century, and a stained glass window, thought to date from the 15th century, depicts King Charles I (described as a martyr) flanked by St Oswald and St Alban.

During restoration work in the 19th century, a small horde of old coins was found. Some accounts say that they dated from the reign of Edward the Confessor (1042-66), which would suggest that the church could have been built on the site of an earlier Saxon church. Other records claim that it was 100 Norman coins that were found, of William the Conqueror and William Rufus.

Beetham Hall, to the south of the village, is dated 1693 (or 1653). Now a farm, it stands on the site of an early or mid-14th-century fortified manor house. The manor was held for many years by the de Beetham family. Much earlier, one of the family fought at the Battle of Hastings (14 October 1066). In the early 14th century, Thomas de Beetham was a knight of Westmorland and was granted a charter for a market and fair.

The **Heron Corn Mill and Museum of Papermaking** is a working corn mill housed in a building that dates from about 1740. A mill is known to have existed on this site before 1096, and in 1220 the Lord of the Manor gave the monks of St Marie's, York, the right to grind their grain at his mill, without payment, or 'multure' as it was then known.

In 1988, to commemorate 500 years of papermaking in England, a barn adjoining the corn mill was converted to house the **Museum of Papermaking**, which shows papermaking ancient and modern. Papermaking was also an important local industry, and one that was founded at Beetham more than 250 years ago.

Beetham Sports, started in 1920 by local farmers, are held on the first Saturday of August.

BEWCASTLE [Carlisle]
NY5674: 9 miles (14km) N of Brampton

Tucked away in the north-east corner of the county, and lying close to the Anglo-Scottish border, Bewcastle, also known as Shopford, has a peaceful, unassuming atmosphere, and was an important place during the days when drovers took sheep and cattle south to the English markets.

About AD120, the Romans built a fort at Bewcastle (Banna), an isolated outpost far north of Hadrian's Wall, to which it was linked by a road. Much of the stone used to build the fort has gone into building the village.

The countryside all around Bewcastle is dotted with the remains of numerous pele towers, which were essential for survival during the time of the Border Troubles that preceded the Act of Union with Scotland.

The **church of St Cuthbert** dates from the early 13th century, and has a tower which was added during Georgian times.

Of greater significance, however, is the **Bewcastle Cross**, which dates from the late 7th century (about AD680). This Anglo-Saxon preaching cross, which stands almost 15ft high, bears an inscription in runes thought to commemorate

Alcfrith, the Deiran king who died c709. What makes the Bewcastle Cross different from all the others in Cumbria are the sacred figures that are carved on it, and the quality of the vine scrolls and knot patterns, surpassed only by the Ruthwell Cross in Scotland.

After the Anglo-Saxons erected their cross, Scandinavian settlers came to the area, one of whom, named Beuth, built the castle from which the village derives its name. Little remains of this, except part of a ruined tower and sections of wall, the castle having received the destructive attentions of Oliver Cromwell in 1641.

BIGGAR [Barrow-in-Furness]

SD1966: 2 miles (3km) S of Barrow-in-Furness

Biggar is a small, isolated village on the windswept Isle of Walney, and so it is a distant suburb of Barrow-in-Furness.

The whole of the Isle of Walney is renowned for its birdlife, and the wealth of sea birds and passage migrants.

BIGRIGG [Copeland]

NY0013: 1½ miles (2km) N of Egremont

A compact village along the road between Whitehaven and Egremont, Bigrigg stands in farmland adjoining the River Ehen, and, like many of the surrounding villages, its development was influenced by the spread of mining in the area.

Its **church of St John** is a modest-sized Victorian church built between 1878 and 1880 in the Decorated style.

BLACKFORD [Carlisle]

NY3962: 4 miles (6km) N of Carlisle

Blackford is a widespread village along the road between Carlisle and Longtown, set in a mainly farming region to the south of the Rive Lyne. The village's most notable feature is the **church of St John the Baptist**, built in 1870 by the Borough of Carlisle.

BLAWITH [South Lakeland]

SD2888: 6 miles (10km) S of Coniston

Blawith is a widespread group of residential and farming properties along the River Crake, at the southern end of Coniston Water.

The church of St John the Baptist, now closed, was built in 1863 in local rubble with sandstone dressings, to replace a chapel built in the 16th century, or earlier. The remains of the chapel can still be found on the opposite side of the road.

North-west of the village rise the Blawith Fells, a wide expanse of bracken-clad hillside, at the foot of which lies the Brown Howe estate, centred on a Victorian mansion house, now converted into flats. The fells conceal Beacon Tarn, a small, natural lake around which there are traces of a prehistoric settlement.

BLENCARN [Eden]

NY6331: 7½ miles (12km) NW of Appleby-in-Westmorland

A modest-sized North Pennine village of stone-built houses in the Eden Valley, Blenearn lies in the shadow of Cross Fell, the highest summit of the Pennines. There is a fine view across green fields to the distant heights, that on a fair day is breathtaking.

Blencarn – its name means 'the summit crag' – was formerly part of the large Norman baronetcy of Adam fitz Swein, held by the Neville family. Later, some of the lands were held by the priory of

Carlisle, while large estates eventually found their way into the hands of Sir Andrew de Harcla, who served Edward I, and was rewarded by being made Earl of Carlisle. Sadly, he was made a scapegoat when Robert the Bruce invaded England in 1323, and was executed at Carlisle (see also Carlisle).

BLENCOGO [Allerdale]

NY1947: 3½ miles (6km) W of Wigton

Blencogo is a small, elongated village set in an extensive area of farmland in the low-lying coastal plain west of Wigton.

Historian **Jonathan Boucher** (1738-1804), a friend of George Washington, was born in Blencogo. He did much work on Hutchinson's *History of the County of Cumberland*, published in 1794.

BLENCOW [Eden]

NY4532: 4 miles (6km) NW of Penrith

Blencow, centred between the road to Wigton and the A66 to Keswick, is divided into two small communites, Great and Little Blencow. It is an attractive village on the River Petteril, which both divides the village, and is the parish boundary. As a result, Great Blencow found itself in the parish of Dacre, and Little Blencow in Greystoke.

The Blencow family has something of a distinguished past. Adam de Blencow was prominent during the Hundred Years' War (1337-1453), and was granted arms by the Baron of Greystoke. Henry Blencow, in 1617, was knighted by James I, and was High Sheriff of Cumberland.

Formerly of great importance to Blencow was its grammar school, founded by Thomas Burnbank in 1577. It was amalgamated with Penrith Grammar School in

1913. Two of Blencow's former pupils achieved some fame. The first, **George Whitehead** (1636-1723), was born in Orton, and became a founder member of the Society of Friends alongside George Fox (see also Orton). The second was **Edward Law**, Baron Ellenborough (1750-1818), born in Great Salkeld, who achieved fame by his successful defence, spanning seven years, of Warren Hastings, Governor-General of India, who had been impeached for corruption. Law later became Lord Chief Justice of England.

Blencow Hall, nearby on the Greystoke road, is an impressive, mullion-windowed building. A hall with a tower at each end, the central part was probably built in the 16th century, the date 1590 is over the door.

To the south of the village is another outstanding country house, **Ennim**, the home in recent times of Viscount William Whitelaw, Member of Parliament and Deputy Prime Minister to Margaret Thatcher.

BLINDCRAKE [Allerdale]

NY1434: 3 miles (5km) NE of Cockermouth

Blindcrake is an elongated village of grey, 18th-century houses and working farms that adjoins a former Roman road, now an A-road, on rising ground above the River Derwent as it flows from Bassenthwaite Lake towards Cockermouth. The village is built on the site of an early British settlement, and is rather isolated from the mainstream of Lakeland villages. It was only supplied with mains water just before the Second World War, while the villagers had to wait for electricity until 1954.

In the south-east corner of the village is

a place where a number of horses have been buried, the villagers preferring to have them buried nearby rather than taken away.

BOLTON [Eden]

NY6323: 8 miles (13km) SE of Penrith

A small village, Bolton stands on rising ground above the flood plain of the River Eden. Its name simply means 'the enclosure with buildings'. There is evidence that a settlement existed here more the 1200 years ago, and the **church of All Saints** is 12th century, a humbly delightful and fascinating building, partly restored in 1848. The north and south doorways are clearly Norman, as is a rare, primitive relief over the blocked north doorway of two knights fighting on horseback (the only other known relief like this is in Dorset).

In 1314 the manor of Bolton was held by Ralph de Greystoke, but it passed through the hands of a number of families until it became the property of the Lowthers.

Between Bolton and Appleby-in-Westmorland lie the ruins of **Bewley Castle**, which dates from the 12th century. It was granted at about that time to the church at Carlisle, but when the second bishop died in 1186 the diocese remained vacant for thirty-two years, during which time the canons decided to appoint their own bishop. Whether such a move would have been tolerated for long is uncertain, but when the bishop and canons swore fealty to the king of the Scots, the king of England, Henry III, applied to the Pope for orders to have the canons expelled. In due course, Hugh, abbot of Beaulieu in the New Forest was appointed Bishop of Carlisle. In 1219, a year after his appointment, the bishop was given the castle, and brought to it the name of his mother-house.

BOLTONGATE [Allerdale]

NY2240: 5 miles (8km) S of Wigton

Boltongate is a small village on a hill above the River Ellen, and has a stunning view of Skiddaw to the south.

The **church of All Saints** is a remarkable building, one bishop remarking that mathematically it ought to have fallen down under the weight of the stone roof. The roof itself is concealed by parapets, but everything seems to be composed of large ashlar blocks, and the traditions and styles of Scotland and Provence in France have been cited as accounting for its ceiling vault in particular.

More unusual are the varying accounts of its building. One relates how it was built by the Earl of Westmorland, a nobleman thought to be among the 'band of brothers' who fought on Saint Crispin's day, mentioned in Shakespeare's *Henry V*. Local legend, however, attributes the building to Michael Scott (c1175-c1230), the Scottish scholar and astrologer, and the wondrous 'wizard' believed to be in league with the devil. The church is said to have been completely built in one night by imps. More prosaically it is possible that the church was constructed by workmen imported from France, hence the possible Gallic influence in the ceiling vault.

BOOT [COPELAND]

NY1700: 6 miles (10km) NE of Ravenglass

Boot is a small village, just off the main valley road, at the Eskdale end of the Ravenglass and Eskdale Railway. Its few buildings and quiet ways contain no hint of the activities that flourished here in years gone by.

Eskdale Mill dates from 1578, though there is evidence of milling having taken place here for almost 700 years. The mill today is one of the few remaining corn mills with two waterwheels. It remained for many years in the same family group, handed down from father to son, and occasionally daughter to son-in-law.

The milling of corn ended in the 1920s, though the machinery continued to be used for some time afterwards to produce electricity for the mill cottage. In 1972, the mill was acquired by the then Cumberland County Council, and the restoration of one waterwheel and a pair of stones was completed in 1975.

The complex today still has some of the original wooden machinery, and features an exhibition of milling machinery and items associated with Eskdale and its people.

About 3 miles (5km) east of the village, the **Hardknott Pass**, undoubtedly Lakeland's most challenging section of highway, forces a way through a mountain gap to Cockley Beck at the head of Dunnerdale. But most motorists, grappling with the twists, turns and gradients of the pass, are unaware of the massive Roman fort only a short distance from the road. **Hardknott Fort** (Mediobogdum) is one of the finest Roman forts in Britain, dramatically built on a shelf above the pass. It was built in the early part of the second century to oversee the road linking other forts at Ambleside (Galava) and Ravenglass (Glannaventa), though that road and the present road are not the same, and it may well have followed a much older, prehistoric thoroughfare.

Although the fort would have been surrounded by trees when it was first built, it nevertheless commanded a good view eastwards to the top of the pass, and down the length of Eskdale. It would certainly

have been a wild and inhospitable place to be garrisoned. Archaeological evidence suggests that the fort was abandoned during the time of Antoninus Pius (138-61), coincidental with the pushing northwards of the frontier of the Roman Empire in Britain, but was later reoccupied when the Antonine Wall was abandoned. The fort itself ceased to be occupied around the turn of the second century.

There are yet more spectacular remains surrounding Boot, notably on Burn Moor to the north of the village. Across the whole of this wild moorland area there is extensive evidence of a large early settlement that is fascinating to explore. On **Brat's Hill** [NY173023], there are stone circles, five in all, the largest being a single ring. There are five cairns within this ring, from which an excavation in 1827 exhumed the remains of burnt bones and the horns of a stag. There are more circles on nearby **White Moss** and **Low Longrigg**, along with a large number of cairns.

Each year in September, Brotherilkeld Farm, near Boot hosts the **Eskdale Show**, a small country show with includes hound trailing, fell racing, and numerous displays and crafts.

BOOTLE [Copeland]

SD1088: 7 miles (11km) N of Millom

Bootle is a very pleasant small village of some antiquity, lying between the swelling mass of Black Combe and the Cumbrian coastline. Its economy today is largely based on farming. The River Annan flows beside the main road, and then disappears under the village en route to the sea. Houses and lanes conjoin in a seemingly haphazard arrangement that lends a unique character to the village.

The village is dominated by the vast,

bracken-clad slopes of **Black Combe**, one of Lakeland's neglected fells, but inspiration both to Wordsworth and Norman Nicholson (see Millom). The mountain and its coastal lands are especially attractive in autumn, though according to W G Collingwood in *The Lake Counties*, there is an old Furness saying that 'Nowt good ever comes round Black Combe' – no doubt the sentiment alludes to the days when raiding was still prevalent. And though Black Combe may have inspired Wordsworth, he was not impressed with Bootle – the weather was inclement and the ocean made too much noise!

There is evidence of a Mesolithic settlement at nearby **Eskmeals**, and a number of Stone Age artefacts, and the remains of a Bronze Age settlement, have been found in the surrounding countryside.

The right to hold a market was originally granted to Bootle by charter of Edward III in 1348, and then renewed by Elizabeth I in 1567. The ancient market cross has been usurped by a more modern one by Paley and Austin next to the churchyard, and erected to commemorate Queen Victoria's Diamond Jubilee in 1897.

The **church of St Michael and All Angels** is an old one with some Norman elements, but extensively repaired and rebuilt in 1837 and 1891. To the north of the church, about a mile away, are the remains of a Benedictine nunnery, dedicated to St Leonard, and founded in the early 13th century.

BOTHEL [Allerdale]

NY1838: 6 miles (10km) NE of Cockermouth

Bothel is a sizeable village with good views over the Solway Firth. In medieval times the inhabitants were required to maintain a sea watch, 'seawake', for the approach of hostile ships, when a fire beacon would be lit.

Associated with the village is the tradition that on the day Charles I was beheaded, the local beck ran red.

To the south-west, near the junction of the Bassenthwaite and Torpenhow roads, is **Caer Mote**, the site of a turf and timber Roman fort, and a smaller, superimposed fortlet, probably from the second century.

BOUSTEAD HILL [Carlisle]

NY2959: 7 miles (11km) NW of Carlisle

Boustead Hill is a small coastal village overlooking the marshlands of the Solway Firth, and immediately adjoining the westward continuation of Hadrian's Wall, here a turf dyke.

A large tract of beautiful coastal marshland and common land near Boustead Hill, known as **Solway Commons**, is owned by the National Trust.

BOUTH [South Lakeland]

SD3285: 5 miles (8km) NE of Ulverston

Bouth is an attractive village perched on a hill, with a fairly modern village green and an old coaching inn, the White Hart, built on the road linking Dalton, then the capital of Furness, and Kendal. Well surrounded by woodland, it is easy to see how the village mainly grew out of traditional woodland industries, which no doubt included a trade in deer.

The village, which has won the prize for the Best Kept Small Village in South Lakeland on a number of occasions, used to form the centre of a thriving agricultural district, and a weekly market was held there, along with two fairs famed for their wrestling matches. It was a major centre in the large parish of Colton, and commonly regarded as the 'capital' of the parish.

The manufacture of gunpowder was also an important local industry, begun in the 19th century, but ended in 1929 after the second of two explosions caused damage from which the business did not recover.

Hay Bridge Nature Reserve to the north of the village is now a deer sanctuary.

BOWNESS-ON-SOLWAY
[Allerdale]

NY2262: 4 miles (6km) N of Kirkbride

Founded by the Romans as Maia, the last fort on Hadrian's Wall, Bowness-on-Solway, is a small, compact village of sandstone cottages and narrow streets.

The original name of the village, Bulness, signifies that this was a 'rounded headland'. Bowness represented the most westerly point of the Solway where it was possible to ford the estuary at low tide, a distinction that saw many travellers using the route, rather at their peril, as a shortcut.

The fordability of the Solway at this point may well have influenced the decision to construct the **Solway Viaduct** here, linking the village by rail to Scotland. The viaduct opened in 1869 for goods, and a year later for passengers. It has been described as 'a gallant monument to an age of reckless enterprise' (Brian Blake, *The Solway Firth*). The viaduct was damaged in the harsh winters of 1875 and 1881. On the latter occasion massive ice blocks crashed into the viaduct as the tide retreated, and broke two large holes in it. The viaduct was re-

paired, and used again, but by 1921 was considered unsafe, and was closed. It was finally demolished in 1934, though a short section of the embankment can still be seen at Herdhill Scar.

The **Solway Coast** itself stretches from the River Esk, near the Scottish Border to Maryport, on the Irish Sea. The name is thought to be derived from two Norse words, 'sul' meaning 'pillar', and probably referring to the Lochmaben Stone, a large ice-borne boulder which marked the Scottish end of a ford, and 'wath' meaning 'ford'. The two words combined mean the crossing at the mouth of the River Esk.

The coastline is a mix of sand dunes, salt marsh, shingle beds and peat mosses, and is immensely popular with birds and other wildlife. The Cumbrian Wildlife Trust and the Royal Society for the Protection of Birds (RSPB) are responsible for the protection and management of most of the coastline, with notable sites at Campfield Marsh, Grune Point and Drumburgh Moss.

There is clear evidence of Roman occupation along the coastline, not only in the form of Hadrian's Wall. Forts stood at Kirkbride, Beckfoot and Maryport, interspersed with milecastles along the entire stretch of coastline.

BOWNESS-ON-WINDERMERE
[South Lakeland]

SD4097: 1 mile (2km) S of Windermere

A sprawling tourist town on the shores of Windermere, which developed following the opening of the railway line to nearby Windermere. Bowness was the nearest accessible point on the lake, and today is the point from which most of the lake cruisers operate.

The village dates originally from the

11th century, when the Vikings settled here, one of the Viking chiefs naming the lake 'Vinand's Mere'. Before the arrival of the railway, Bowness was little more than a group of cottages and huts used by fishermen, but once the railway made travel into the Lake District considerably easier and quicker, so the tourists flooded in, and wealthy industrialists came to live in the area. Many of the large, almost palatial houses found in Bowness and neighbouring Windermere date from this time, and provided much work for local builders.

Found in Rayrigg Road, the **Windermere Steamboat Museum** houses a unique collection of historic steamboats and motorboats, including the *Dolly*, reputedly the oldest mechanically-powered boat in the world.

The **church of St Martin** was consecrated in 1483, and contains glass thought to come from Cartmel Priory. It replaces a previous church destroyed by fire. Under the chancel is a mass grave containing the bodies of almost 50 people drowned in 1635, when the ferry on which they were returning from Hawkshead capsized.

In 1870, St Martin's was enlarged into the form it is today. Behind the church is the oldest part of Bowness, a delightful web of narrow streets, known as Lowside, which give a better idea of what the village would have been like before the railway.

BRAITHWAITE [Allerdale]

NY2323: 2 miles (3km) W of Keswick

Braithwaite today is a quiet place with few residents employed locally, but in the past it had more than 1000 inhabitants and its own coterie of tradespeople – butcher, baker, blacksmiths, millers, shoemaker, grocer, joiners and builders – and was closely associated with the village of Thornthwaite to the north. Formerly the seat of a thriving woollen industry, Braithwaite was the first location of the Cumberland Pencil Company formed in 1868, a business that only moved to its site in Keswick thirty years later when the buildings burned down.

The village lies just off the Keswick to Cockermouth road, at a point where the choice arises of crossing into the Vale of Lorton via the Whinlatter Pass, or into Buttermere through the Newlands valley.

BRAMPTON [Carlisle]

NY5261: 9 miles (14km) NE of Carlisle

The sandstone village of Brampton, pleasingly attractive and oddly laid out, with two parallel main streets, was founded by the Augustinian monks of Lanercost Priory in 1166. Less than 200 years later it was destroyed by Robert the Bruce, and later still regularly plundered by Scottish reivers. It was during such a raid, or as a retreat was being made from Penrith to the south, that a raider is thought to have dropped and lost the original brass town seal of Penrith. It lay undiscovered until found in a ditch in the mid-19th century.

In the centre of the town stands the octagonal **Moot Hall**, built in 1817, with an external staircase to its main upper entrance.

The **church of St Martin** mostly dates from the 19th century. It is the only church built between 1874 and 1878 by architect Philip Webb (1831-1915), who met, and had a long association with the work of, William Morris. The church contains a fine collection of stained glass by Morris and Burne-Jones, notably the

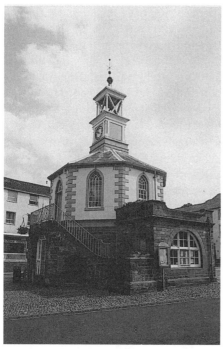

Moot Hall, Brampton

east window. Pevsner remarks that although the church has none of the 'blis-
sful beauties' of a church of the same era
by other architects, it is, nevertheless, a
remarkable church.

The old parish church on the outskirts
of the town was built from parts of
Hadrian's Wall, and was in use until
1878, when the present church replaced
it.

In High Cross Street is a building that
Bonnie Prince Charlie used as his headquarters in 1745. Nearby is a monument
on the site of the **Capon Tree**, from
which luckless supporters of the Jacobite
cause were hanged following Culloden.

Naworth Castle, about 2 miles (3km)
east of Brampton, is the family home of
the Howards, earls of Carlisle, and an ancient border fortress. In the 17th century
it was the home of Lord William Howard,
known as 'Belted Will', from his habit of
wearing a broad, studded belt, mentioned

by Walter Scott in the *Lay of the Last
Minstrel*. The oldest part of the castle,
Dacre Tower, an old pele tower, is from
the 14th century. Lord William converted the building to a mansion, which
was damaged by fire in the mid-19th
century, and later restored.

Birdoswald Roman Fort, Gilsland,
Brampton, is one of the finest Roman
forts on Hadrian's Wall. The museum
also has displays about Border reivers,
Victorian antiquaries and archaeological discoveries.

Each year the village stages the important **Brampton Sheepdog Trials** in
September.

BRANTHWAITE [Allerdale]
NY0524: 5 miles (8km) SW of
Cockermouth

Branthwaite, the 'broom-covered clearing', stands on the steep banks of the
River Marron, a pleasant old village
spread along three minor roads.

Branthwaite Hall, between the village and Dean, is now a farm. It was built
around a pele tower with a tunnel-
vaulted basement. From 1422 to 1757, it
was the home of the Skeltons, and later of
William Hetherington (1788-1865), a
local poet, who lies buried in Dean
churchyard.

BRIDEKIRK [Allerdale]
NY1133: 2 miles (3km) N of Cockermouth

A small village on the outskirts of Cockermouth, Bridekirk consists mainly of
old farms and modern houses, the latter
meeting a commuter need.

The **church of St Bride** (St Bridget) is
a neo-Norman church which was largely
rebuilt between 1868 and 1870, incorpo-
rating parts of a much older church, in

particular, two genuine Norman doorways. The church contains a 12th-century font covered with fascinating sculptures. The name Bridekirk means 'the church of St Bride', who was a 5th-century Irish saint.

The politician **Sir Joseph Williamson** was born in the vicarage at Bridekirk, and later became Secretary of State in 1674. He spent some time in the Tower of London, on the orders of Parliament, but later became President of the Royal Society, and on his death was buried in Westminster Abbey.

The poet **Thomas Tickell** (1686-1740) was also born in the vicarage at Bridekirk. He became a fellow of Queen's College, Oxford from 1710 to 1726, and was especially skilful in occasional poetry. His complimentary verses on *Rosamund*, written in 1709, coupled with his own virtues, brought him to the favour of Joseph Addison (1672-1719), the English essayist and politician. On becoming Secretary of State in 1717, Addison made Tickell his under-secretary.

BRIERY [Allerdale]

NY2824: 1 mile (2km) NE of Keswick

Once famous for its manufacture of bobbins for use in the industrial mills, notably of Lancashire, Briery is a small, sequestered community in the narrow ravine fashioned by the River Greta on the outskirts of Keswick. Low Briery Bobbin Mill was the first mill opened during the Industrial Revolution, and at the height of its production made up to 40 million bobbins per year. In addition to bobbin mills, there used to be a 'Fancy Bottoms Mill' here, a specialist textile mill producing the intricate bottom edgings for waistcoats.

BRIGFLATTS [Eden]

SD6491: 1 mile (2km) SW of Sedbergh

Brigflatts, on the outskirts of Sedbergh and the banks of the River Rawthey, not far from its confluence with the Lune, was once a flax-weavers' settlement. Here stands a **Friends' Meeting House**, a small and beautiful white cottage, built as a cooperative effort in 1675, making it the oldest meeting house in the north of England.

The house was built at a time when nonconformist meetings were illegal, and failure to attend parish church brought persecution. It is said that one local man never attended the meeting house services without taking his nightcap, against the possibility of being apprehended and taken off to prison. One local farmer, Alexander Hebblethwaite, for meeting here was fined eight shillings, an enormous sum, which he refused to pay, and forfeited his cow. A blacksmith, guilty of the same offence, had his tools of trade taken from him.

BRIGHAM [Allerdale]

NY0830: 2 miles (3km) W of Cockermouth

A sizeable village community along the River Derwent on the outskirts of Cockermouth. The name means 'the meadow by the bridge'.

The **church of St Bridget** is part Norman, with a variety of styles, having been restored between 1864 and 1876. It has an attractive ceiling, and a piscina with faces. The stained glass in the east window is in memory of Wordsworth's son, John, who was vicar here.

George Fox relates how he preached in the church for three hours, standing on a seat.

Moorland Close, a farmhouse at Brigham, was the birthplace of **Fletcher**

Christian (c1764-c1794), the English seaman and ringleader of the mutiny against Captain Bligh on the *Bounty* in 1789. He was educated at St Bees School and Cockermouth Grammar School.

Christian declined to go to university, but instead joined the navy at the age of 18. He served with Bligh on a number of ships, and was selected by Bligh to sail as midshipman with him on the *Britannia*, sailing to the West Indies in 1787. They became close friends, and Bligh appointed him as first mate on the *Bounty* on a voyage to Tahiti. After the mutiny, Christian and eight other mutineers took refuge on Pitcairn Island, where, with some Tahitian men and women, they founded a settlement. Christian was probably killed by Tahitians, along with other mutineers.

BRIGSTEER [South Lakeland]
SD4889: 3 miles (5km) SW of Kendal

A sizeable village at the foot of Scout Scar and on the borders of the beautiful Lyth Valley, Brigsteer stands on the edge of drained mosses, an area formerly more densely wooded than today. Peat cutting was, therefore, a popular pursuit, and may well have influenced the settlement here of Scandinavian invaders.

The name Brigsteer was first spelt 'Bryggstere', and describes a bridge over which 'steers' were driven. It could, and logically might, also refer to a causeway across the moss.

The roughcast **church of St John** lies just outside Brigsteer in Helsington parish and is thought to date from 1726, with restorations in 1898 and 1910.

BRISCO [Carlisle]
NY4252: 3 miles (5km) SE of Carlisle

Brisco is a small linear village along the road between Upperby, on the edge of Carlisle, and Wreay. It is primarily based on a farming economy.

St Ninian's Well dates back to AD400, and is believed to be the place where St Ninian baptised Christians.

BROMFIELD [Allerdale]
NY1746: 5 miles (8km) WSW of Wigton

The name means 'broom-covered land', and this small village is set in low-lying agricultural lands on the Cumbrian Plain.

The **church of St Mungo** is part Norman, but largely restored in 1860. Mungo is an affectionate name for St Kentigern, who is said to have baptised converts in a well to the north of the church. There is evidence to suggest that there have been as many as five places of worship on the site. The first, a pagan site, was replaced by the Romans in the second century. A new church from the time of St Kentigern, followed, then a Norman church, and finally the present one.

Cockfighting used to take place in the churchyard with the approval of the vicar, who supported the sport.

BROUGH [Eden]
NY7914: 4 miles (6km) N of Kirkby Stephen

This natural trading point has seen activity since Roman times. Modern Brough (pronounced 'Bruff') comprises Market Brough, Church Brough and Brough Sowerby.

The town is divided by the Barnard Castle to Appleby road. Below the castle, close by St Michael's Church, is Church Brough, a collection of stone houses and a village green that used to have a market cross. Market Brough, where a market cross tops a clock tower, grew around a

14th-century bridge spanning Swindale Beck.

The prosperity of the town grew during the 18th and 19th centuries, when the town was on the important stagecoach routes from London to Carlisle and Glasgow, and from York to Lancaster. Inevitably, the town was a bustle of people employed to service the needs of travellers – stableboys, ostlers, cooks, innkeepers, blacksmiths, wheelwrights, and leathersmiths. At one time there were seventeen inns in Brough, but only a few have survived, and some now wear different guises.

Brough declined when local landowners opposed the development of a railway line. The promoters of the line simply switched the route of the line and went via Kirkby Stephen, which became an important rail junction, and thrived on the new-found prosperity that had hitherto been Brough's.

The **church of St Michael** is a long and low church, typical of north country churches; the tower dates from 1513, the rest from the late 14th to early 16th centuries.

Brough Castle, was originally one of William Rufus's royal castles, built around 1095, and largely destroyed by William of Scotland in 1174, and later rebuilt. The castle ruins, now under the control of English Heritage, stand in a dominant position above Swindale Beck, and occupy the northern part of the Roman fort of Verterae. In Fitzwilliam Museum in Cambridge is the **Brough Stone**, a memorial to a 16-year-old Roman soldier, and virtually all that remains of Verterae.

During the 15th century, Brough Castle, having in 1204 been granted to Robert de Vipont, and through him to the lords Clifford, was inhabited by an unsavoury character known, with good cause, as 'The Butcher'. Also known as Bloody (or Blackfaced) Clifford, he was John, the 9th Baron Clifford (1435-61), a ruthless Lancastrian and merciless persecu-

Brough Castle

tor of the Yorkists in the Wars of the Roses (1455-85/7), immortalised in Shakespeare's *Henry VI*. He was killed at the Battle of Towton, near Tadcaster, taking an arrow through his throat, and his castle seized by Richard Neville, the kingmaker, Earl of Warwick (1428-71).

The castle was, however, regained by John's son, Henry (1455-1523), known as 'The Shepherd Lord', who lived there until it was burned down two years before his death. Nothing was done to reinstate the castle until Lady Anne Clifford repaired it in 1659, though it was destined to survive only for a further seven years before fire once again brought it to ruins, from which it has never recovered

Brough Hill Fair is an annual gathering of gypsies which has taken place for 600 years, and is held in September. A charter was granted to hold a weekly market and annual fair in 1331.

BROUGHAM [Eden]

NY5328: 2 miles (3km) SE of Penrith

Evidence still remains at Brougham of Roman occupation, and here stand the ruins of Brougham Castle. Both these factors, the importance of the site to the Romans, and the building of Brougham Castle, show that the Normans were no less adept at strategic sitings, and contributed significantly to Brougham's illustrious history.

The manor was first granted to Ranulph de Meschines, but in the late 12th century passed to the Vipont family when King John (1199-1216) granted it to Robert de Veteripont, as part of the confiscated estates of Hugh de Morville, one of the murderers of Thomas à Becket.

Brougham Castle, under the care of English Heritage, dates from the time of Henry II (1133-89) and the late 13th and early 14th centuries. It is built largely in the traditional red sandstone of this region. During the latter part of the 13th century, it came into the possession of the Clifford family, and remained with them until the death here of Lady Anne Clifford, Countess of Pembroke (1590-1676).

Ann Radcliffe (1764-1823), the English romantic novelist, visited Lakeland in 1794 on part of a great tour, and described the castle as having 'Dungeons, secret passages and heavy iron rings...to hint of unhappy wretches, who were, perhaps, rescued only by death from these horrible engines of a tyrant's will'. The castle dungeons, she went on were 'the dens of serpents and other venomous reptiles'.

The **Roman fort**, Brocavum, lies at the junction of an old Yorkshire-Lancashire route. The castle has removed the northern quarter of the fort, but the rest of the fort is visible as a bank and ditch in the field to the south of the castle. It is believed that the fort was occupied from the second century to the end of the fourth, and probably housed up to 1000 troops of infantry and cavalry.

Above the River Eamont, and northeast of the castle, stands the **church of St Ninian**, also known as Ninekirk. It stands on the site of a Saxon church, replaced by a Norman one, which was then completely rebuilt by Lady Anne Clifford in 1660, and is regarded as a fine example of a Gothic structure. It is a delightful, unspoiled relic of its time, with a pleasing altar rail, box pews and screen.

St Wilfred's Chapel, which is easily missed, stands south-west of the castle, and contrasts remarkably with St Ninian's, although it, too, was restored by Lady Anne Clifford in 1658. This is a long, rectangular chapel, containing an

Countess Pillar, Brougham

built between 1830 and 1840, and was the home of the Brougham family, which included Henry Peter Brougham (1778-1868), 1st Baron Brougham and Vaux, who later became Lord Chancellor. The fourth lord became immortalised in song as the man who (twice) broke the bank at Monte Carlo. But it wasn't enough to save the hall, which he was forced to sell. The hall was demolished in 1934.

BROUGHTON BECK [South Lakeland]

SD2882: 2½ miles (4km) N of Ulverston

Broughton Beck is a small community set in farming land among the low, rolling fells north of Ulverston. Once it was a small, self-contained farming community with a water mill powered by the beck that has given the village its name.

The slate and red sandstone **church of St John the Evangelist** was consecrated in 1874 by the Bishop of Carlisle as a chapel-of-ease to the parish church of St Mary in Ulverston. It is another Paley and Austin church, but is not outstanding.

BROUGHTON-IN-FURNESS [South Lakeland]

SD2187: 8 miles (13km) NW of Ulverston

At the southern edge of the Lake District National Park, the market town of Broughton-in-Furness, a name that means 'stronghold', was of strategic importance during the times of the Border Troubles and much earlier, lying as it does where the River Duddon broadens into an estuary. The town serves a large rural community of hill farmers, and was once very important for the woollen and cattle trades. A market charter was

amazing collection of carved oak, including a screen thought to date from the early16th century, collegiate stalls and pulpit, and large parts of a Flemish triptych of about 1520. Its finest carving, however, a stunning Flemish reredos, is now displayed in Carlisle Cathedral.

About equidistant between the two churches of Brougham is the **Countess Pillar**, erected in 1656 by Lady Anne Clifford to commemorate her last farewell from her mother forty years before. Margaret Clifford (née Russell: 1560-1616) had been betrothed to George Clifford (1558-1605), the 13th Lord Clifford and 3rd Earl of Cumberland, when they were both children, in the presence of Queen Elizabeth. The pillar is a fine decorative monument which Defoe admired as 'the best and most beautiful piece of its kind in Britain', and which inspired Wordsworth to write a poem.

Brougham Hall, now in ruins, was

granted during Elizabethan times. The town square, where the market was held, is surrounded by chestnut trees, and its set of stocks and fish slabs are reminders of the past.

On the south side of the square is the town hall, which dates from the 18th century and was once a market hall; it now houses the tourist information office. In the middle of the square stands an obelisk erected in 1810 to commemorate the Golden Jubilee of George III, underlining the fact that many of Broughton's houses are Georgian.

For over 400 years only two families held the lordship of Broughton – the earls of Derby, from 1487 until 1651, and then the Sawreys, who were instrumental in building the town hall and market square in 1760.

The importance of Broughton's charter is perpetuated and celebrated to this day when, on the first day of August, at noon, the charter is read out at the Market Cross. Councillors and other civic dignitaries process from the Old King's Head pub – an old coaching inn – and after the **Reading of the Charter**, coins, normally 5p or 10p, are carefully cast into the assembled crowd. Following this everyone repairs for refreshments at the expense of the lord of the manor, these days the county council.

The **church of St Mary Magdelene**, located to the south of the town, was consecrated in 1547, though the doorway is late Norman. Restoration work was carried out in 1874, when the north aisle was built in neo-Norman style. The church has an Elizabethan Bible, and a 15th-century bell, which was rung following the defeat of the Spanish Armada.

Broughton Tower, a spacious mansion, was built around a 14th-century tunnel-vaulted pele tower by the Gilpin Sawreys in the mid-18th century. This and the dungeons are all that remain of an old castle.

An annual **agricultural show**, a combined effort between Millom and Broughton, is held in Broughton during August.

BROUGHTON MILLS [South Lakeland]

SD2290: 2 miles (3km) N of Broughton-in-Furness

The small, quiet, mainly farming community of Broughton Mills lies enfolded within the Dunnerdale Fells along the River Lickle.

The river, which in the past provided power for local woollen, corn and bobbin mills, joins the River Duddon just west of Broughton-in-Furness before reaching the nearby Duddon Estuary. Like so many small villages in Cumbria, Broughton Mills was a quietly industrious place, part of the larger woollen trade of Furness. The remains of kilns can still be found on the surrounding fellsides. These were used both to produce lime for building and use on the land, and to burn bracken to produce potash, which was used to clean wool.

BROUGHTON MOOR [Allerdale]

NY0533: 2 miles (3km) SE of Maryport

Once known as Wyndham Row, Broughton Moor is a former mining village on the outskirts of Maryport.

The **church of St Columba** is a rock-faced structure, built from locally quarried material in 1905 by W D Caröe, an architect who, as Pevsner commented, 'had the virtue of originality'. The church is plain, but pleasingly attractive.

BURGH-BY-SANDS [Carlisle]

NY3259: 5 miles (8km) NW of Carlisle

Pronounced 'Bruff', this small village on the Solway, is noted for the massive tower, thought to date from the mid-14th century, attached to the **church of St Michael**. The dedication of the church goes back at least to the late 12th century, but the exact date of the present building is not known with certainty. The church and its lands and revenue were given to Holme Cultram Abbey around AD1200, and this would suggest that the first building existed here in the mid-12th century.

The church is built within a Roman fort on Hadrian's Wall, and is thought to occupy the site of one of the central buildings of the fort, possibly the granary. The imposing tower, built using stones from the wall, although originally constructed as a belfry, clearly had defence as a primary consideration: it has no doorway to the outside, enormously thick walls, and only small windows. Probably, it is the earliest of three surviving examples in Cumbria of the fortification of churches during the 14th century – other examples exist at Newton Arlosh and Great Salkeld. It was restored in 1883.

The site of the Roman fort of Aballava is now lost beneath the village, with the church almost in its centre.

In its early days many of the village's cottages would have been 'clay daubins', built using the plentiful local supply of clay. Traditionally, the thatched roofs were supported by large tree branches, and the cottages built with thick walls and small windows. There are still a few clay daubin cottages in the village.

Out on the Solway Sands is a **monument** to Edward I (1272-1307), erected in 1685 by the Duke of Norfolk, and restored in 1803 (by the Earl of Lonsdale) and 1878. It commemorates the king, who died on Burgh Sands on 7 July 1307, as he prepared yet again to invade the Scots. The death of Edward I was a turning point in the fortunes of the English army. During the 14th century, the border became difficult to defend, and war was endemic, giving rise to the need for self-help in matters of defence. A need that manifested itself in a spread of pele towers throughout the region, and much further south.

Edward I monument, Burgh-by-Sands

BURNBANKS [Eden]

NY5016: 1½ miles (2km) SW of Bampton

The small, and now partially derelict, village of Burnbanks was originally built to house the workers on the Haweswater Reservoir.

Once described as a most primitive and secluded dale, the most charming and restful in all Lakeland, Mardale, as the valley above Burnbanks is called, is now under water, flooded in 1936 to quench the thirsts of Mancunians. Ironically, the description of the dale was given by a Manchester city councillor, in 1921. In her *Guide to the English Lakes*, Harriet Martineau describes the path to the drowned village of Mardale at the head of the valley, which "winds...round the bases of knolls, past the ruins of the old church, and among snug little farms".

Sheep and dairy cattle had been the mainstay of the dale community for hundreds of years, and early descriptions of the valley mention buildings with huge chimneys in which meat was hung to dry for winter food. It was these selfsame farms that supplied butter and other produce to the distant cities, Manchester included. But it was not enough. As Manchester grew, the need for water exceeded that which could be supplied by Thirlmere, and so Mardale and its farms, its popular Dun Bull Inn, its quiet lanes, and the church of the Holy Trinity (where the last service was held on 18 August 1935), were drowned. During subsequent droughts it is still possible to see the old village lanes and the ruins of its buildings.

BURNESIDE [South Lakeland]
SD5095: 2½ miles (4km) N of Kendal

Closely associated with the manufacture of paper at Croppers Paper Mills, Burneside is now mainly a dormitory suburb of Kendal, and sits astride the River Kent, just outside the Lake District National Park boundary. In earlier times, Burneside was a mainly agricultural and milling settlement. With both the River Kent and the River Sprint embracing the village, there was a plentiful supply of water, which enabled farming and milling to co-exist in harmony. When James Cropper bought the paper mills in 1845, Burneside experienced a period of rapid industrialisation.

The **church of St Oswald** is a quite large church, and has a history that mirrors the increase in Burneside's population as industry expanded. Formerly, the church was no more than a small chapel, superseded in 1826, and added to in 1869. Finally, in 1880-1, the church was almost entirely rebuilt in Westmorland slate.

Tolson Hall, just outside the village, is a large house dated 1638, while **Burne-**

Haweswater reservoir

side **Hall** to the north-east, is a hall-house built around a 14th-century pele tower, that was lived in by the Under Sheriff of Westmorland.

BURTON-IN-KENDAL [South Lakeland]

SD5376: 5 miles (8km) W of Kirkby Lonsdale

Burton-in-Kendal, a pleasing jumble of old cottages and houses and much new building, pre-dates the Domesday Survey. It is chiefly one main street leading into a square flanked by Georgian houses, in a setting that blends easily with the extensive sheep-farming countryside all around.

A market was established here in 1661, to become in time probably the most extensive corn market in the county (then of Westmorland), and only later replaced by sheep farming. It was, too, the improvement of communications with the larger towns of Westmorland and Cumberland that brought about the decline of Burton's market. The 18th-century limestone market cross bears traces of leg irons used to hold lawbreakers.

The village was clearly an important staging post, a place to gather one's resources before setting off for the unknown ordeals of the rugged countryside that surrounds the village. Stone mounting steps outside the King's Arms pub betray its former role, and that of the nearby Royal Hotel, as coaching inns. The first stagecoach came this way in 1763. It is a place where imposing buildings that speak of wealth and prosperity stand (almost) side by side with less prominent buildings, concealed in the nooks and crannies of stabling yards and attractive old streets.

Just west of the village runs the disused

Lancaster Canal, 57 miles of waterway linking Preston and Kendal, mainly in use between 1819 and 1942. The canal wharf, where coal was brought, still exists.

The **church of St James** was originally a Norman church, thought to date from 1180. Most of the church today, which has a Jacobean pulpit, is Perpendicular in style (14th-16th century), and was extensively restored in 1844 and 1872. There are parts of a Saxon cross in the churchyard, which suggests there may have been an earlier church on this site.

BUTTERMERE [Allerdale]

NY1716: 7 miles (11km) SW of Keswick

The delightful village of Buttermere stands between the lake of Buttermere and Crummock Water, both most attractive stretches of water, and surrounded by the high fells of Grasmoor, Robinson and the High Stile ridge. The name Buttermere, however, applies not only to the village, but to the valley, and one of its two lakes.

The whole scene is one of Nature in her most benevolent mood, for here she has bestowed great riches of scenic beauty – swelling peaks, wooded fellsides, grey crags, oases of vivid green, making this one of the most endearing valleys in Lakeland. The poet Robert Southey wrote of Buttermere: 'The hills that, calm and majestic, lifted their heads in the silent sky... Dark and distinct they rose. The clouds have gathered above them, High in the middle air, huge, purple, pillowy masses.' W G Collingwood (1854-1932), sometime private secretary of John Ruskin, in *The Lake Counties*, said 'Buttermere and Crummock are Nature's art for art's sake,' a very apt description.

The village is dominated both by the great fells of Robinson, Hindscarth and Dalehead on the one hand, and the magnificent High Stile ridge on the other. It is down from a small tarn below Red Pike and High Stile that Sour Milk Gill flows, one of the most stunning cascades in Lakeland. At times it is almost dry enough to scramble up, on other occasions the gill is a foaming torrent of white, sweeping all before it as it hurtles headlong for the valley.

The village of Buttermere, however, is renowned for something of a scandal, which occurred at the beginning of the 19th century. At that time, one of the village hotels, The Fish, was kept by a couple called Robinson. They had a stunningly beautiful daughter, Mary, who used to wait at table. When only fourteen, she was remarked upon by Captain Budworth in his book *A Fortnight's Ramble in the Lakes*, and she became something of a local celebrity as the 'Beauty of Buttermere'. When she was twenty-four, Mary caught the eye of a personable visitor to Buttermere, the Honourable Alexander Augustus Hope, Lieutenant-Colonel in the 14th Regiment of Foot, and brother to the Earl of Hopetoun. The colonel wooed and won the **Beauty of Buttermere**, and they were married in Lorton church on 2 October 1802 (coincidentally, only two days before William Wordsworth and Mary Hutchinson were married). Ironically, Coleridge, a long-standing admirer of Mary, wrote a piece on the wedding for the *Morning Post*, where it eventually came to the notice of the genuine Colonel Hope, who had been abroad all summer, for Mary's husband was an impostor.

Inquiries followed which led to the detection of the imposture, when Mary's Colonel Hope was found to be one John Hatfield, who had only recently failed to win the hand of a young lady of fortune in Keswick, but who already had a second wife still living, and children from two marriages. He was eventually hanged in Carlisle in September 1803, not for bigamy, but for forgery. As for Mary, who bore him a child which died, her sorry tale became the stuff of melodrama on the London stage. She married again and lived into old age in the village of Caldbeck, where she is buried in St Kentigern's churchyard.

Scale Force, overlooking and feeding Crummock Water, is the highest waterfall in the Lake District, and was a popular place with Victorian visitors who would reach it by boat, and a short walk, from Buttermere.

The tiny parish **church of St James**, built in 1841, is perched on a hillock above the village, and is a small and peaceful place of repose. For hundreds of years, Buttermere was part of a much larger parish, that of Brigham, and could not justify an ordained priest of its own. Like many other chapels, Buttermere was served by non-ordained readers, one of whom, **Robert Walker** of Seathwaite in Dunnerdale, gained some notoriety as a formidable man in more ways than one. He acquired the name 'Wonderful', becoming the Wonderful Walker, and served Buttermere until 1736, dying at the age of 93 in 1803. He was a painfully frugal man, and in spite of a very low stipend of five pounds per year, managed to leave over £2000 in his will. His character and constitution enabled him to augment his stipend by ploughing fields, spinning cloth, and writing letters for those who could not read or write. He also availed himself of a number of local customs known as clog-shoes, hardensark, whittle-gate and goose-gate, which gave a man in his position the right to claim shoes, clothing, food and lodging from the parish, as well as grazing on the common for his geese.

CALDBECK [Allerdale]

NY3239: 11 miles (17km) SW of Carlisle

Most widely renowned for its association with huntsman John Peel, Caldbeck is nevertheless an attractive and pleasing village in its own right, and has some fine scenery around it. It is an old community, and for centuries was entirely self-sufficient, having almost 2000 inhabitants at the end of the 18th century. The name Caldbeck means 'cold stream' in Old Norse, and indicates that the village evolved where two hill streams meet in the valley below the northern fells. Not surprisingly, the waters were harnessed to provide energy for mills, which once numbered more than a dozen, including a corn mill, built in 1740, and exclusively used by the church.

The church, dedicated to **St Kentigern** (or St Mungo, Bishop of Glasgow, who is said to have preached in Caldbeck in AD553 on his journey from Scotland to Wales), is medieval, and though restored in the 1930s, dates from the 12th century. John Peel lies buried in the churchyard, as does Mary, the Beauty of Buttermere (see Buttermere).

Overlooking the church is the rectory, built in 1785. It has two interesting tripartite Gothic windows.

John Peel (1776-1854), was a Caldbeck man, one of 13 children, who himself fathered 13 children. He and his wife, the 18-year-old daughter of a wealthy farmer from Uldale, were married at Gretna Green after his mother-in-law to be had objected to their marriage. Begrudgingly, the family accepted that the two were indeed married, but insisted on a service of remarriage at Caldbeck church.

It was about this time that Peel started hunting with his own pack of hounds, and often followed them on foot, in the traditional Lakeland manner. He is forever

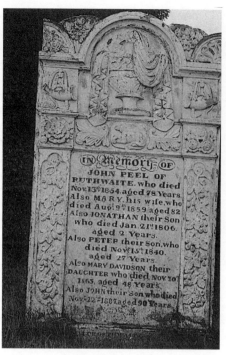

John Peel's grave

immortalised in the verses of *D'ye ken John Peel* written by his friend John Woodcock Graves and set to music by William Metcalfe, organist at Carlisle Cathedral.

A little to the east of the village bridge is a three-bay, single-storeyed cottage, built in 1698 as a **Friends' Meeting House**. Behind the church, **Friar Row** is comprised of stone cottages tiled with Cumberland slate, and built around 1800.

CALDER BRIDGE [Copeland]

NY0305: 3 miles (5km) SE of Egremont

This former agricultural village, between Gosforth and Beckermet, lies on the River Calder, and is now largely a residential area for workers at the Sellafield Nuclear Power Station. Here, as Collingwood describes '...the river tumbles over flat tables of sandstone, very picturesque in its quiet, lowland way'.

During the 12th century, **Calder Abbey** just outside the village, was founded by Ranulph fitz William de Meschines, Lord of Copeland, for the Order of Savigny, an order that was united in 1148 with the Cistercians. The abbey is now in ruins, and on private land. In 1138, less than four years into their possession of the site, raiders burned down the abbey, and drove the twelve resident monks away. They walked to Furness Abbey, but apparently met with a less than welcoming reception, so continued into Yorkshire where, at Byland, they founded another abbey.

The second attempt at building an abbey, probably of wood, was replaced by a stone building in 1180. About 1220, a new stone structure was built, but this, too, received the attention of Scottish raiders, in 1322, following which it was restored. In 1536, at the hands of Henry VIII, Calder Abbey suffered much the same fate as many others, and has changed hands times to reach the present ownership.

The **church of St Bridget** is the parish church of Beckermet, and was built in 1842, to replace the church of the same name at Beckermet.

The village also has the parish church of Ponsonby, mid-way between the two villages. The red sandstone church, which has no dedication, was built in 1840 and added to in 1874. The east window contains glass by William Morris and Sir Edward Burne-Jones. Ponsonby is a small group of houses on the lower slopes of Ponsonby Fell, with a seaward view consumed by the complex of Sellafield.

CALTHWAITE [Eden]

NY4640: 9 miles (14km) S of Wetheral

The isolated community of Calthwaite is set in farmland adjoining the M6, between Penrith and Carlisle.

The name means 'the clearing where calves are kept', a clear indication of the importance of cattle in the area, for a long time the main source of employment.

The church is 20th-century, clean and simple. Before it was built, services were held in the nearby school.

CAMERTON [Allerdale]

NY0330: 3 miles (5km) NE of Workington

Beautifully set on the north bank of the River Derwent, Camerton, like many of its neighbours, was built as a mining village, though the village also prospered by manufacturing bricks.

The **church of St Peter**, extensively restored in 1892, and set in a loop in the river, is built on a site where a church was first erected at least 1000 years ago. Rebuilding took place in 1694 and 1796, and the tower and spire were added in 1855.

The church contains an effigy (early 16th century) in black stone of a knight who died about 1500. He was known as Black Tom of the North or Black Tom Curwen – a descendant of the Curwen family of Curwen Hall, Workington – and was buried at Shap Abbey.

CARK-IN-CARTMEL[South Lakeland]

SD3676: 2 miles (3km) SW of Cartmel

The village of Cark takes its name from the Celtic word 'carrec', meaning rock, and is a compact place overlooking Ulverston sands. The village was the site of a 17th-century paper mill, not far from which a cotton mill was added in 1782. The cotton mill was one of the earliest in England, and cotton was brought by sea to Cark, a busy port at the time.

Cark Hall is a late 16th-century building with mullioned windows and a magnificent late 17th-century doorway with Ionic columns. George Fox was once held prisoner here. The hall was built by Thomas Pickering, and eventually passed by marriage into the Curwen family, and then the Rawlinsons.

CARLISLE [Carlisle]

NY3956: 19 miles (31km) NNW of Penrith

The City of Carlisle, in its present form, came into being in 1974. At that time the Border Rural District, which covered much of the area around the town of Carlisle, was amalgamated with the County Borough of Carlisle, giving the new creation the distinction of being England's largest city (104,010 hectares) in terms of area. Carlisle District now stretches from the Scottish borders in the north almost to the Lake District National Park boundary in the south, and from the Solway coast in the west to the North Pennines in the east, bordering Northumberland.

Throughout its long history, Carlisle's prosperity has pivoted around its position, and continues to do so. The strategic importance of the city goes back over 2000 years. Few other English cities could have experienced as much strife as Carlisle, and there were many times when the words 'border' and 'frontier' were synonymous, indeed, the very name of the city is derived from the Celtic word 'caer', meaning fort. Carlisle was, and had to be, a stronghold if it were to survive.

It is still obviously a Border town where Scottish and English names and accents flow easily together, though there is little today to hint at the troubles the city faced. Nor is it easy to see from ground level how well defended the site of Carlisle was. On one side flows the River Eden, while two other sides are protected by tributaries, the River Petteril and the River Caldew.

For the Romans, the city effectively marked their northern frontier, with their most important monument, Hadrian's Wall, stretching the whole width of England from the Solway Firth to the North Sea.

Agricola and his forces reached Carlisle in about AD80, and built a base which they called Luguvalium; it was during this time that Carlisle acquired the status of a town and administrative centre. Luguvalium was built of turf and wood on the site of the present-day cathedral, but about AD125, the Emperor Hadrian was compelled to consolidate the frontier of his Empire, and did so by commanding the building of the wall that bears his name. During construction of the wall the fort of Luguvalium was demolished, and the city completely replanned as a civil settlement. A new fort, housing the transferred military garrison, was built at Stanwix on the northern outskirts of the city, and was called Petriana.

During the time of the Roman presence in Carlisle, the city experienced a period of peace and prosperity, along with high standards of living not again matched until the 20th century. But by the beginning of the fifth century the Romans had gone, and the years that followed are poorly documented. It was during this time that the British kingdoms were set up, of which Rheged, with its capital at Carlisle, was the most important. Its earliest ruler was Coel Hen, who has travelled down through history to become the 'Old King Cole' of the children's nursery rhyme.

The early Celtic missionaries had converted the people of the region to Christianity, and the place of Carlisle as an important religious centre is evidenced by the existence here of a monastery visited by St Cuthbert in 686, though the exact location is not known.

Towards the end of the 9th century, the Danes destroyed Carlisle, burning it down, demolishing the walls, and killing every man, woman and child, leaving it in such a state that the city was indistinguishable from the surrounding countryside. After this brutal assault, what remained of Carlisle was linked with the Scottish kingdoms of Galloway and Strathclyde in the larger kingdom of Cumbria. In 945, the kingdom came under the control of the Scottish king, Malcolm I, and remained under Scottish jurisdiction until 1070, at which time Carlisle was held by Dolfin, son of Earl Gospatrick of Northumbria. It is because Carlisle was part of Scotland that it escapes mention in the Domesday Book instigated by William the Conqueror.

In 1092, William Rufus, the son of William the Conqueror, advanced on Carlisle in response to one of many raids, and drove out Dolfin, restored the town and built a castle, probably of wood – of which nothing now remains. He brought in people from the southern parts of England – Essex, Kent and Middlesex – to establish the town's economy and develop the surrounding land.

A priory was founded in 1122 by Henry I, William's brother and successor, who recognised the strategic importance of Carlisle. However, by the time Stephen (1135-54) succeeded Henry, a succession that was disputed, Carlisle was once again being fought over. Under King David, the Scots captured it and strengthened its defences during the long Scottish occupation of the northern counties. David died in Carlisle Castle in 1153, and was succeeded by his grandson, Malcolm IV (known as 'The Maiden'), who was forced to surrender the city to Henry II,

who also seized three northern counties, and granted a charter to Carlisle in 1158. Attempts, unsuccessful, were made to recapture Carlisle by Malcolm's successor, William, who also demanded the return of Northumberland. Henry II was back in Carlisle in 1186, and had rooms built for him at the castle, clearly intending its continued use as a royal residence. But from his death, the people of Carlisle never saw their king, Richard I, who was preoccupied with the crusade in the Holy Land.

It was not until the reign of King John (1199-1216), who taxed his Carlisle subjects punitively, and was a most unwelcome visitor, that the Scots, under Alexander II, regained Carlisle when King John's barons rose against him. Meanwhile, the new county of Cumberland subsumed the Norman Honour of Carlisle (1177), following which a basic local government structure evolved based on medieval trades' guilds. The first Mayor of Carlisle, Walkelin de Carlisle, sat from 1240 to 1270, but civic life was very much dominated by a Royal overlord, the Sheriff of Cumberland. The city campaigned to set itself free from this encumbrance, preferring the right to self-government, directly under the Crown itself. In 1277 Carlisle became a bailiwick, or administrative ward in the county of Cumberland, with the right to hold courts in the city. The importance of the city to the Crown cannot be underestimated, and for over 500 years royal interest in local affairs even extended to the appointment of the town clerk, which had to be approved by the monarch.

Under Edward I, Carlisle once again became an important Border fortress and a major military centre, now as part of the king's campaign to impose English sovereignty on Scotland. In March 1296, a surprise attack on Carlisle was one of the opening moves in the Wars of Independence that were to bedevil the next fifty years.

Three Parliaments (1298, 1300 and 1307) were held in Carlisle Castle, by then a royal palace. The last was shortly before the death of Edward I, when the king again visited Carlisle because Robert the Bruce had been crowned King of Scotland.

Edward II was not as strong as his father in resisting the Scots, and Robert the Bruce managed a number of devasting raids across the Border in 1311 (when Lanercost Priory was sacked) and after Bannockburn in 1314. He was, however, unable to take the castle, contenting himself with raids all over Cumbria, including as far south as Furness Abbey. The second stand against Robert the Bruce was made by Sir Andrew de Harcla, constable and Earl of Carlisle. So great, however, was the damage caused by the Bruce's subsequent raids that de Harcla began negotiations aimed at sparing the county from complete destruction. To do so, alas, was treason, and though Edward II was later to enter into a similar arrangement, Sir Andrew was arrested, and in 1323 hanged, drawn and quartered on the charge of conspiracy and treason.

The Border Troubles continued for many years, through the reigns of successive kings – Edward III, Richard II, Henry IV, V and VI, Edward IV, and so on – and during these times the city and its castle received its share of attention. Only after Edward IV had sent Richard of Gloucester to carry out repairs and fortify the stronghold, which he seems to have done with commendable skill, did the Scots start taking less interest in Carlisle. But, as with the countryside that surrounds it, the city felt the impact of years of destruction. As a result, there are few medieval buildings in or around Carlisle today.

Elizabeth I adopted a policy of reconciliation with the Scots, and, apart from a few minor disturbances, a time of relative peace ensued, until, that is, the Civil War heaped more anguish on the city.

Carlisle became the chief Royalist stronghold in the north of England, and held out against a siege by General Lesley with 4000 troops. Cattle and horses consumed, the inhabitants of the castle were in the end reduced to eating hempseed, rats and dogs. Only when they heard of the defeat of the Royalists at Naseby (14 June 1645) did the people of Carlisle finally surrender. By 1647 Carlisle was 'a model of misery and desolation'. George Fox, who visited Carlisle in 1653, commented that the city was, 'A filthy, nasty place…where men and women were put together in a very uncivil manner and the prisoners [were] so lousy that one woman was almost eaten to death by lice.'

After the surrender, the Royalist forces repaired the castle using stones from the abbey and the cathedral, and, with a few minor interruptions, a period of peace ensued, for almost 100 years. During this time, however, the reiving, north of the city, still went on, in spite of legislation that ought to have brought it to an end.

In 1707, during the reign of Queen Anne, the Act of Union finally brought England and Scotland together. James I (1603-1625) had unified the crowns of the two countries, but had not united the countries themselves. In 1707, the last Scottish Parliament assembled, and on 1 May 1707, the 'United Kingdom of Great Britain' came into being. When Daniel Defoe undertook his great journey around England in the early part of the 18th century, he found Carlisle to be 'strong, but small, the buildings old, but the streets fair; the great church is a venerable old pile, it seems to have been built at twice, or, as it were, rebuilt, the upper part being much more modern than the lower'.

Defoe's description was written before Prince Charles Edward Stuart (Bonnie Prince Charlie) had landed in Scotland to set about claiming the thrones of England and Scotland for his father. The 1745 rebellion began with capture for Carlisle, by now a city with poor defences and even poorer spirit among its inhabitants. In November 1745, the prince's men, commanded by the Duke of Perth, took the city after only a week, and on the day of surrender, the 17th, the prince entered Carlisle and King James III was proclaimed from Carlisle Cross. Less than a week later the prince marched on Penrith, but returned on 19 December, defeated, and retreated northwards across the Border. He was hotly pursued by the Duke of Cumberland ('The Butcher'), who took the castle without difficulty against the mere 400 troops the prince had left to make a stand.

The aftermath of the subsequent defeat at Culloden was an appalling time. The castle and the cathedral were filled with prisoners, many of whom died from disease, or by hanging, others were transported. Troops billeted in the town added to the overcrowding and further reduced already sparse food supplies.

But after all this trouble, peace finally returned to Carlisle. By 1773 life in the city had changed considerably for the better; the streets were clean and tidy, and modern houses had been built. Just before Christmas of that year, the first Sunday stagecoach service to London ran, a journey that took three days. Twelve years later the first mail coach arrived in Carlisle.

Carlisle is today the 'capital' of Cumbria, housing most of the administrative offices, and a range of other important services, including television, radio, and airfield and a main line railway station.

Its industries today are wide-ranging, from machinery construction to food production and textile manufacture. At the start of the 19th century, the textile trade in particular was well established in Carlisle, but there were then many more trades including soap manufacturers, tanners, banks, breweries and foundries. The business of weaving did not prosper for long, and ended when in 1819, the weavers petitioned to be sent to America because of the poor conditions in which they lived and worked.

By the end of the 19th century, the population of Carlisle had increased fourfold, and substantial improvements were to be found both in the appearance of the city and in the conditions in which people lived. Streets now had lighting, the first theatres were being built, a police force operated within the city, a gas supply was connected. It was from this time that the embryo city administration as it exists today was born, and the last of the squalid conditions observed down the centuries finally banished.

Today, the city and its surrounding villages lie in a high-quality rural environment dominated by the Solway Plain, across which the landscape is primarily one of farmland with hedgerows and woodlands. The river valleys – the Eden, the Caldew and the Petteril – are a distinctive feature of the urban scene, and provide a visually rich and attractive environment, within which there are several important 'green' areas of open space, predominantly agricultural and parkland.

The wider rural area comprises open countryside of high landscape value, and includes two Areas of Outstanding Natural Beauty, the North Pennines and the Solway Coast, along with Sites of Special Scientific Interest (SSSI) and important nature reserves. The King's Forest of Geltsdale, to the east and on the edge of the North Pennines, is both a SSSI and a Royal Society for the Protection of Birds Nature Reserve, characterised by wild heather moorland, blanket bog and acid grassland.

In the west the Solway Coast largely comprises open salt marsh, the Upper Solway Flats, an area that is also a SSSI, and a Special Protection Area under the EC Directive on the Conservation of Wild Birds. Along with wetland sites of international importance, Carlisle maintains 26 SSSIs, some of which are found in the upland area of the Bewcastle Fells and the woodland gorges of the River Lyne, and others near the River Irthing, a river forming the boundary between the North Pennines and the Bewcastle Fells.

Carlisle Cathedral was founded in 1122 as a Norman priory for Augustinian canons. Its most outstanding feature is its small size, among the English cathedrals only Oxford is smaller. It was not always thus.

Around 1102, Henry I granted a site at Carlisle for the foundation of a religious building, but this may not have been started until Ranulph de Meschines had left Carlisle and Henry had taken over. He it was who established the Augustinian canons, and in 1133 Henry made the town the see of a bishop. The priory accordingly became a cathedral, the only Augustinian house in England to achieve such a status. It was at this time that the greatest period of building took place, and, at one time, the nave had as many as eight bays, of which only two survive. The attentions of Parliamentarian forces during the Civil War, preceded by a serious fire in 1292, combined with friable

stonework, has meant that very little of the original building survives; what does remain can be found in the south transept and the nave. Much of the building material for the cathedral probably came from Hadrian's Wall or the remains of the Roman fort, Luguvalium. These parts of the building are of dark grey stone, contrasting with the more extensive red sandstone of later building periods.

In the 14th century the cathedral still had its nave, and much of the building was in the form seen today. The north transept and the crossing tower is attributed to Bishop Strickland (1400-19), along with other internal works, including some outstanding misericords.

It was the Civil War, of course, that led to much of the devastation of the cathedral, though it is certain the building was already structurally poor after years of neglect. Long after the nave was demolished, a parish church of St Mary was built in its place, but this was pulled down in 1954. Much of the cathedral was restored during Victorian times, bringing it into the state in which it stands today.

The **church of St Cuthbert**, off the Market Place, is the principal parish church of Carlisle. It was built in red and grey stone in 1778, with a tower, a nave of eight bays and a low chancel. Next to appear was the Georgian **church of the Holy Trinity** in Wigton Road, built between 1828 and 1830 as a Commissioners' church, and costing £6894. This was built in beige stone and considered to be an excellent example of its type. There are more churches, mainly Victorian, in the city, notably the **church of St Aidan** in Warwick Road (1899-1902), built in the Decorated style; the **church of St James** (1865-7), in St James's Road, built in a prime suburb of Carlisle; the **church of St John the Evangelist** in London Road (1867); the Roman Catholic **church of Our Lady and St Joseph** in Warwick Square (1891-3) and the **church of St Paul** in Lonsdale Street (1868-75). All are fine examples of their type, for those who are students of architecture or churches in particular.

Carlisle Museum (Tullie House), in Carlisle Street, is an award-winning museum and art gallery, with displays telling much of the history of the city from Roman times and beyond. A rich collection of regional importance includes archaeology, natural history and Carlisle's social history.

The story of **Carlisle Castle**, now in the custody of English Heritage, is inevitably linked with that of the town. The keep is the oldest surviving building, and dates from the 12th century, though there were much earlier fortifications on the site. The castle has seen 800 years of military use. It commanded the western end of the Anglo-Scottish border, and was besieged on many occasions.

Carlisle's loss of status as a frontier town was compensated by its increasing importance as a place of regional government, and the castle became the headquarters of the Warden of the Western March. The rebuilding of the castle began in 1378, during the reign of Richard II. More rebuilding, restoration and additions followed over the ensuing centuries. In 1568 the castle effectively became the prison of Mary, Queen of Scots, until she was taken to more secure imprisonment at Bolton Castle. The castle, clearly, was not the greatest of strongholds as a prison. Indeed, in 1596 one of the Border reivers, Kinmont Willie, was rescued by Walter Scott of Buccleugh. When surveyed by the Crown in 1604, it was in a very sad state and by the time of the Civil War, the castle had to be refortified, yet again. After the Jacobite rebellions, custody of Carlisle was given to its

civilians, and the castle may well have crumbled had not the French Revolution occurred. When the Bastille fell, no English 'tory' felt safe, and Royalist Carlisle became a place of radicals. Anti-slavery campaigners came in 1792, corn rioters in 1795, and machine breakers in 1809. As a result, a large armoury was built at the castle and filled with arms. Such a 'prize' then needed to be guarded, and so in 1819, with the radicals marching on the city, soldiers returned to Carlisle Castle. The new armoury was converted to barracks in 1827, a military prison was built in 1840, and yet more additions and alterations took place.

When the castle was no longer under threat, a reorganisation of the army district took place, and Carlisle became the training centre of the 34th Cumberland and 55th Westmorland Regiments, which were to amalgamate in 1881 as the Border Regiment. Ever since, the castle has been home to the military. In 1959, another amalgamation took place, and the centre was closed, but the castle today remains the headquarters of the King's Own Royal Border Regiment.

Located within Carlisle Castle, the **Border Regiment and King's Own Royal Border Regiment Museum** relates the history of Cumbria's County Infantry Regiment from 1702 to the present time. Displays comprise uniforms, weapons, equipment, medals, memorabilia, dioramas, and so on.

Carlisle boasts the only museum to be located at a 'live' airport; the **Solway Aviation Museum** houses a range of exhibits that largely date from the Second World War.

Carlisle Canal, which linked the city with Port Carlisle on the Solway, was opened on 12 March 1823, and reduced the cost of transportation of goods such as cotton, sugar, wine, cheese and coal.

The canal represents part of Carlisle's attempts to reach the sea, and was built at a time of canal mania, when it may well have been possible to envisage ships sailing across the width of England from the Solway to the east coast. The canal, originally intended to be built as far as Maryport, only reached a small hamlet called Fisher's Cross, just east of Bowness-on-Solway, which later assumed the title of Port Carlisle. But the prosperity of the canal was short-lived, and its end signalled by the coming of the Maryport and Carlisle Railway, which benefited from the boom times of the coal, iron and steel industries of West Cumberland. The canal was filled in, and the railway track laid over it in 1854.

Hadrian's Wall, much of which has subsequently gone into building large parts of the city, was built from AD122 under the supervision of Aulus Platorius Nepos, and stretched from coast to coast across England, a distance of 80 Roman miles (73 imperial miles). It was dotted along its length by small forts, each a mile from the next, with turrets built between them. In front of the wall was a deep ditch, and behind the wall, a great earthwork, the Vallum. The wall is the product of Emperor Hadrian's desire '...to separate the Romans from the barbarians'. This comment, in Latin '...qui barbaros Romanosque divideret', is the only surviving comment on the reason for the building of the Wall.

Around AD140, when the Antonine Wall was built further north, Hadrian's Wall was evacuated. But when the Brigantes revolted in 155, the Antonine Wall was evacuated, and Hadrian's Wall soon recommissioned. This process was repeated a few years later, and by about 163 Hadrian's Wall was fully regarrisoned.

Carlisle is a focal point for the wall, which ran through the northern part of the city. Not all of the wall remains, nor is there much in a good state of preservation. The western part was constructed not of stone, but turf, and so was more susceptible to collapse, though it was less likely to be vandalised by later generations, who pillaged the stone sections for building.

CARTMEL [South Lakeland]

SD3878: 13 miles (20km) SW of Kendal.

Cartmel is an attractive village on the River Aye, and stands on a broad peninsula projecting into the tidal River Kent and Morecambe Bay. The village gathers about a square with tiny, cobbled forecourts, while elsewhere the architectural merit of the village is displayed in bow-windowed cottages and others of considerable character and charm. Not surprisingly the village is popular with artists, and in its heyday as a market town was the focal point for the commerce of neighbouring villages.

During the 7th century the lands of Cartmel were granted to St Cuthbert by the king of Northumbria, Ecgfrith, for the sole purpose of establishing a monastery. No trace of the monastery remains, but the village has much of historical interest.

Its most notable feature is the **Priory church of St Mary and St Michael**, a noted monastic church, built with the style and grandeur that elsewhere hallmarks cathedrals. It is without doubt one of the wonders of England, and the largest intact medieval church between Chester and Carlisle. It dominates the village, and dates from about 1190, when the Baron of Cartmel, William Marshall (who later became the 2nd Earl of Pembroke), had a vision in which he saw St Cuthbert, who ordered him to build a priory next to water. Consequently, he founded an Augustinian priory in Cartmel, and endowed it with the manor and all the lands of Cartmel, as well as some lands in Ireland. He ordained that the priory should be free from subjection to other religious orders, and that there should be a priesthood established to serve the people.

Most of the priory buildings were destroyed during the Dissolution of the Monasteries (1536-9), though part of the building was left to serve as the parish church, thanks to that apparently minor condition imposed by William Marshall. When the monasteries were being demolished, the people of Cartmel claimed a parochial right, and appealed to London for guidance. When the decision came it explained that Henry VIII's law concerned the dissolution of monasteries, not parish churches, and that if the people could prove a parochial right, as, indeed, in Cartmel they could, then the right would be respected.

Holes in the south-west door of the church, known as Cromwell's Door, are said to be bullet holes made by locals firing at Cromwell's soldiers who had used the church as stabling for their horses.

Today, only the picturesque gatehouse of the priory remains, standing in the village square, and this is in the custody of the National Trust. From 1624 to 1790 it was used as a grammar school.

The church is well endowed with fine examples of carved oak, a 15th-century stained glass window, and the mid-14th-century tomb of the 1st Lord Harrington, inserted in an arch between the chancel and the south chapel, and one of the most interesting of its time.

Cartmel was for many years the northern end of the treacherous cross-sands route over Morecambe Bay, and an old-fashioned fingerpost, giving the 'over-the-sands' distance to Lancaster and Ulverston, serves as a reminder of days when travellers preferred to engage the risks of the tidal estuary rather than embark on lengthy detours. In spite of guidance from the priors of Cartmel, many travellers who failed to beat the incoming tide are buried in the churchyard.

According to legend, it was the monks of Cartmel Priory who started the Cartmel Races as their Whitsuntide recreation, an event that continues to this day in May and August. The village also holds an annual **agricultural show** in August.

CARTMEL FELL
[South Lakeland]

SD4188: 5½ miles (9km) S of Bowness-on-Windermere

Cartmel Fell is a small, unspoilt hamlet concealed among the wooded fells above the River Winster, at the southern end of Windermere, and formerly in the county of Lancashire. There is a good view of Whitbarrow Scar in one direction and the Coniston Fells in the other.

The **church of St Anthony** is a fascinating and thoroughly delightful pre-Reformation church, thought to have been built around 1505 to serve the community of hill farmers. It is solidly built and contains a rare triple-decker pulpit of 1698, and a pew that was made in 1571 out of the old chancel screen. The church, which is believed to be the only church in northern England dedicated to St Anthony, also contains some very attractive stained glass from the early 15th century, showing St Anthony, St Leonard and the seven sacraments. In *Helbeck of Bannisdale*, Mrs Humphry Ward (1851-1920), Tasmanian-born English novelist, described the church, 'Above the moth-eaten table that replaced the ancient altar there still rose a window that breathed the very *secreta* of the old faith – a window of radiant fragments, piercing the twilight of the little church with strange, uncomprehended things...'

CASTERTON [Eden]

SD6279: 1 mile (2km) NE of Kirkby Lonsdale

Casterton is an attractive village of grey stone houses among the hills above the River Lune. The name of the village means 'the place by a fort', and suggests that there may have been a Roman fort along the road that runs nearby.Charlotte Brontë and her sisters are known to have received some of their education at nearby Cowan Bridge in 1824 at a School for Clergymen's Daughters. The school moved to Casterton in 1833, and is referred to by Charlotte in *Jane Eyre*.

The grey stone **Holy Trinity** church was built by William Carus-Wilson in 1831-3 as a chapel for the school. It contains large wall paintings and stained glass in pre-Raphaelite style by Henry Holiday (1839-1927), a friend of Edward Burne-Jones.

The name of the Carus family features regularly in the history of this region. The family acquired the manor of Kirkby Lonsdale in the 16th century, while a descendant married Elizabeth Wilson, and in the process regained Casterton Hall. From that time on, he used the name Carus-Wilson, and it was his eldest son who founded the school at Cowan Bridge and built Holy Trinity.

CASTLE CARROCK [Carlisle]

NY5455: 4 miles (6km) S of Brampton

Built on rising ground on the western edge of the north Pennines, the village of Castle Carrock has a fine view across the Eden valley. The high vantage point may well have influenced the first settlers in this area, for there is evidence of a Bronze Age burial site on Cardunneth Pike to the south of the village.

The **church of St Peter** was rebuilt on its original site in 1828, and, according to Pevsner, 'violently normanized' internally sixty years later.

It has been suggested that a large stone in a field near the village is all that remains of an early pele tower, the stonework of which may well have gone into the building of the church. There was certainly no castle here, or at least no evidence of one, in spite of the name. It may be that 'carrock' is a corruption of 'currack', a name for a large pile of stones, such as that on Cardunneth – but this is pure conjecture.

CHAPEL STILE [South Lakeland]

NY3205: 4 miles (6km) W of Ambleside

Chapel Stile, the main village of Langdale, has many older houses of slate, built mainly to house quarrymen, though new houses were built during the 1980s.

The population of the village increased dramatically during the 19th century with the opening of a gunpowder works, introduced to meet the needs of the local quarries, when their beautiful green slate was in great demand.

The **church of Holy Trinity** is a large church built, in 13th-century style in 1857, of green slate from the nearby Silver How quarry. It replaced a chapel built a century earlier, the curate of which was so poor he found it necessary to sell ale to support himself and his family. Nor was the old chapel much better off, for, as Harriet Martineau recorded in her *Guide* *to the English Lakes*, the pulpit collapsed with the minister in it, just after he had started his sermon. Apparently the text was 'And, behold I come quickly' (Revelation 22:12), undoubtedly more prophetic than he intended.

CLAPPERSGATE
[South Lakeland]

NY3603: 1 mile (2km) SW of Ambleside

Clappersgate is a small residential and farming suburb of Ambleside on the River Brathay, at the head of Windermere. Strange as it may seem, the village was once classified as a port, because it had a wharf on the Brathay, from which slate was taken to Windermere and on down the lake.

CLEATOR [Copeland]

NY0115: 2 miles (3km) N of Egremont

The village of Cleator lies to the south of Cleator Moor, and shares much the same history. It, too, is an old village that expanded with the iron industry boom, and in so doing lost what charm it had, though it still retains its village character. Many of the houses, built in long, unattractive terraces to a common pattern, provided for the demand of incoming miners.

But Cleator was not alone in bearing the impact of industrial expansion; other nearby villages – Frizington, Arlecdon and Cleator Moor – also developed rapidly. Between 1840 and 1880 they accommodated a population expansion that went from 835 to more than 17,000, with the number of miners rising one hundredfold from the sixty that lived there in 1840. Statistics, alas, tell little of the real story of this beautiful part of Cumbria, a story of social problems and of hard-drinking men who brought with them, whether from Ireland, Scotland, Cornwall, Northumberland, Lancashire or Yorkshire, an atmosphere closer to the Klondike days that North America had yet to face, than to the true character of northern England.

The **church of St Leonard** is a red sandstone building, off the main street. It was built in 1841, with additions in 1900-4, though a church has been on this site since the 12th century, and the possibility exists of an even earlier church here. The same can be said of the ornate Roman Catholic **church of Our Lady of the Sacred Heart** at the northern end of the village. It was built by Pugin in 1856, and is thought to be on the site of a pre-Reformation chapel.

CLEATOR MOOR [Copeland]

NY0115: 2½ miles (4km) N of Egremont

The former iron mining, now largely agricultural, village of Cleator Moor is bordering on a small town. It has a rectangular market place and adjoins the River Ehen, known locally as Hen Beck, at the western edge of the high Lakeland fells.

The **church of St John the Evangelist** is a neo-Norman church built between 1870 and 1872.

The **church of St Mary** (RC) was designed, like the nearby church at Cleator, by August Pugin (1812-52), the London-born son of a French architectural draughtsman, Auguste Pugin, and has a grotto similar to the one at Lourdes in France. Each September, a pilgrimage to the grotto attracts visitors from far and wide.

CLIBURN [Eden]

NY5824: 6½ miles (10km) NW of Appleby-in-Westmorland

The village of Cliburn is a small farming community on the River Leith, a tributary of the River Eden. The name means 'cliff stream', aptly so since the Leith has worn a way through rock to form a river cliff about 30ft (10m) high. Attractive sandstone houses, most of which are 18th or 19th century, flank the main street, though the area was probably well settled before the Normans arrived.

The largely Norman **church of St Cuthbert** was restored in 1886-7, and contains one of the best-preserved Jerusalem Crosses in Britain. The cross is made from Gethsemane olive inlaid with ebony and mother of pearl, and is believed to have come from the Vallambrossa Monastery in Italy, where it had been for 700 years. It was given to the church by Admiral Christopher Cleborne of the US Navy, a descendant of the Cliburns of Cliburn Hall.

Cliburn Hall, now a farmhouse, was built around a 14th-century pele tower by the lord of the manor, Robert de Cliburn.

CLIFTON [Eden]

NY5326: 2 miles (3km) S of Penrith

Only the 15th-century pele tower remains of Clifton Hall, at the northern end of the village of Clifton. The 13th-century Norman **church of St Cuthbert** is older, but had the benefit of restoration with original materials in 1846. The church is traditionally one of the numerous places where the monks of Lindisfarne rested with the saint's body as they fled from the Danes in the 9th century.

The west coast railway line passes through the village, which used to have two stations. At one, Lord Lonsdale, of nearby Lowther, had a private waiting room and a personal siding for loading his household luggage. Now the village also echoes to the sound of traffic on the A6 and M6.

On nearby **Clifton Moor** the advance party of the Duke of Cumberland's army caught up with the rearguard of Bonnie Prince Charlie's forces as they retreated from Derby to eventual defeat at Culloden in 1746. The battle at Clifton was, therefore, the last on English soil of the Jacobite Rebellion. A stone in the churchyard marks the spot where some of Cumberland's men were buried, while at the southern edge of the village, at Town End, stands an old oak tree, called the Rebel Tree, under which the Highlanders were buried.

Collingwood, in *The Lake Counties*, records the custom of Penrith folk to indulge in 'well-wakings', when they used to meet at local wells – Clifton was the second Sunday in the month – to drink the water with 'Spanish juice' (presumably sherry). By the early 19th century, the practice had stopped because 'they led to mischief'.

Clifton was the birthplace of **John Wilkinson** (1728-1808), the son of a farmer who by 1750 had become an ironmaster near Wrexham. John followed his father into iron founding, and by 1770 was in charge of three furnaces manufacturing grenades, shells and cannon, as well as castings for domestic and industrial use. Wilkinson was one of the principal promoters of the iron bridge at Coalbrookdale in Shropshire.

COCKERMOUTH [Allerdale]

NY1230: 8 miles (13km) E of Workington

The town of Cockermouth is renowned today as the birthplace of William Wordsworth on 7 April 1770, and his sister, Dorothy, the following year. The house, known as Wordsworth House, still stands in Main Street, a north-country Georgian town house built in 1745, and then owned by Sir James Lowther of

Lowther Castle. William and Dorothy's father was an agent for Sir James, and in consequence lived in the house rent-free. The house is today in the care of the National Trust, and includes furniture and effects of the family. The original staircase, fireplaces and panelling also remain. The River Derwent runs behind the house, and is referred to in *The Prelude*, by William. Elsewhere Wordsworth tells how as a child he played among the ruins of Cockermouth Castle, chased butterflies on the green, and climbed on the walls.

Then, as now, Cockermouth, which stands between two hills, was a bright and cheerful little market town. Its name comes from the River Cocker, which flows into the River Derwent. The town is a complex arrangement of old streets, alleyways and yards, in many of which the weekly market is held.

Above Market Place stands the **church of All Saints**, a Victorian church, with a stained glass window that commemorates Wordsworth, whose father's grave is in the churchyard. Near the church, a hall stands on the site of the old grammar school, where Wordsworth was educated for a time.

On one of the hills between which Cockermouth is sandwiched, stands the castle, largely dating from the 14th century, but built on the site of an earlier castle thought to have been constructed in 1134 by Waltheof, a Scottish noble and son of the Earl of Dunbar. It is now largely in ruins.

In 1221, Henry III ordered the Sheriff of Westmorland to destroy the castle at Cockermouth, then held by the Earl of Albemarle, William de Fortibus. Subsequently, the earl found favour again, and was able to rebuild his castle, a triangular structure, though it appears to have been done rather hurriedly: either against the

vagaries of Royal favour or in readiness for assault from the north.

This early castle had a number of distinguished occupants – Edmund Crouchback, the Crusader, Earl of Lancaster and brother of Edward I; Piers Gaveston, the favourite of Edward II; then Sir Andrew de Harcla, the Earl of Carlisle (see also Carlisle). Sir Andrew was taken prisoner on a charge of conscpiracy and treason by Anthony de Luci, who received Cockermouth as his reward, in 1323.

The Scots attacked the castle in 1387, and burned it down, but not so efficiently that Henry Percy, Earl of Northumberland, was prevented from completing work on it, including a gatehouse and dungeons.

In 1568, Mary, Queen of Scots spent a night here on her way from Workington to temporary imprisonment at Carlisle.

The castle was besieged by Royalist forces in 1648 during the Civil War, and though relieved, began a steady decline into ruin.

Winner of the 1995 National Heritage Shoestring Award, the **Cumberland Toy and Model Museum**, at Banks Court, Market Place, specialises in mainly British toys from 1900 onwards.

At 102 Main Street is **The Working Museum of Printing**, which contains a varied range of printing presses and equipment brought together from all over Britain.

COLBY [Eden]

NY6620: 1 mile (2km) W of Appleby-in-Westmorland

An extended linear village on Hoff Beck, Colby is close to but not quite part of the market town of Appleby-in-Westmorland.

The village dates from at least the 11th

century, when the Colby family owned it – hence the name. Most of the properties today are in the familiar red sandstone of the region, and some date back to the 17th century. It was the practice here, as elsewhere, to block up windows in excess of seven to avoid the penalty of the unpopular 'Window Tax' introduced by William Pitt the Younger, when he was Prime Minister between 1783 and 1801.

COLTHOUSE [South Lakeland]
SD3598: ½ mile (1km) E of Hawkshead

Very much in the shadow of nearby Hawkshead, the tiny village of Colthouse, hard pressed against the slopes of Latterbarrow, would undoubtedly pass its days in happy oblivion had not two events made it forever a place of modest pilgrimage. The first was the visit of George Fox to Hawkshead in 1653, following which Colthouse became an important Quaker centre. It still has a Friends' Meeting House, built in 1688. This was a time of persecution, the Toleration Act, granting freedom of worship, was still a year away, and religious meetings such as those inspired by Fox had to be held in secret.

The second, probably less momentous, but still responsible for gathering a few visitors each year, is the fact that while attending school in Hawkshead, William Wordsworth lodged at Colthouse with Ann Tyson (see Hawkshead).

COLTON [South Lakeland]
SD3186: 5 miles (8km) N of Ulverston

Colton is a tiny hamlet, no more than a handful of farms and cottages, tucked away among the unspoilt folds of the Furness Fells, east of the southernmost tip of Lake Windermere.

The **church of the Holy Trinity**, by far the most ancient of the buildings in the village, also serves the nearby village of Bouth. It is a delightful church, on the site of a chapel that existed in the 15th century. After the dissolution of the abbey, the church was enlarged and consecrated in 1578 by Archbishop Sandys, who was born at Satterthwaite in Grisedale Forest. Holy Trinity was rebuilt in 1600, enlarged in the 18th century, and extensively altered in 1840, 1890 and 1952. As a result, the overall impression is of a Victorian church.

CONISTON [South Lakeland]
SD3097: 6 miles (10km) SW of Ambleside

Dominated by the Coniston Fells, which rise to the summit of the **Old Man of Coniston** (2634ft/803m), the village of Coniston is one of the most popular places in the Lake District. Its name derives from the Anglo-Saxon for the 'king's village'. The fells that surround it have the characteristic ruggedness of Borrowdale Volcanics, yet the village is built on slates and shales.

In spite of the development nearby of slate quarries and copper mines that in the 19th century brought the village much of its prosperity, the character of the village, which gathers about its fine church of St Andrew, remains largely unaffected. A number of the terraced cottages date from the mid-18th century. At that time, the cottages and the whole of the area of Furness formed part of the county of Lancashire, which lost its portion of Lakeland to Cumbria in the local government reorganisation of 1974.

The **copper mines**, for which the area is renowned, probably date from Norman times, but were primarily worked

from the 16th century, when, as at Newlands, German miners were used. The
main valley rising along Church Beck
into the fells is still known as Coppermi-
nes Valley, and was the scene of considerable mining activity until the end of the
First World War. The ore was taken out
of Coniston on a railway opened in 1859,
which linked with the Furness Railway
near Broughton-in-Furness; now only the
trackbed remains.

The beauty of both the village and the
valley of Coniston has attracted many
people since the days of the first Viking
invaders. **Tennyson** (1809-92) spent part
of his honeymoon in Coniston; **William
Gershom Collingwood** (1854-1932),
the English artist and archaeologist,
moved to Coniston to be private secretary
and collaborator to John Ruskin, and **Arthur Ransome** (1884-1967), the journalist and writer of children's books, made
Coniston the setting for *Swallows and
Amazons*, and used Peel Island at the

southern end of Coniston Water as his
'Wild Cat Island'.

Poet, art critic and social reformer
John Ruskin is closely associated with
Coniston. He lived at Brantwood, on the
shores of Coniston Water, from 1871 until his death in 1900, and brought a pro-
found and enduring influence to bear on
the world of art of his time. Spending the
last years of his life at Brantwood,
Ruskin declined the prospect of burial in
Westminster Abbey and lies buried in the
churchyard in Coniston. Brantwood now
houses a museum commemorating his
life and work.

Brantwood is one of the most beautifully situated houses in the Lake District,
and enjoys fine views both of Coniston
Water and the Coniston Fells. During
Ruskin's time there – he bought it in
1871 for £1500 – Brantwood became one
of the greatest literary and artistic centres
in Europe. Ruskin himself was one of the
most respected figures of the Victorian

Coniston: village street

The grave of John Ruskin

long, and was used during Donald Campbell's ill-fated attempt at the world water-speed record in 1967. His jet-powered boat, *Bluebird*, went out of control as he attempted to become the first man to break 300mph on water, and Campbell was killed; his body has never been found.

Before the arrival of cars, Coniston Water was an immensely popular lake with visitors who would use the Furness Railway. This was an especially attractive proposition, as the railway company operated a steamer service on the lake using, *The Gondola*. First launched in 1859, *The Gondola* stood unused for a long time at the southern end of the lake, but it was restored and brought back into service in 1980. Arthur Ransome, as a child, was allowed to steer the boat, and the experience was turned into Captain Flint's houseboat in *Swallows and Amazons* and *Winter Holiday*.

There is evidence of human settlement around Consiton since Bronze Age times, with considerable expansion of human presence in Norse times. Indeed, the lake was formerly known as Thurston's Mere, the mere of the lord Thurston.

Following the Norman Conquest, much of the land where Coniston now stands came under the control of Furness Abbey, which heralded a period of much exploitation of woodland, for charcoal, and the fells themselves, for minerals. Charcoal, needed for iron-smelting, was a major industry in these parts, and made enormous demands on the woodlands. So vital was the charcoal to this process that iron ore was often carried to the woodlands, rather than the other way round, and as a result a number of small smelting sites, or bloomeries, were established, traces of which can still be found along the lakeside. This industry

age, a social revolutionary, as well as a poet, artist, prophet, critic, and first Slade Professor of Fine Art at Oxford, who counted among his disciples such notables as Tolstoy, Marcel Proust and Mahatma Gandhi. A keen conservationist, Ruskin foresaw the 'greenhouse effect' more than 100 years ago, and many people have been as inspired by him, as he was by the landscape around his home.

Further examples of Ruskin's work are gathered in the **Ruskin Museum** in Yewdale Road, alongside features of local interest, including Sir Malcolm and Donald Campbell and *Bluebird*.

The nearby **Coniston Water** is one of the longest straight stretches of placid water in the Lake District, 5 miles (8km) seems to have gone on from the 15th to the 17th century, and resulted in the fell-sides, once densely wooded, being denuded of great swathes of their tree cover. Now there is no natural woodland left; what trees are seen were planted during the 19th century and later.

Coniston Hall, a short way to the south of the village, is a 16th-century farmhouse, with, as Coleridge noted 'four Round Chimneys'.

A short distance to the north of Coniston is **Tarn Hows**, a popular beauty spot. The tarn is strictly an artificial pond created by damming a stream and a few pools of marshland. The area around Tarn Hows is now in the care of the National Trust, and was once owned by Beatrix Potter (Mrs William Heelis: 1866-1943), the author and illustrator of books for children, including Peter Rabbit, Jemima Puddle-Duck, Mrs Tiggy-Winkle and others. She sold half of the Tarn Hows area to the National Trust at cost, and bequeathed the other half.

The first accepted tourist ascent of the Old Man of Coniston is accorded to **Captain Joseph Budworth**, in 1792. On what he described as a 'rest day' from his travels in Lakeland, Budworth walked from Ambleside to look at Coniston Water, but could not resist the challenge of the high fells above the village. Sustained only by brandy, he made the first ascent...and then walked back to Ambleside.

CORNEY [Copeland]

SD1191: 2 miles (3km) N of Bootle

The small coastal village of Corney lies at the foot of the fell that takes its name. There is ample evidence on the fells and along the coastal lands that prehistoric man settled here, and remained here for some time.

The village today is almost entirely given to farming, and it was a self-contained community during the 18th and 19th centuries, centred on its inn, which was built c1800.

The **church of St John the Baptist** is an old church of simple design but in mixed styles, and largely restored in 1882. It is built on the site of an older church, probably of the 12th century.

The village is the birthplace of **Edward Troughton** (1753-1835), an instrument maker who left Corney to make his fortune in London. With his brother, John, they produced a number of precision surveying and measuring instruments. It was Edward who developed the equatorial mounting for astronomical telescopes, which soon became the standard mounting for all large instruments.

COTEHILL [Carlisle]

NY4650: 4 miles (6km) S of Warwick Bridge

Cotehill is a pleasant village set on farmland slopes above the River Eden, south of the town of Wetheral. As its name suggests, it stands high on a hillside, and has good views of the north Pennine hills.

The **church of St John the Evangelist** was built in 1868, and has an attractive east window, possibly influenced by the work of William Morris, and a beehive-shaped bell tower, an unusual design.

CROGLIN [Eden]

NY5747: 8½ miles (13km) SE of Warwick Bridge

Croglin is a small, pleasant village, one of many along the western base of the north Pennines, where Croglin Water flows down from Black Fell. It is an ancient village, attacked by Scottish raiders in 1346, and has had a church since Norman times. The present **church of St John the Baptist** was rebuilt in 1878 on the site of the Norman church, and opposite it is the old rectory pele tower of uncertain date.

Built around the village is the tale of the **Croglin Vampire** which appears in *The Story of my Life* by Augustus Hare, and is claimed to have been told by a man whose family once owned Croglin Grange. One summer's evening, so the story goes, a woman was attacked by a hideous creature with flaming eyes, which entered her room and bit into her neck. When she screamed, the creature fled. A year later the creature again appeared, but this time one of the woman's brothers managed to shoot it in the leg as it fled. They followed it into the churchyard, and the next day opened the vault into which they had seen it disappear. It held a dead, withered, hideous figure, which inexplicably bore the marks of a fresh pistol shot in its leg!

CROOK [South Lakeland]

SD4695: 4 miles (6km) NW of Kendal

Crook is a pleasant village along the road between Kendal and Bowness-on-Windermere. It is a linear village, with no real centre, and these days functions mainly as an accommodation centre within the Lakeland tourism industry. In the past the village supported a number of mills, manufacturing worsted cloth. Almost all traces of this industry are, however, now gone, along with corn mills, bobbin mills and wood-related businesses.

The roughcast, almost barn-like **church of St Catherine**, was built in 1887, and contains a bell from the 14th century, the only thing that remains of the earliest church here, the site of which is unknown. The bell is almost certainly one of the oldest in northern England. Not far from St Catherine's, on a hill to the south-west, stands the unbuttressed tower of a second church, formerly the manor chapel, and used from the early 16th century until about 1880.

CROOKLANDS [South Lakeland]

SD5383: 5½ miles (9km) S of Kendal

A small village enfolded in undulating hills near the crossing point of the Lancaster Canal and Peasey Beck, Crooklands is inextricably linked with the neighbouring hamlets of Endmoor, Milton and Preston Patrick.

The **Lancaster Canal** runs close by the village and was used primarily to transport coal from south Lancashire to Westmorland, and stone from Westmorland, southwards. At Crooklands there used to be coal wharfs, and stables to accommodate the canal horses.

The author of the noted *Cyclopaedia, or A Universal Dictionary of Arts and Sciences*, **Ephraim Chambers**, was born near Crooklands, in the adjacent hamlet of Milton; he is buried in the cloisters of Westminster Abbey.

Each year in September the village stages the **Westmorland County Show**, a full-day agricultural show with up to 200 trade stands.

CROSBY [Allerdale]

NY0738: 3 miles (5km) NE of Maryport

Crosby is a large farming village along the main road from Maryport to Carlisle, and though much of it comprises modern residential development, there are still a few houses that date from the early to mid-18th century. The village, like many in this region, developed as a result of mining, notably during the 19th century.

CROSBY GARRETT [Eden]

NY7209: 3 miles (5km) W of Kirkby Stephen

The village of Crosby Garrett, mainly agricultural in its economy, is dominated by the Smardale Viaduct of the Settle - Carlisle railway line, and has been a settlement since Saxon times. It contains a number of old houses, and has an ancient church, the **church of St Andrew**, perched high on a hill. As a result, it commands a fine view. Legend has it that when the Devil saw the stones in readiness to build the church at the foot of the hill, he carried them to the top in order to make pursuit of the true way as irksome as possible, especially as the village population grew older.

Parts of the church, for example, a blocked narrow arch above the chancel, are believed to be Saxon. A north aisle was added around 1175, and the chancel was rebuilt in the 14th century.

A number of the moorland fells to the south and south-west of Crosby Garrett show traces of prehistoric settlements, ranging from simple cairns to a much larger cairn on Rayseat Pike. These all indicate that the area was settled from Stone Age times.

CROSBY RAVENSWORTH [Eden]

NY6114: 4½ miles (7km) SW of Appleby-in-Westmorland

The development of sheep rather than arable farming has helped to preserve a wealth of prehistoric remains around this attractive village on Lyvennet Beck, and it is clear that the banks of the Beck have been attractive to those looking for somewhere to settle from the earliest times.

The village is surrounded by low, open fells on which numerous burial mounds and traces of settlements can be found. The most notable of these is **Ewe Close**, or Ewe Lock, a complex arrangement of rectangular enclosures and ditches containing the remains of circular huts, including one measuring 50ft (15m) in diameter.

Long after prehistoric man, the Vikings came, finding the fertile ground to their liking, and a wooden Saxon church is known to have stood in the village. It was replaced with a Norman church, that itself was demolished during a Scottish raid in the 12th century.

The present **church of St Lawrence** is a large church of considerable beauty surrounded by ancient oak trees, and although extensively rebuilt in the 19th century, is of great architectural interest. Some parts of the church, which was granted to the abbey at Whitby, date from the late 12th century, though near the 13th-century doorway is part of a medieval cross, from the seventh century or earlier. The first Bishop of York, St Paulinus, is thought to have worshipped here.

On land above Lyvennet Beck, set in beautiful grounds, is the towered, Victorian **Flass House**.

To the south, high on the moors, stands a monument at **Black Dub**, claimed to mark the source of Lyvennet Beck. Erected in 1843, it also commemorates the passage this way in 1651 of Charles II, who is said to have "regaled his army and drank of the water on his march from Scotland". Although Cromwell's Commonwealth did not end until 1660, Charles had allowed himself to be crowned king in 1650, in order to gain allies. Two campaigns were initiated by Charles; the first at Dunbar in 1650, which was defeated by Cromwell, and the second a year later, when Charles marched south into England, pursued by Cromwell. His route, which ended in Worcester, crossed the moors above Crosby Ravensworth.

The moors today are a particularly favoured breeding ground for birds, and Crosby Ravensworth Fell is designated a Site of Special Scientific Interest (SSSI), and important for nature conservation. Golden plover, that most evocative of high moorland birds, breed here, as do red grouse, redshank and curlew.

Featuring sheep, cattle, goats, poultry, ponies, fell racing and **sheepdog trials**, the village holds an annual **agricultural show** in August.

CROSSCANONBY [Allerdale]

NY0739: 3 miles (5km) NE of Maryport

Just a short way inland from the coast, the compact village of Crosscanonby was once the site of a satellite house of the Augustinian church in Carlisle, now the cathedral.

Today, what remains is the delightful Norman **church of St John the Evangelist**, largely restored in 1880. Parts of the church, notably the chancel arch, are taken from the Roman camp at Maryport. The square font, on five supports, is 13th century.

CROSTHWAITE [South Lakeland]

SD4491: 5 miles (8km) W of Kendal

The name of the village means 'a cross in a clearing', and probably indicates the site of a former chapel or church. The church today is dedicated to **St Mary**, built in 1878, and much of the cost of building was sustained by a local family, the Argles.

The village lies at the head of the Lyth Valley, beside the River Gilpin, which provided power for a corn mill, later converted to a field studies centre.

Crosthwaite was the birthplace of **William Pearson** (1780-1856), a Quaker naturalist, folklorist, banker and friend of Wordsworth. The author of *The Natural History of Crosthwaite and Lythe, and the valley of the Winster*, he was renowned for his lively sketches on wildlife and the human goings-on of the area.

CULGAITH [Eden]

NY6029: 7½ miles (12km) NW of Appleby-in-Westmorland

A modest-sized village set in farmland in the Eden Valley, and in the shadow of Cross Fell, Culgaith enjoys the best of both worlds, gazing east to the northern Pennines and west to the fells of Lakeland. The village developed with the coming of the railway (Settle - Carlisle line) in the 1870s. The third longest tunnel on the line (660yds/m) was constructed through a hill on which the village stands.

The external appearance of the cruciform **church of All Saints**, consecrated in 1758, seems to be entirely Victorian. It stands on the site of an earlier chapel-of-ease. In 1456, the Pope instigated an inquiry into the failure of the incumbent to offer weekday Masses at the chapel, the sole reason for which seems to be the excessive distance (3 miles!) from the adjacent church at Kirkland.

CUMDIVOCK [Carlisle]

NY3448: 5½ miles (9km) SW of Carlisle

Cumdivock, the name means 'black valley', is a straggling rural community entirely surrounded by farmland, between the adjacent villages of Thursby and Dalston. At the centre of the village stands the plain **Church St John the Evangelist**, built in grey stone in 1871.

Stone from the nearby Shawk Quarries was extracted to help build Hadrian's Wall, and later Carlisle Cathedral and the city walls. Roman inscriptions were found in the 18th century on a rock above the adjacent beck, though the rock appears now to have been destroyed.

CUMREW [Carlisle]

NY5550: 6 miles (10km) SE of Warwick Bridge

Cumrew is a small farming village, its name means 'the valley by the hill', concealed among winding lanes on the edge of the northern Pennines and the ancient Royal Forest of Geltsdale.

The **church of St Mary** is rock-faced, rebuilt in 1890 and stands on a site occupied by a church since 1291. At the time of the Civil War, the church register reveals a large number of children not of the village to have been baptised. This is thought to indicate that they were the children of Scots who were on the side of the Parliamentarian forces, and who laid siege to Carlisle Castle in 1644-5.

On nearby Cumrew Fell is a large prehistoric cairn, which was partially excavated in the 19th century and found to contain a number of cremation burials in urns.

CUMWHINTON [Carlisle]

NY4552: 3½ miles (6km) SE of Carlisle

A small farming village of red sandstone houses along the Wetheral road, in the Vale of Eden, Cumwhinton was previously recorded as Combe Quinton. Until the building of the M6, a vein of alabaster nearby was extensively mined, providing local employment; today most inhabitants work in Carlisle.

CUMWHITTON [Carlisle]

NY5052: 3½ miles (6km) SE of Warwick Bridge

Cumwhitton is a small, attractive village of red sandstone houses in the Vale of Eden, entirely surrounded by farmland. The original village was almost certainly Celtic, and there is evidence to show that there has been a settlement here since Saxon times.

The delightful **church of St Mary** dates from the 12th century, and contains both Saxon and Norman work.

The sometime local blacksmith, Robert Robinson, was found guilty, together with his son, of killing a river bailiff who, in 1862, caught them poaching salmon.

DACRE [Eden]

NY4526: 4 miles (6km) SW of Penrith

The village of Dacre is thought to have been the site of a Saxon monastery from as early as 698, and it is believed to have been at Dacre that the king of England, Aethelstan (c895-939), grandson of Alfred the Great, verified the Peace of Dacre with Constantine, the king of Scotland, and Eugenius of Cumberland. Here the pagan kings swore allegiance to Aethelstan, by all accounts a mighty warrior king, and were baptised into Christianity. The meeting, thought to have taken place in AD927, was not recorded until the 12th century, by the medieval historian William of Malmesbury in *Gesta Regum Anglorum*. If it did take place in Dacre – a precise detail overlooked by the historian apparently, the *Anglo Saxon Chronicles*, identify Eamont Bridge as the place – then it must surely have been the most important occasion in the village's long history. A stone on the south side of the chancel in the church is said to represent this so-called 'Peace of Dacre'.

The name Dacre derives from the Welsh for tear, *daigr*, though there is nothing to be sad about in this quiet village along the crystal waters of Dacre Beck, set in splendid isolation among the low fells north of Ullswater. Dorothy Wordsworth describes in her *Journals* how she and William explored the countryside hereabouts at the beginning of July in 1802, writing: 'The trees are left scattered about as if intended to be like a park, and these are very interesting, standing as they do upon the sides of the steep hills, that slope down to the Bed of the River, a little stony bedded stream that spreads out to a considerable breadth at the village of Dacre.'

A little over a mile (2km) east of Dacre stands **Dalemain House**, a largely 18th-century mansion built around an earlier house and, possibly, a pele tower thought to date from Norman times. The house has remained in the same family since 1680, when Sir Edward Hasell, the son of the rector of Middleton Cheney in Northamptonshire, purchased it from the de Laytons. Hasell was secretary to Lady Anne Clifford until her death in 1676, when he settled in Cumberland. He married Jane Fetherstonhaugh of Kirkoswald, and, after sitting as Member of Parliament for Cumberland, was knighted by William III. Pevsner explains that the Georgian east front, which he describes as 'exceedingly fine', was added by the son of Sir Edward (also Edward), and has nine bays with the middle five separated by rusticated quoins.

Like most Cumberland castles, **Dacre Castle** began life as a pele tower, and was built in the 14th century. In 1354 a licence for a chapel in the castle was

Dalemain House

granted by Bishop Welton of Carlisle, and a new tower was added in 1485. By 1688, however, little remained of the castle but the walls, and in 1716 it was sold to Sir Christopher Musgrave, who had little interest in it, and sold it to the Hasell family of Dalemain House. In times of trouble, villagers would take refuge in Dacre Castle, which would have afforded considerable security, with its massive walls and battlements.

The **church of St Andrew** has a Norman west tower and a late 12th-century chancel, though the church was largely rebuilt in 1810. The church is believed to have been built on the site of the Saxon monastery mentioned by the Venerable Bede in his Ecclesiastical History of 731, as being 'built near the River Dacre'. Little remains of the Saxon structure except some foundations and a drain.

Also of interest in the church is the lock on the south door. It is dated 1671, and is one of a number of locks presented by Lady Anne Clifford to those who had shown her particular kindness. The locks were made for Lady Anne by George Dent of Appleby, and cost £1 each.

The church also contains a memorial tablet to Edward Hasell, bearing a kneeling female figure, which is thought to be the only work in the county of Sir Francis Legatt Chantrey (1781-1841), Derbyshire-born English sculptor, famed for his portrait statues and busts.

At the four corners of the churchyard stand the enigmatic **Dacre Bears**, four large sculptures cut in stone, now largely weathered, and thought to commemorate the marriage between Thomas de Dacre and Philippa Neville, though their true origin is unknown. The monuments seem to depict an encounter between a bear and a cat: one shows the bear sleeping, then the cat awakens the bear, which seizes the cat, kills it and promptly eats it.

A Dacre Bear

DALSTON [Carlisle]

NY3650: 4 miles (6km) SW of Carlisle

Dalston is largely a dormitory suburb of Carlisle, but its earlier prosperity was based on the cotton and flax industries, largely introduced by industrialist George Hodgson of Manchester.

The red sandstone **church of St Michael**, at the end of the Square, has a chancel that dates from the 13th century and the graves of two bishops of Carlisle – Edward Rainbowe (1608-84) and Hugh Percy (1784-1856). The present church, approached through a modern lych-gate commemorating a former vicar, was built in 1750, and restored in 1890, and contains a small window to Hugh de Lilford, a hermit who used to live in the parish.

The font cover was designed by Sir Robert Lorimer (1864-1929), the Scottish-born architect, and depicts the four elements. Along the south wall of the church runs a bench, originally intended for the elderly and infirm in the days before church seating was provided. It has been posited that the saying 'The weak go to the wall' stems from this custom.

The village holds an **agricultural show** early in August each year.

DALTON-IN-FURNESS [Barrow-in-Furness]

SD2273: 3 miles (5km) SE of Askham-in-Furness

For more than 400 years the monks of Furness Abbey held their courts in Dalton, which was then an important market town, and, indeed, the principal town in Furness. The decline of the town is thought to have begun when the plague broke out, although some better fortune returned when iron mining began at the Park Mine.

The town was the birthplace of portrait painter **George Romney** (1734-1802). For ten years Romney worked with his father as a cabinetmaker, but in 1755 he was articled to Count Steel of Kendal to be taught how to paint. From 1757 he specialised in portraiture, and was influenced by Joshua Reynolds, and, to a lesser extent, Gainsborough. Having left his wife and children to go to paint in London, he later returned to Kendal in 1798 in poor health, and died. He is buried in St Mary's churchyard, near Dalton Castle. His gravestone is marked simply, 'Pictor Celeberrimus'.

The **church of St Mary** stands in a fine, elevated position behind Dalton Castle and the market place. It dates from 1882-5, but replaces a pre-Reformation church, and is regarded as one of the most spectacular buildings designed by the renowned architects Austin and Paley.

Dalton Castle, standing above the town, is a 14th-century pele tower. Precisely when a castle was first built at Dalton is unknown, but in 1127 King Stephen conferred on the Abbot of Furness the power to hold courts and administer justice. It seems certain then that it was built by the abbot – especially since it stands on the site of the abbey's civil administration – most probably as protection against marauding Scots. Again the exact date is uncertain. As part of his power to administer justice, in 1292 the abbot claimed the right to build gallows at Dalton, and in addition was allowed the pillory and ducking stool.

By 1545, the castle was in a ruinous state, in spite of repairs ordered by Henry VIII. The castle is now owned by the National Trust, to whom it was given by the 8th Duke of Buccleuch in 1965, and was restored in 1968-9. It is open on summer Saturdays for a few hours.

DEAN [Allerdale]

NY0725: 4 miles (7km) SW of Cockermouth

Dean is a charming village with a mix of both old and new houses, and once boasted a grammar school founded in 1596, and that survived for almost 300 years. Farming is the basis of the local economy these days, and all that prevents the village from becoming exclusively residential.

There is an ancient preaching cross outside the **church of St Oswald** dating from the 12th century, though the church itself is of uncertain date. Some authorities point to gargoyles that decorate the south wall, which are thought to be from the 14th or 15th century; others suggest the church is 17th century.

DEARHAM [Allerdale]

NY0736: 2 miles (3km) E of Maryport

Dearham is a large, uninspiring former mining village in the great Cumberland coalfield, on the outer fringes of Maryport. Its finest feature is the **church of St Mungo**, a splendid Norman church restored and enlarged in 1882 when the north aisle was added. The church contains some interesting Anglo-Danish sculptures. One, a wheel-head cross, bears the Yggdrasil, the great ash tree of Scandinavian mythology; the second, the Adam Stone, bears a runic inscription, rosettes, figures and the word ADAM, upside down at the bottom; the third, the Kenneth Cross, shows a man on a horse, a bird, and scrolls and plaiting, said to represent the legend of a 6th-century hermit.

Translator **John White** (1866-1933) was born in Dearham, but spent most of his life in Southern Rhodesia (now Zimbabwe), and translated the New Testament into tribal languages.

DENDRON [South Lakeland]

SD2470: 2½ miles (4km) E of
Barrow-in-Furness

Dendron is small village on the outskirts of Barrow-in-Furness, and is now largely agricultural. The name means 'the clearing in the valley'.

The **church of St Matthew** was built in 1642 by Robert Dickinson, a Londoner born in nearby Leece, and rebuilt in 1795, with a tower added in 1833. Between 1642 and 1833 the school, attended by artist George Romney (see also Dalton-in-Furness) until he was eleven, was held in the church, which was built with such use in mind. A plaque in the present church, and formerly above the door, reads: 'This chappell was built and fin-

ished in…1642…to have divine service read…according to the church of England and in the weeke day to have children brought upp (sic) in learning and taught therein.' When the tower was added, the wall dividing the church from the school was removed. The building was restored in 1891.

DENT [Eden]

SD7086: 4 miles (6km) SE of Sedbergh

The remote village of Dent, properly Dent Town, is a place of quiet beauty close by the River Dee. Although in the county of Cumbria, it lies within the boundaries of the Yorkshire Dales National Park; the village was once described as 'Terestrial Paradise', and is visited as a 'typical Dales village'.

Following the Wars of the Roses, Dentdale was in the hands of owner-farmers, 'Four and Twenty' of whom constituted a form of local government that started as long ago as 1429. This practice continued until the late 19th century when the system of parish councils took over most of their functions. The 24 was a version of the parish vestry found elsewhere, but constituted in a manner which appears to be a relic of Norse settlement – other 24s occurred in a number of Norse-settled areas, though Dent may well be the only place where it has survived. The 24 consisted of men who represented the longest-established and more prosperous families, vacancies among them being filled by nomination – usually the eldest son or nearest kinsman of the member who had died. Today the 24 of Dent exists as a registered charity meeting at least once a year, and their pews can still be found in the church.

It was wool that made Dent. Many of the natural stone-built houses in the main, cobbled street of Dent used to have first-floor galleries, where 'the terrible knitters i' Dent' (described by Robert Southey), who formed a thriving cottage industry, would sit knitting simple garments from which Dentdale ultimately derived its share of fame. Everyone, it seemed, young and old alike, knitted.

In 1800, with a population a little under 2000, Dent was very much a self-contained settlement, with many trades flourishing, including marble quarrying, horse-breeding and coal mining. Now only the cobbled streets, the church and a few plaques and monuments tell of those distant times.

The 12th-century **church of St Andrew** was rebuilt in 1417, and probably came under the care of the monks at Coverham Abbey, near Middleham. More restoration followed in 1590, 1787 and 1889.

On one street corner near the church, a huge fountain, carved from a block of granite, commemorates **Adam Sedgwick** (1785-1873), son of the township, born at the Old Parsonage. He was a great Victorian geologist whose work laid the foundations for modern geological studies, and for more than 50 years he was Woodwardian Professor of Geology at Cambridge. One record does suggest, however, that at the time the professorship became vacant, Sedgwick was practically ignorant of the subject, and only on his election as professor did he begin to study the subject. He was later elected President of the Geological Society, President of the British Association, and, in 1834, became a Canon of Norwich Cathedral. Sedgwick is buried at Trinity College, Cambridge.

A little further up the valley, at the foot of Whernside, stands **Whernside Manor**, now a cave and fell centre. The manor was built in the late 18th century by a Liverpool merchant, who was a noted slave trader, and kept a sizeable household of enslaved servants.

DISTINGTON [Copeland]

NY0023: 3 miles (5km) S of Workington

Distington is a much-enlarged village, developed by the addition of modern housing; the older part of the village is just one main street.

The **church of the Holy Spirit** was built in 1886, and stands on a hill overlooking the village and the surrounding countryside. The chancel arch of its predecessor, dating from the 17th century, stands in the churchyard. There are thought to have been at least two other churches on this site.

DOCKRAY [Eden]

NY3921: 9 miles (15km) SW of Penrith

A small, mainly farming community, with a hotel and a number of premises offering bed and breakfast accommodation, the village of Dockray stands on the western edge of Gowbarrow Fell.

The grounds around nearby **Aira Force**, now in the ownership of the National Trust, provide an idea of a landscaped Victorian park, with impressive waterfalls formed by Aira Beck. It was along the shores of nearby Ullswater and at the foot of Gowbarrow Fell that Dorothy Wordsworth noted the daffodils that later inspired William to write his famous poem.

DOVENBY [Allerdale]

NY0933: 2½ miles (4km) NW of Cockermouth

A small village of farms, cottages and a

few new properties on the Maryport to Cockermouth road, and about halfway between the two. The main feature of the village is **Dovenby Hall**, now a home for elderly and mentally handicapped people.

The front of the hall is Georgian, but behind it, not easily noticed from the outside, is a very early, tunnel-vaulted pele tower with a Norman window. The hall is said to be haunted by the spectre of a girl who committed suicide when her family disapproved of the man she wanted to marry.

DRIGG [Copeland]
SD0699: 2 miles (3km) NW of Ravenglass

The small village of Drigg is set in low-lying land on the coast north of the Esk Estuary.

The **church of St Peter**, built in red sandstone in 1850, stands on the site of an older church. The lych-gate is dated 1887.

On the boulder clay and gravel shoreline of Drigg, between the River Irt and the coast, a number of flint-knapping sites have been discovered, believed to have been occupied in Mesolithic, Neolithic and Bronze Age times.

DRUMBURGH [Allerdale]
NY2659: 8 miles (13km) WNW of Carlisle

A small coastal village overlooking the Solway Firth. The remains of a Roman fort were discovered on the top of a hill, beside which there is a stretch of Hadrian's Wall. The fort was partially excavated in 1947.

Drumburgh Castle was built in the early 16th century by Thomas, Lord Dacre, from Roman stones. Four hundred years ago Leland recorded that, 'the stone of the Pict Wal were pulled down to build

Dumbuygh...a prety pyle for defens of the contery'. All is now in ruins.

DRYBECK [Eden]
NY6615: 3 miles (5km) E of Crosby Ravensworth

Taking its name from the stream along which it lies, and set amid the limestone landscape south of Appleby-in-Westmorland, Drybeck is a small hamlet of farms that have existed for hundreds of years.

To the south-west stands **Gaythorne Hall**, an interesting, probably Jacobean house with mullioned windows. The house was partly rebuilt in 1702.

DUFTON [Eden]
NY6825: 3 miles (5km) N of Appleby-in-Westmorland

Built around a broad village green, with an avenue of trees down the middle, the quiet and attractive village of Dufton was, during the 18th and 19th centuries, a major centre of lead mining activity. There is evidence to support the claim that Romans worked lead ore in the area, notably on the opposite side of the Pennines, in the South Tyne valley.

The village was built by the **London Lead Mining Company**, a Quaker concern, to house its workers. The company was founded by Royal Charter in 1692, and acquired a number of mines and, later, the estate of the 3rd Earl of Derwentwater, James Radcliffe Derwentwater (1689-1716), against whom a warrant was raised at the time of the 1715 Jacobite Rising. The earl later pleaded guilty to high treason and threw himself, unsuccessfully, on the mercy of King George I: he was beheaded on Tower Hill.

The **church of St Cuthbert** is shared with the neighbouring village of Knock, and stands between the two villages. It dates largely from at least 1784, and stands on the site of an older church; records go back to the late 13th century.

The village has an attractive **Georgian village pump** on the oblong green, while on Castle Hill are the remains of an ancient fort, roughly circular in shape and enclosed by a ditch and external banking.

There are two prominent landmarks not far from the village. **Dufton Pike**, to the north, is of limestone capped by resistant volcanic rocks, and as a result retains its distinctive shape, one of the few real peaks in the Pennines. To the east, **High Cup Nick** in the Whin Sill escarpment is a notable feature, and one used by the Pennine Way as it crosses from Teesdale to Dufton, bound for Cross Fell.

One of the noted peculiarities of the area, from which the village suffers from time to time, is the **Helm Wind**. This curious phenomenon is a ferocious and localised gusting of wind caused when the air from the east rises across the nearby mountains, Cross Fell in particular, and is cooled. Once over the summit plateau, the cold air rushes down the other side with tremendous force. As to that force, Thomas Wilkinson of Yanwath, a Quaker friend of Wordsworth said, 'if I advanced it was with my head inclined to the ground, and at a slow pace; if I retreated and leaned against it with all my might, I could hardly keep erect; if I did not resist it, I was blown over'.

In late August each year Dufton holds an **agricultural show**, including fell racing, drystone walling competitions, and **sheepdog trials.**

EAGLESFIELD [Allerdale]

NY0928: 2 miles (3km) SW of Cockermouth

The village of Eaglesfield was the birthplace of **John Dalton** on 5 September 1766. A chemist and originator of the atomic theory, Dalton effectively elevated chemistry to a science. It was Dalton who, in 1794, first described colour blindness ('Daltonism'). He developed a number of laws and theories, as well as recording over 200,000 meteorological observations. In 1793 he was appointed teacher of mathematics and science in New College, Manchester, where he died on 27 July 1844.

Eaglesfield was also the birthplace of **Robert Eaglesfield**, confessor to Queen Philippa (c1314-69), second cousin and wife of Edward III. He was also a founder of Queen's College, Oxford.

EAMONT BRIDGE [Eden]

NY5228: 1 mile (2km) S of Penrith

The attractive village of Eamont Bridge lies just to the south of Penrith, and contains many historic houses, and former inns used by drovers and travellers for whom the village was the crossing point of the river and the county boundary.

The village stands at the confluence of the rivers Eamont and Lowther. The first mention of a bridge seems to be in the 14th century, when the vicar of Edenhall, John Marshall, left a shilling (5p) in his will for the maintenance of six bridges, including that at Eamont. By 1380, it was necessary to impose a toll on anyone carrying goods over or under the bridge, so that funds were available for its repair. This same 'right of pontage' also extended to the crossing at 'Loutherbrig' and the 'Castlewath of Burgham', the ford at Brougham Castle. The early bridges would have been wooden affairs, for the first stone bridge was not built until 1425. In those days when one could buy remission from sins, the Bishop of Durham made a grant of forty day's indulgence to anyone who contributed towards the building of the stone bridge. It is not clear how many people availed themselves of this concession, but 20th-century records show that the bridge, which has segmental arches with triangular cutwaters, was regarded as a monument of national importance, and comparable to other great structural feats of the Middle Ages.

Eamont Bridge was the birthplace of **Isaac Ritson** (1761-89), a poet, classical translator and author of a number of works, including a ballad cataloguing twenty-five Cumbrian mountains.

Not far from the centre of the village are the remains of two ancient fortifications: **Mayburgh Henge** [NY519284] dating to about 2500BC, and **King Arthur's Round Table** [NY523282], of about 1800BC. Both are regarded as excellent examples of Neolithic henge monuments.

The Mayburgh Henge, which formerly contained an inner stone circle, may well stand along the line of Neolithic trade routes. The site has been extensively despoiled, and by the early 18th century the centre of the site was under cultivation, the stones having been blasted apart with gunpowder. This destruction is said to have given rise to a number of tragedies: one man hanged himself, and another became insane. Predictably, this caused people to link the misfortunes to the wrath of some ancient gods, angered by the sacrilege.

EDENHALL [Eden]

NY 5632: 3 miles (5km) NE of Penrith

There is little about the village of Edenhall other than the good-looking **church of St Cuthbert**, parts of which are Norman, though much of the building dates from the 14th century.

The original Edenhall, demolished in 1934, was the mansion of the Musgrave family, who improved the village in 19th century.

Associated with Edenhall is a rare glass goblet, known as the **'Luck of Edenhall'**. It is a slim beaker with flaring rim, painted in brilliant red, blue, green and white enamels, with gilding. It was made in Syria about the middle of the 13th century, and is said to have been brought back from the Crusades. Its early history is untraced, but it seems to have descended by the female line into Musgrave possession in the Middle Ages: legend has it that it was one of the Musgraves who brought it back. The earliest printed mention of 'The Luck' was in 1729 in the so-called 'Wharton Ballad', which refers to a drinking match instigated by the first Duke of Wharton (1698-1731), at Eden Hall. The poem contained the lines:

God prosper long our Lord the King
And also Edenhall

This was later changed to:

God prosper long from being broke
The Luck of Edenhall.

A printed account of 'The Luck' appeared in *The Gentleman's Magazine* for August 1791. The passage, signed 'WM', probably Sir William Musgrave, concludes 'Tradition, our only guide here, says, that a party of Fairies were drinking and making merry round a well near the Hall, called St. Cuthbert's well; but, being interrupted by the intrusion of some curious people, they were frightened, and made a hasty retreat, and left the cup in question: one of the last screaming out

If this cup shall break or fall
Farewell the Luck of Edenhall'.

The goblet remained intact in the possession of the Musgrave family until it was put on loan to the Victoria and Albert Museum in London, by whom, in 1958, it was finally acquired.

EGREMONT [Copeland]

NY0110: 5 miles (8km) SE of Whitehaven

Egremont is a small market town, having held a charter since 1267. Each September, the town holds a **Crab Apple Fair**, a tradition started in the year it was granted its charter. In the past the Lord of Egremont used to give away crab apples to the local population, but today apples are simply thrown from a lorry as it drives through the streets.

The fair has an interesting history, deriving from medieval times when, after harvesting, serfs of the lord of the manor gathered wild fruits, and with their vegetables, corn and animals went to pay their dues. From this sudden congregation of serfs, the opportunity was taken to celebrate the completion of harvesting, and to forget for a while the customary poverty and tribulations by taking part in a series of crude but arousing and sporting games.

Traditional sports still feature as part of the day, including wrestling, terrier racing, pipe-smoking competitions, and hound trailing, in which hounds pursue a laid trail, usually aniseed scent, over hills and across the river. The highlight of the day, however, is the **World Gurning Championships**, a contest in which each 'gurner' places his head through a horse collar, a 'braffin', and pulls a face; the ugliest wins. To 'gurn' means to snarl like a dog, look savage, or distort the countenance', and the competition to do so is extremely popular.

The town, like many in Cumbria, has a wide main street. It is overlooked by the ruins of a Norman castle, built on a grassy hill between the River Ehen to the south

and the town's tree-lined streets to the north. Indeed, the name Egremont derives from a Norman French name for a sharp or pointed hill, and here clearly refers to the hill on which the castle stands.

Egremont Castle was built on the site of a Danish stronghold between 1130 and 1140 by William de Meschines. Little remains of the castle, which was destroyed in the 16th century, but the Norman drawbridge arch is still intact. The story of the lords of Egremont Castle is a fascinating one.

The heir to the Lord of Egremont, Eustace de Lacy, left for the Crusades with his younger brother, both of whom were captured by the Saracens. The younger brother, however, was released and sent home with a ransom message, but on reaching Egremont he discovered that his father had died. Casting aside any concern for his brother, and the rightful heir, he assumed the title of Lord of Egremont, proclaiming that his brother had died in the Crusades.

Wordsworth's poem *The Horn of Egremont Castle* takes up the story, and is based on a medieval legend that a great horn hanging in the castle can only be blown by the rightful lord. The poem recounts how the impostor, Hubert de Lacy, arranged to have his brother murdered while on a crusade. The plot, however, was foiled, and the brother, Eustace, returned to blow the horn and so establish his rightful claim to the castle. Hubert, it is said, on hearing the horn, fled to the sanctuary of a monastery.

A rather more romantic conclusion tells how the Saracens tied Eustace to a beam by his long hair, and waited for the ransom to be delivered. The daughter of the Saracen lord, however, fell in love with Eustace, and plotted to release him. One night she came and cut him down, but in doing so cut too deeply and partially scalped him. Hiding him away secretly, she nursed him back to health until he was well enough to return to England. On his return, Eustace blew the horn of Egremont and asserted his rightful place. And though Hubert may well, indeed, have fled in terror, his brother eventually forgave him, and even made him Lord of Millom.

As for the Saracen lord's daughter, she made her own way to England and Egremont Castle, where she and the rightful lord were married. As a sign of his guilt, and his brother's forgiveness, Hubert took as his emblem a horn and a 'hatterell' of hair. The emblem can be found on the Huddlestone Tomb at Holy Trinity Church in Millom.

The **church of St Mary and St Michael**, built in the early 1880s, is considered a splendid example of Victorian Gothic architecture, with slender pillars supporting the roof and nave arches. The capitals at the top are carved in floral designs, of which there are almost 100, each different from the others.

On the outskirts of Egremont, the **Florence Mine Heritage Centre** includes the opportunity to visit a real iron ore mine, the last such working mine in Europe.

ELTERWATER
[South Lakeland]

NY3204: 3 miles (5km) W of Ambleside

Standing at the entrance to Langdale, and with the craggy Langdale Pikes as a backdrop, Elterwater is a cluster of attractive cottages, shops and an inn. The name of the village is said to mean 'Swan Lake' in Norse, and swans do indeed grace the nearby Elter Water from time to time. Surrounded by waterfalls, volcanic crags and tree-clad slopes, the village is largely built of the attractive, local grey-green

stone, and centres on a small green with an ancient maple tree.

The village was once the focus of a thriving charcoal burning industry that used juniper wood, which was especially suitable for making gunpowder. The manufacture of gunpowder came to be an important Lakeland industry during the 18th century, and the gunpowder works at Elterwater did not close until the early 20th century.

EMBLETON [Allerdale]

NY1730: 3 miles (5km) E of Cockermouth

Embleton is a scattered village strung out along rising ground and a minor road above the main road linking Cockermouth and Bassenthwaite Lake.

On Setmurthy Common, to the north of the village is a small circle of fifteen stones of volcanic ash. Originally there were thirty stones, along with an outlier to the south-west. In 1488, the site, now usually referred to as **Elva Plain**, was known as Elfhow, possibly a corruption of 'elfshot', meaning a prehistoric axe. Since the circle does lie near an ancient trackway along which stone axes would have been carried from the 'factories' in Langdale, this is a possibility. The name may also derive from Old Norse, 'elfhaugr', the hill of the malignant elves.

ENNERDALE BRIDGE
[Copeland]

NY0615: 3 miles (5km) E of Cleator Moor

Quiet, winding roads lead to the small agricultural community of Ennerdale Bridge, a collection of largely modern dwellings, spanning the River Ehen at the western end of Ennerdale.

In prehistoric times, iron was smelted here, and much later haematite was mined along the valley of Ennerdale. There were also a number of small industries here related to weaving, and Ennerdale Bridge grew as a result.

The **church of St Mary** was built on the site of a medieval chapel originally founded in 1534, between 1856 and 1858, and enlarged in 1885.

There is a small stone circle on **Blakeley Moss**, south-west of Ennerdale Bridge, consisting of eleven small stones, each about 2ft (0.75m) high. The stones are fixed in concrete, having been re-erected in 1925 [NY060140].

FARLAM [Carlisle]

NY5558: 5 miles (8km) ENE of Warwick Bridge

Farlam means 'a fern clearing', in this case a small village on the north-western slopes of the Pennines overlooking the Vale of Eden. Its **church of St Thomas à Becket** was built in 1860, at a cost of £1570, and has an attractive pulpit reached by a doorway in a wall.

FARLETON [South Lakeland]

SD5380: 2½ miles (4km) E of Milnthorpe

Farleton is a small village of grey houses adjoining the Lancaster Canal, at the foot of Farleton Fell, and reached along narrow, winding lanes.

The summit of nearby **Farleton Fell**, along with neighbouring Hutton Roof Crags, is a most extensive plateau of limestone pavement.

FAR SAWREY [South Lakeland]

SD3795: 3 miles (5km) SW of Bowness-on-Windermere

- see Near Sawrey

FIELD BROUGHTON [South Lakeland]

SD3981: 2 miles (3km) N of Cartmel

This small farming village has a lime kiln used until 1922 to produce quicklime. A number of coppices were grown to produce the wood for charcoal burning.

Just to the north of the village, the spire of the **church of St Peter** is a prominent landmark for miles around. The church was consecrated in 1894, replacing an earlier one built in 1745.

FINSTHWAITE [South Lakeland]

SD3687: 1 mile (2km) N of Newby Bridge

This attractive, small village of whitewashed and grey-stone cottages is surrounded by woodland of oak, birch and hazel, and can trace its ancestry back to Viking times. The proximity of so much wood was ideal for the growth of a small industry manufacturing bobbins for the growing textile industry of the early 1800s.

On nearby **Finsthwaite Heights** is a tower commemorating the 'Officers, seamen and marines of the Royal Navy, whose matchless conduct and irresistible valour defeated the fleets of France...and promoted and protected liberty and commerce, 1799'.

The **church of St Peter** is among the best by those fine architects Paley and Austin, and was built in 1873-4 on the site of a church consecrated in 1724. Built of slate with sandstone dressings, it lies discreetly concealed in a hollow from which its tower projects strongly.

The church has no aisle, and the chancel is separated from the main body of the church by a large tower vault. There are some fine examples of stained glass, and a mosaic reredos by Salviati of Venice.

In the churchyard is a **simple cross**, inscribed, not very legibly, to Clementina Johannes Sobiesky Douglass of Waterside, who died in 1771. Though believed by some to be a Polish princess, she is also thought to be the natural daughter of Prince Charles Edward Stuart (Bonnie Prince Charlie) by his mistress Clementina Walkenshaw.

Just below the village stands **Finsthwaite Mill**, one of the last working bobbin mills in Cumbria. There used to be a great many of these mills in the county. They were built wherever there was a plentiful supply of water power.

FIRBANK [Eden]

SD6293: 2½ miles (4km) NW of Sedbergh

Firbank is an elongated, mainly farming community strung out along a road running through the Lune valley.

A small rocky outcrop on the fellside above Firbank is traditionally one of the numerous places where George Fox (1624-91), preached his Quaker faith, and to this day retains the name **Fox's Pulpit**.

FLETCHERTOWN [Allerdale]

NY2042: 3½ miles (6km) E of Aspatria

A small part of the scattered community of Mealsgate, Fletchertown is set in farmland to the north of the River Ellen. Its **church of All Hallows** was built between 1869 and 1899, and known as New All Hallows to distinguish it from Old All Hallows attached to nearby Mealsgate.

FLIMBY [Allerdale]

NY0233: 2 miles (3km) S of Maryport

Flimby is a sizeable coastal village that grew considerably during the 19th century, in harmony with the demand for coal from the nearby coalfields. Ultimately it increased its population almost tenfold. The area was originally settled by the Vikings.

The lands around Flimby were given to Holme Cultram Abbey in 1279, but after the Reformation Henry VIII granted the lands to Thomas Dalston of Carlisle, who sold them a few years later to John Blennerhasset. The traditional old Flimby is around Flimby Cross.

The **church of St Nicholas**, in the old part of the village, was originally built in 1794 on the site of an earlier church. It was restored in 1862, and renovated in 1897.

FLOOKBURGH [South Lakeland]

SD3675: 3 miles (5km) SW of Grange-over-Sands

Flookburgh is an ancient, coastal market town between the Kent Estuary and the Cartmel Sands. It was devastated by the Plague in 1669 and a fire that destroyed much of the town in 1686, though houses still remain with dates preceding this. The importance of the town, which in reality was little more than a village, rested on the fact that it lay on a cross-sands route that linked Lancaster and Furness. It was also renowned for cockle gathering and flat fishing (flukes), which is still carried on along the Kent Estuary.

The town was granted a market charter in 1278 by Edward I, which was renewed by Henry IV (1412) and Charles II (1675). The market cross was erected in 1882 on the site of a 13th-century cross.

The **church of St John** is a large church built, as the gift of the Cavendishes of nearby Holker Hall, between

1897 and 1900 by Paley and Austin. The general style is Romanesque, with a broad west tower that opens out towards the nave in a low arch.

One of the houses in Market Street (number 32) is of an interesting design, having a symmetrical façade of mullioned windows and a Yorkshire lintel.

Wraysholme Tower, about a mile (2km) east of Flookburgh, is an oblong pele tower attached to a farmhouse. It is probably late 15th century, and stands guard, overlooking Morecambe Bay.

FRIZINGTON [Copeland]

NY0316: 4 miles (6km) E of Whitehaven

Frizington is a large village of two-storey cottages, inland from Whitehaven, that owes its existence to mining. Until the early part of the 20th century, oil was still used for public lighting here.

The **church of St Paul** is a simple, rock-faced church built in 1867-8, with a fine east window depicting scenes from the life of Christ.

GAMBLESBY [Eden]

NY6039: 9 miles (15km) NE of Penrith

Gamblesby is a secluded, small and spacious village of red sandstone buildings, mostly houses and farms, many of them 18th century.

The **church of St John** was built in 1868 in the late 13th-century style. The churchman **John Wesley** designed and built a chapel in Gamblesby in 1784; and is known to have preached in the village in 1751 and 1780.

GARRIGILL [Eden]

NY7441: 3 miles (5km) S of Alston

Formerly known as Gerrard's Green, the community of Garrigill focuses on its village green. It stands on the River South Tyne, not far from its source, and below Cross Fell, the highest summit of the Pennines. The Pennine Way passes through the village. The verdant loveliness of Garrigill stands as a stark contrast to the grey, bleak mountains that surround it, and though the layout of the village is not outstandingly attractive, it is a homely place.

The **church of St John** was built in 1790, probably on the site of an earlier church thought to have been here in the 12th century.

GILCRUX [Allerdale]

NY1138: 2½ miles (4km) SW of Aspatria

Gilcrux is a large and long farming village where it is said John Wesley once preached, indeed, its chapel is said to mark the very spot.

The grey-stone **church of St Mary** was originally a Norman church built and restored over a long period, starting in the 12th century. It is a simple structure of nave, chancel and bellcot, and with a reredos that is a copy in glass of Leonardo's *Last Supper*.

Philosopher and scientist **Joseph Jackson** was born in Gilcrux. He tried to disprove Newton's theory.

GILSLAND [Carlisle]

NY6366: 7 miles (11km) NE of Brampton

With a foot in two counties, Cumbria and Northumberland, Gilsland is unique; Poltross Burn, running through the centre of the village marks, the boundary. At the beginning of the 20th century, the village was a self-contained community, building its economy on agriculture, mining and quarrying, all of which have seen a steady decline. The village was once a popular spa, and often visited by

Walter Scott. Just upstream of the village are the 'Popping Stones', where Scott is supposed to have asked Charlotte Carpenter to marry him. Whether the sulphur spring influenced her decision is not recorded, but they did later marry, on Christmas Eve 1797 in Carlisle Cathedral.

Hadrian's Wall passes close by the village, and the remains of both the wall and its turrets flank can be seen along the road to Greenhead. There is the site of a Roman fort on high ground to the south of the village.

To the north of the village is the **church of St Mary Magdelene**, of simple construction and built between 1852 and 1854.

Cumberland and Westmorland wrestling feature alongside with sheep showing and a large horse and pony contingent at the annual **Gilsland Agricultural Show** each September.

GLASSONBY [Eden]
NY5738: 6½ miles (10km) NE of Penrith

The small village of Glassonby is set in lovely countryside along the Vale of Eden. Its name means 'Glassan's settlement'.

Tucked away from the village, the **church of St Michael** is old, possibly 15th century, and on the site of a church washed away when the River Eden changed its course. The present church may well contain parts of its 14th-century predecessor. One of the church's vicars was **William Paley** (1743-1805), the English theologian born in Peterborough who became Archdeacon of Carlisle, and published a number of widely popular theological works.

On a hill just north of the village is a small cairn circle which contains decorated stones, similar to Long Meg, near Little Salkeld [NY575393].

GLEASTON [South Lakeland]
SD2570: 3 niles (5km) E of Barrow-in-Furness

Recorded in the Domesday Book as 'Glasserton', Gleaston is large and scattered, with a high proportion of new properties.

The remains of **Gleaston Castle**, originally built in the 14th century by the lords of Aldingham as a defence against reivers, are now incorporated into a farmhouse.

GLENRIDDING [Eden]
NY3817: 1 mile (2km) NW of Patterdale

Glenridding is a small, largely tourist village on Ullswater, though it grew in importance with the development of the Greenside Lead Mine.

Lead ore was first discovered at what became the **Greenside Lead Mine** in the 1650s, the first levels were driven by Dutch adventurers in the 1690s and dressed ore was carried to the Stoneycroft smelter at Keswick. Production at the mine, however, did not really begin until the late 18th century, and the mine was not extensively worked until 1825, when the mining activity reached its height. Power was originally provided by waterwheels, with the water being supplied by the damming of nearby tarns. One of them, Keppel Cove, burst its banks in 1927, bringing disaster to the village below. Much the same happened four years later, when flood waters smashed through the concrete of High Dam.

By the early 1960s it had become uneconomic to continue to extract lead from the mine, and it closed. But that was not entirely the end of the story for the mine was then used to test instruments designed to detect underground nuclear explosions. Most of the mine buildings are now gone, but a few remain and see service as a youth hostel and mountain huts.

GOSFORTH [Copeland]

NY0603: 5 miles (8km) NW of Ravenglass

Gosforth is the gateway to Wasdale and the ancient Forest of Copeland, and is an interesting and busy village that combines old and new dwellings. It lies on the road south from Whitehaven, and in former times was a staging post, where stagecoaches changed horses. Its earlier economy was based on agriculture, and the village had its own group of trades, enough to make it self-sufficient. Today most people in Gosforth either commute to nearby towns to work, or are in employment at the British Nuclear Fuels plant at Sellafield.

It is, however, mainly known for its Viking cross, in addition to which there is a Viking fishing stone and Viking carved stones built into a toolshed, now a listed building. The oldest buildings in Gosforth date back to 1628.

At 14ft (4.5m), the **Gosforth Cross**, in the churchyard, is the tallest sandstone monolith in Britain. It is carved with pagan and Norse symbols on one side and Christian motifs on the other; both relate the story of the triumph of good over evil. The cross is believed to date from the late 10th century, and is thought to be a relic of the Vikings or their descendants. The base of the cross is carved to represent a tree bole, Yggdrasil, the ash tree of Norse mythology, that supported their universe.

The **church of St Mary** has a simple Norman doorway, and a chancel that is thought to date from the 14th century, but standing on Norman columns with figured capitals, including one of a Green Man's head. Essentially, however, the church was built in red sandstone between 1896-9. The church is regarded as having the finest collection of Anglo-Saxon and Anglo-Danish work in Cumbria.

The village still maintains its ancient farming traditions, and each year in August holds an **agricultural show**.

GRANGE-IN-BORROWDALE [Allerdale]

NY2517: 8km (5 miles) S of Keswick

At the southern end of Derwent Water, where Borrowdale closes in, the village of Grange sits to the west of the clear-watered River Derwent, separated from the main valley road by a great and graceful double-arched bridge. Above rise the grass, bracken and scree slopes of Maiden Moor and High Spy which look down on the neat gathering of cottages and farms that, until the road was built, could only be reached on foot or horseback.

To the south rises **Castle Crag**, the 'tooth' in the Jaws of Borrowdale, a National Trust property, given to the Trust in 1920 by Sir William Hamer and his family in memory of their son, John Hamer, killed in action in 1918.

Thomas West, author of *Antiquities of Furness* and *A Guide to the Lakes* wrote of Castle Crag, 'From the top of Castle-crag in Borrowdale, there is a most astonishing view of the lake and vale of Keswick, spread out to the north in the most picturesque manner...a beautiful mixture of villages, houses, cots and farms, standing round the skirts of Skiddaw, which rises in the grandest manner from a verdant base and closes this prospect in the noblest style of nature's true sublime. From the summit of the rock the views are so singularly great and pleasing that they ought never to be omitted... This truly secreted spot is completely surrounded by the most horrid, romantic mountains that are in this region of wonders; and whoever omits this *coup d'oeil* hath probably seen nothing equal to it.'

GRANGE-OVER-SANDS [South Lakeland]

SD4077: 2 miles (3km) SE of Cartmel

As with many towns and villages in the Furness region, Grange-over-Sands developed significantly with the coming of the railway in 1857. It was then that wealthy business families from industrial Lancashire and Yorkshire settled here to benefit from the bracing air and equable climate. This charming Edwardian seaside resort, now a holiday centre and place of retirement, has a long promenade and ornamental gardens, and was once the site of the grange, or granary, for Cartmel Priory. The surrounding countryside is especially beautiful, and popular with birdwatchers and walkers. It possesses a wide variety of habitat ranging from limestone to peat moss and salt marsh, as well as the underlying slate rocks on which Grange stands.

Like other villages across the Cartmel peninsula, Grange was once part of Lancashire, an area known as Lonsdale North of the Sands, or Lancashire over the Sands. Indeed, before the main turnpike road was built, the principal route was across the sands to Kents Bank, now a suburb of Grange. The way across the sands is still legally a public right of way, but it is a foolhardy person who attempts to cross the sands without either the benefit of considerable local knowledge or the company of the official guide (see Kents Bank). Over the years the sands have claimed many victims, as the memorials in Cartmel churchyard will testify.

Above the town rises **Hamps Fell**, on the summit of which is a hospice built by a former vicar of Cartmel parish as a shelter for those who wandered about the fell.

GRASMERE [South Lakeland]

NY3307: 3 miles (5km) NW of Ambleside

Associated forever with Wordsworth, who lived at Dove Cottage on the edge of the village, Grasmere is a delightful place, where cottages, houses, shops and inns, most made of grey-green or purple-hazed local stone, gather in a vast natural hollow at the foot of the steady rise to Dunmail Raise. All around, fells of varying heights and steepness enfold the village, and provide by far the best view of it, while the nearby lake of Grasmere, adds a sparkle that is missing from less blessed Lakeland villages.

The London-born poet **Thomas Gray** (1716-71) visited the Lake District in 1769, and wrote of Grasmere that, 'The bosom of the mountains, spreading here into a broad bason (sic), discover in the midst Grasmere-water; its margin is hollowed into small bays with iminences; some of rock, some of soft turf, that half conceal and vary the figure of the little lake they command...a little unsuspected Paradise.'

The rough-hewn, pebble-dash structure of the **church of St Oswald** stands on the banks of the River Rothay. It is a fine building of unusual beauty, and occupies a site where man is thought to have worshipped since Saxon times, though the oldest part of the present building dates from the 13th century. Oswald was a Northumbrian king and a powerful advocate of Christianity, who was killed in battle with Penda, the heathen King of Mercia, at Maserfield near Hexham in AD642. Tradition has it that Oswald preached on the site of the present church.

Every year, on the first Saturday in August, a **rush-bearing** ceremony is held in Grasmere, an ancient tradition kept alive in only a few Lakeland villages (Ambleside, Urswick and Warcop are the others). The custom dates from the time when the church floor, since 1841 covered with local flagstones, was strewn with another local, but less durable covering, rushes.

It is thought that rushbearing ceremonies may be a relic of Roman traditions. At Grasmere, not only was the floor of the church still earthen into the 19th century, but bodies of parishioners were buried in the church until 1823. It was important then to keep the atmosphere in the church fragrant, and so it seems likely that rushes were laid at times other than just on St Oswald's Day (5 August).

The church is indeed a marvellous structure, characterised by Wordsworth in *The Excursion*:

'Not raised in nice proportions was the pile,
But large and massy; for duration built;
With pillars crowded, and the roof upheld
By naked rafters intricately crossed,
Like leafless underboughs in some thick wood,
All withered by the depth of shade above.'

Wordsworth is buried in a quiet corner of the churchyard, along with Mary, his wife; Dorothy, his sister; and three of his children, Dora, Catherine and Thomas. The grave shelters beneath one of eight yew trees planted in the churchyard by Wordsworth.

Also in the churchyard, near the wall and west of the lych-gate, is the grave of **Sir John Richardson** (1787-1865), the distinguished Scottish-born naturalist and Arctic explorer.

Immediately adjoining the church is the **Gingerbread Shop**, built in 1660, and formerly the village school. It was attended by the Wordsworth children when the family lived at the Rectory (1811-3).

Dove Cottage, where the Wordsworths lived from December 1799 until 1808, when they moved to Allan Bank, was originally an inn called the Dove and Olive Bough. In Wordsworth's time it had no name, however, and was simply looked on as part of Town End, a small

Rush-bearing ceremony, Grasmere

hamlet. The name, Dove Cottage, has only been in use since the Wordsworth Trust acquired the cottage in 1890.

The Wordsworths repaired and decorated the cottage themselves, and it was here that Dorothy kept her *Journals*, written between 1800 and 1803, an almost daily account of the goings-on in their lives. Here, too, William wrote many of his finest works. The view, now obscured by newer housing, must have been fine, for Dorothy wrote: 'We played at cards – sate up late. The moon shone upon the water below Silver-how, and above it hung, combining with Silver how on one side, a Bowl-shaped moon the curve downwards – the white fields, glittering Roof of Thomas Ashburner's house, the dark yew tree, the white fields – gay and beautiful. William lay with his curtains open that he might see it.'

A short distance away, in a former barn, stands the **Dove Cottage and Wordsworth Museum**, which contains many of Wordsworth's personal belongings, paintings and drawings. When the Wordsworths moved on, Dove Cottage became

the home of **Thomas de Quincey** (1785-1859), the Manchester-born critic and essayist, a close friend of theirs, and author of *The Confessions of an English Opium Eater* (1822).

Allan Bank, where the Wordsworths lived from 1808 until 1811, is owned by the National Trust and privately let. It was acquired by the Trust under the will of Canon H. D. Rawnsley, one of the Trust's founding members. The next two years saw the Wordsworth household in the Rectory, opposite St Oswald's, before they moved to Rydal Mount, between Grasmere and Ambleside, where Wordsworth lived until his death in 1850.

Also owned by the National Trust is **Church Stile**, opposite the church, a 16th-century cottage, and one of the oldest in the village. It is now a studio, flat and information centre. In Wordsworth's day it was an inn, conveniently placed for churchgoers, who would hitch their horses to the rail outside. The building was restored in 1969, when a cockpit was unearthed in the yard behind.

The Wordsworth graves

The **Grasmere Sports**, a popular event that regularly attracts thousands of visitors, are customarily held in late August, and include such events as Cumberland wrestling, hound-trailing, and a fell race to the summit of Butter Crag. Each year, too, Grasmere holds a **Weekend Book Festival** in January, two days of talks, discussion and workshops about books, their writing, printing, illustration and upkeep.

The **Annual Art Exhibition of Cumbria Local Arts** is also held in Grasmere in April, and features exclusively the work of artists living or working in Cumbria.

GRAYRIGG [South Lakeland]

SD5796: 4½ miles (7km) NE of Kendal

Grayrigg is an isolated, small village, midway between Kendal and Tebay, with fine views of the Howgills and embracing the adjoining hamlets of Docker, Whinfell, Patton and Dillicar. The Quakers met here for over 200 years from 1696, when they built a Friends' Meeting House at Beckhouses.

The **church of St John** stands on a site which has been used for worship for centuries. The present church was built in 1837-8, and renovated in 1910. The tower dates from 1869.

Churchman **Francis Howgill** was born in Grayrigg. Howgill was instrumental in introducing George Fox to the people of Westmorland, who later formed the core of the Society of Friends.

GREAT ASBY [Eden]

NY6813: 5 miles (8km) S of Appleby-in-Westmorland

An attractive village with a long village green set in a wooded hollow. In reality,

Asby is a widespread parish that contains the two villages of Great and Little Asby. The name Asby comes from Norse, 'askr' for 'ash', and '-by' meaning 'a farm'.

Little Asby, just over 2 miles (3km) south-east of Great Asby, is the older of the two villages, though it is little more than a hamlet. Its remoteness may be attributed to the fact that there used to be a chapel here dedicated to St Leonard, the patron saint of lepers. Now only a few farms remain.

Great Asby sprawls across Asby Gill, and in the 19th century sustained a number of shops and its own coterie of tradespeople, from tailors and weavers, to butchers and cobblers, in the self-sufficient way of many of these remote hamlets. Today, in addition to its role as a 'retirement' and holiday place, its farming activities are mainly concerned with sheep and cattle.

The **church of St Peter** set on an island site on the village green, was rebuilt in grey stone in 1863-6, when the former church, first mentioned in 1160, was in need of extensive repair and in consequence demolished. The new church reflects the style of the old.

The rectory to the south of the church, contains one wing that used to be the pele tower of the house, and dates from the 14th century. Preserved in the church is a door lock from the rectory, presented by Lady Anne Clifford after she and her companions were given shelter there during a storm; the practice of giving locks was one that Lady Anne frequently undertook as a token of her gratitude.

Below the church is **St Helen's Well**, a natural spring, its waters said to possess healing properties. Nearby is a group of almshouses, built in 1811 for widows and widowers.

On the moors south of the church are a

number of small **prehistoric sites**, notably a stone bank with a roughly oval area and inner grass banks, thought to be Iron Age or Roman [NY682122]. A group of small rectangular and oval enclosures about 1½ miles (2km) south-south-west of the church; also probably Iron Age or Roman [NY673109]. Three miles southwest of the church is a triangular enclosure on **Great Asby Scar**, which is surrounded by a stone bank and contains a number of hut circles [NY650093].

GREAT BLENCOW [Eden]

NY4532: 4 miles (6km) NW of Penrith

- see Blencow

GREAT BROUGHTON [Allerdale]

NY0731: 3 miles (5km) W of Cockermouth

Great Broughton is a large village, including Little Broughton, notable for the untidy layout of many of its older properties. The traditional occupations of the village were copper smelting, coal mining, pipe making and weaving. The name is Norse, from 'broch' and 'ton', meaning 'a fortified place', which it needed to be during the times when raids by Scots were part of the way of life.

The village church, **Christ Church**, which was built in 1856, contains some Art Nouveau stained glass, and an 18th-century pulpit.

The village's most celebrated son was **Abraham Fletcher** (1714-1793), a self-taught mathematician, largely denied an education by his father, who kept the boy busy making clay pipes. Fletcher also taught himself to read and write, and is distinguished for having subsequently published two definitive works on mathematics, *The Universal Measurer* (Whitehaven, 1753) and *The Universal*

Measurer and Mechanic (1762). He seems also to have been the village schoolmaster, lawyer and doctor, prescribing herbal remedies.

GREAT CORBY [Carlisle]

NY4754: 4½ miles (7km) E of Carlisle

Great Corby is a large village of Scandinavian origin on the right bank of the River Eden, and contains a number of unusual and attractive houses, from one of which (Ferry Cottage) passengers used to be rowed across the river to Wetheral. The village was originally a farming community, but is now largely a commuter suburb.

Corby Castle sits across the river from Wetheral, and defies precision: it probably dates from the 13th century, when it may have been a pele tower, possibly built by the Salkeld family. Little is visible of the tower today. In 1611 the Salkelds sold the tower to Lord William Howard, third son of the Duke of Norfolk, and he it was who built a house onto the existing tower. Later, Henry Howard commissioned an architect to modernise the house. The grounds (occasionally open to the public) were laid out by Thomas Howard, who died in 1740.

The **Great Corby Viaduct**, 600ft (180m) long and 100ft (30m) high, was constructed by Francis Giles between 1830 and 1834 and connects Great Corby to the railway station at Wetheral.

GREAT CROSTHWAITE [Allerdale]

NY2524: ½mile (1km) N of Keswick

Great Crosthwiate is a large residential suburb of Keswick, from which it is separated by the River Greta. It is a place of great antiquity where St Kentigern preached in the 6th century on the spot where the church dedicated to him now stands.

The **church of St Kentigern** is mainly a Late Perpendicular church (it dates from 1523), and has many features, including the font, that date from the 14th century and into the 16th. It has aisles that run the entire length of the church from east to west. The north chapel is from the 14th century, and survives from the original church. The church walls display sets of consecration crosses that mark the spots where the bishop anointed the walls at its consecration. The church was restored in 1844.

In the church there is a white marble memorial to the Poet Laureate (1813), **Robert Southey** (1774-1843), who is buried in the graveyard. Southey lived out his later years at Greta Hall in Keswick with his friend Coleridge, whose sister-in-law, Edith Fricker, Southey had married in 1795. Southey's epitaph was composed by Wordsworth. There are also effigies of Sir John and Lady Ratcliff, who were responsible for having the church rebuilt.

Elizabeth Linton (née Lynn: 1822-98), a novelist and writer about the Lake District as well as a journalist, was born in Keswick, and is also buried in St Kentigern's graveyard.

Canon H. D. Rawnsley (1851-1920), founder of the National Trust, was vicar of Crosthwaite for 34 years; he, too, lies buried in the graveyard. Rawnsley's accomplishments were great, and his name crops up frequently throughout the story of Cumbria. He was a disciple of Ruskin, a minor poet, a patron of the arts, conservationist, access campaigner, biographer, local historian, lecturer, and a generous, socially-concerned churchman who appears to have lived life very much to the full.

GREAT MUSGRAVE [Eden]

NY7613: 2 miles (3km) SW of Brough

Great Musgrave is a quiet and peaceful village on a hill above the River Eden and Swindale Beck, surrounded by winding lanes and with good views over the extensive open countryside adjoining the northern Pennines. On the opposite side of the river stands the neighbouring hamlet of Little Musgrave.

A path leads down from the village to its **church of St Theobald**, above the banks of the river. The present church was built between 1845 and 1846 to replace a church so closely positioned to the river that at times it flooded. For a couple of years in the 1770s, the rector was **William Paley** (1743-1805), a noted author of theological writings, who later became Archdeacon of Carlisle, and was also vicar at Glassonby for a time.

GREAT ORMSIDE [Eden]

NY7017: 3 miles (5km) SE of Appleby-in-Westmorland

A small village in the Vale of Eden, Great Ormside gathers around a triangular village green, and was formerly the seat of a Viking warrior, Orm.

The grey-stone **church of St James** is a Scheduled Historic Monument, and stands on a hill beside the River Eden. It is certainly Norman and possibly earlier; some authorities suggest it is on a site that has been a place of burial for 2000 years. Some of the walls contain Roman stones and the remains of an altar. In the churchyard is an ancient cross socket dated 1643, and here, in the early 19th century, the Ormside Bowl was found – an outstanding piece of Saxon metalwork dating from the 9th century which is now in York Museum.

Ormside Hall is now a farm. It stands by the church, and has a 14th- or 15th-century tower, almost certainly built for defensive purposes.

The ten-arched **Great Ormside Viaduct**, on the Settle - Carlisle Railway Line, spans the river and was built in stone between 1870 and 1875.

GREAT ORTON [Carlisle]

NY3254: 5 miles (8km) W of Carlisle

Great Orton is a large and varied village strung out along a lane, where the entrances to the village used to be closed with chains at night, probably to prevent cattle from straying.

The **church of St Giles** is delightful. Being late 11th or early 12th century, St Giles's Church is certainly ancient, and the only church in the Carlisle diocese dedicated to the French saint.

St Giles is the patron saint of cripples, and his church in Cripplegate in London is well known. A local legend tells how a white deer fled to his protection while being hunted by a king. An arrow, intended for the doe, pierced the saint's hand, for which the king apologised, and later was persuaded to found a monastery. The legend is depicted in one of the stained glass windows in the church.

Churchman and antiquary **William Nicolson** (1655-1727), later Bishop of Carlisle, was born in the church porch in Great Orton.

GREAT SALKELD [Eden]

NY5536: 5 miles (8km) NE of Penrith

In Great Salkeld, one of the most attractive of Cumbrian villages, red sandstone barns blend tidily with neat cottages and farm buildings in a manner characteristic of the Eden valley. Here they line the road

before gathering, almost protectively, around the ancient village church. A number of the buildings still have external stone staircases, and the local pub, *The Highland Drove*, recalls days when the village saw much coming and going of cattle being driven south to the English markets.

The **church of St Cuthbert** has a strong, ivy-clad tower, constructed in the 14th century as a refuge against reivers from across the border with Scotland. It is one of three remaining examples in Cumbria of 14th-century fortified churches; the others are at Burgh-by-Sands and Newton Arlosh.

Monks are said to have rested here in the 9th century as they fled from Viking raiders with St Cuthbert's coffin. The south doorway of the church is a fine example of Norman handiwork, possessing heavy, dog-tooth carving and many heads. The church stands on the site of an older, possibly Saxon, church.

Great Salkeld was the birthplace of **Edward Law** (1750-1818), sometime Lord Chief Justice of England, who achieved fame by his successful and very extended defence of Warren Hastings, Governor-General of India, on grounds of corruption (see also Blencow).

GREAT STRICKLAND [Eden]

NY5522: 5 miles (8km) SE of Penrith

Listed in the Domesday Book as Stircaland – a stirk being a young bullock – Great Strickland is quite large and set amid numerous pastures on the east bank of the River Leith.

There is little of note in the village. Its church, dedicated to **St Barnabas**, was built in 1872 as a chapel-of-ease to the church in Little Strickland.

GREAT URSWICK [South Lakeland]

SD2774: 2½ miles (4km) SW of Ulverston

- *see Urswick*

GREENODD [South Lakeland]

SD3182: 3 miles (5km) NE of Ulverston

The village – its name means a 'green promontory' – stands at the mouth of the River Leven, and was an important port in times gone by, though the only evidence of this remains in the form of the Ship Inn, built in 1772 alongside the former quay.

GREYSOUTHEN [Allerdale]

NY0729: 3 miles (5km) W of Cockermouth

A large, former mining village with rows of miners' cottages, Greysouthen is set in farmland to the south of the River Derwent and retains much of its original character. The village is renowned for its high stone walls surrounding the mansion in its centre. The mansion was originally a 17th-century farm, but was gradually extended over the years; it has since been converted into flats.

GREYSTOKE [Eden]

NY4330: 5 miles (8km) W of Penrith

Greystoke is a pleasant unassuming village with 17th-century cottages with cobbled forecourts, where the late Sir Gordon Richards (1904-86), who trained the Grand National winners *Lucius* and *Hallo Dandy* in 1978 and 1984 respectively, had his racing stables.

The nearby **Greystoke Castle**, which stands in a vast wooded park, is an impressive sight, though little remains of its medieval origins. It was built in the 19th century in the Elizabethan style for the Howard family (but it is not open to the public).

The village **church of St Andrew** still contains elements that date from the 13th century, concurrent with the original castle, though much of the church was changed in the 15th century. It, nevertheless, is a venerable building, predominantly in the Perpendicular style. It was once collegiate and has twenty canons' stalls with carved misericords, a man mounting a horse, two young men and a donkey, and St Michael and a dragon, for example. The east window tells the story of St Andrew, and is largely 15th-century glass reassembled in 1848.

To the east of the village are three follies, built by the 11th Duke of Norfolk as amenity features to enhance the landscape in the 18th century. **Fort Putnam** and **Bunkers Hill** are built like forts, while **Spire House** looks like a church.

GRINSDALE [Carlisle]

NY3758: 2½ miles (4km) NW of Carlisle

Grinsdale is a small farming village in a cul-de-sac off the road between Carlisle and Burgh-by-Sands, immediately adjoining the River Eden. Although agriculture was the mainstay of the economy of Grinsdale, weaving and the production of linen also played its part.

The **church of St Kentigern** lies a short distance away, positioned immediately above the wide River Eden. It was built in 1740 and restored in 1895, though there has been a church on this site since the 12th century.

HALLBANKGATE [Carlisle]

NY5859: 4 miles (6km) ESE of Brampton

The hamlet of Hallbankgate is a small, former lead mining community at the foot of the northern Pennines. It is the focal point of a number of scattered hamlets and farms, and was once a thriving settlement with its own coal mines, quarries and railways. It even had a small industrial estate complete with gas works, foundries and blacksmiths, which occasionally managed to build the odd steam engine or two. The village 'shop', too, was on a grand scale. Originally called the Naworth Collieries Co-operative Society, it occupied a three-storey building, and catered for all the needs of the people in the surrounding parishes, including those who needed a hearse.

The local pub, **The Belted Will**, is named after the 17th-century Lord William Howard, of Naworth Castle (see also Brampton). It was closed for some years, but reopened in the 1970s. It was once a temperance hotel.

HARTSOP [Eden]

NY4013: 2 miles (3km) S of Patterdale

The small hamlet of Hartsop, once renowned for wool spinning, lies in a cul-de-sac at the southern end of Patterdale. A number of its grey-stone cottages, some of which date from the 17th century, still have their spinning galleries, and are typical of Lakeland fell-side villages.

The village is within a vast hunting forest used for sport by ancient kings, and Hartsop's name may derive from the deer that once populated the area extensively.

On the other side of the main valley from the village of Hartsop stands **Hartsop Hall**, a National Trust property. There has been a dwelling of some kind on this site since the 13th century, though the hall seen today dates from the 16th, being extended in the following century by the de Lancasters family. Towards the end of the 17th century it passed to Sir John Lowther, the first Lord Lonsdale.

HAVERIGG [Copeland]

SD1578: 1 mile (2km) SW of Millom

Haverigg is a small village at the end of a lane leading to an extensive area of sand dunes; a large RSPB reserve has been developed on an old iron mining site.

HAVERTHWAITE [South Lakeland]

SD3483: 2½ miles (4km) SW of Newby Bridge

Standing beside the River Leven, the picturesque village of Haverthwaite was the location of the Low Wood Gunpowder Works, which dated from 1849; the river serving as a convenient, and safe, means of removing the gunpowder.

The unremarkable **church of St Anne** was built during the reign of George IV, though the architect is not known, and, as one writer put it, 'no one would want to claim it'.

HAWKSHEAD [SouthLakeland]

SD3598: 4 miles (6km) S of Ambleside

Set midway between Ambleside and Coniston, and flanked by the wooded hills of Grizedale Forest, Hawkshead is a timeless place of great character, a place that has flourished since Norse times. Until the 12th century it was under the rule of Furness Abbey, though it was little more than a waterlogged and wooded valley. The village later grew up at the junction of packhorse trails that were developed to link the Windermere ferries with the Coniston valley.

The focal point, as in any market town, is the market place, with the town hall on the north side, and on the south side houses that pre-date the building line requirements of modern planning legislation. It was not until the 19th century that roads penetrated as far as the village, and even today the village centre, a snug arrangement of narrow streets, squares and cobbled pavements with low archways leading to secluded courtyards, is banned to vehicular traffic.

As evidenced by his initials on one of the desks, Wordsworth attended the **grammar school** here (1779-1787). Endowed in 1585 by Edwin Sandys, a local man later to become Archbishop of York, the rebuilt school is now a museum and library. Although Wordsworth was born in Cockermouth in 1770, he went to school in Hawkshead, following his mother's death, when he was only eight. He spent a good deal of his time there, lodging with Ann Tyson, until he went to Cambridge in 1787, and it is easy to see how the village and its setting would have inspired the young mind in his earlier works.

Ann Tyson, but for her care of William Wordsworth, would be unknown today. She used to run a shop in Hawkshead, selling food and clothing, but by 1779, with both herself and her husband in their sixties, they could no longer manage to run the shop. and decided to take in boys from the local grammar school as boarders, among them Richard and William Wordsworth.

For many years, students of Wordsworth endeavoured to identify with certainty which cottage in Hawkshead was Ann Tyson's. Local and other opinion pointed to a small cottage in the centre of town, today called **Wordsworth's Cottage**. But it was discovered by Mrs William Heelis (better known as Beatrix Potter), that the Tysons lived at Green End Cottage in Colthouse, a short distance away on the edge of town. Historians appear now to have reached a compromise, and have deduced that the Tysons, with their lodgers, lived in the centre of town until 1784, when Mr Tyson died, following which Ann Tyson moved to Colthouse.

Several properties in and around Hawkshead, along with land overlooking Esthwaite Water, were bequeathed to the National Trust by Beatrix Potter, who lived only a few miles away at Near Sawrey.

The **Beatrix Potter Gallery**, owned by the National Trust, contains a selection of original drawings by Beatrix Potter, together with a display telling the story of her life. The building was once the office of her husband, solicitor William Heelis, and remains largely unaltered since his day.

The **church of St Michael**, stands in an elevated position on a grassy hillock above the school. It is a church of the 16th to mid-17th century, long and low in profile, quite plain, but sturdy, with a low west tower. In the church can be found a 'Burial in Woollen' certificate. Burial in woollen was a national requirement during the 17th and 18th centuries, and wool merchants prospered handsomely from it.

In the north aisle of the church is the **Sandys Chapel**, commemorating William and Margaret Sandys of Graythwaite, whose son, Edwin, founded the local grammar school.

Hawkshead Courthouse, also in the care of the National Trust, at the junction of the Ambleside and Coniston roads to the north of the village, is mainly a 15th-century building and has stepped gables.

Each year in August, the village stages an **agricultural show** which features show jumping events, numerous competitions and hound trailing.

HAYTON [Carlisle]

NY5057: 3 miles (5km) SW of Brampton

The name of the village of Hayton means 'hay farm', and it is a quiet and delightful place, now mainly a commuter village for those working in Carlisle. In former times it was very much a lively farming community, centred on its **church of St Mary Magdelene**, built in 1780. Next to the church stands a private house which used to belong to the Graham family of Edmond Castle, so that they could spend Sunday there and conveniently attend services in the church.

HAYTON (Aspatria) [Allerdale]

NY1041: 2½ miles (4km) W of Aspatria

Hayton, near Aspatria, is a small and attractive village in idyllic surroundings on the coastal plain inland from Allonby.

The **church of St James** was built in 1867-8, and has an iron rood screen of about the same date. The pulpit is hand carved, and the font is believed to be over 800 years old, and came from the chapel at Hayton Castle.

Hayton Castle, the oldest building in the village, probably dates from the 15th century, though some authorities suggest the 11th century. It is now a farm, and stands on an elevated site surrounded by extensive farmland. It was besieged by Cromwell's soldiers during the Civil War, at which time it was the home of the Musgrave family.

The military leader Sir Thomas Musgrave, British Commandant of New York, who fought in the American War of Independence, was a member of the Musgrave family who lived at Hayton Castle.

HENSINGHAM [Copeland]

NX9816: 1 mile (2km) SE of the centre of Whitehaven

Although formerly of village status, Hensingham is now almost entirely part of Whitehaven.

The Gothic **church of St John the Evangelist** is a rock-faced, red sandstone church built between 1911 and 1913. Poet Thomas Blackburn (1916-77) was born in the rectory, the Victorian house on the south side of the church.

HESKET NEWMARKET [Allerdale]

NY3338: 1 mile (2km) SE of Caldbeck

The village of Hesket Newmarket is a delightful gathering of mainly 18th-century houses built around a green and a market cross. The cross indicates that this was once an important market 'town', known to have been visited by Charles Dickens and Wilkie Collins in 1857.

Hesket Hall is a square house with gabled wings and a large central chimney projecting from a pyramidal roof. It is believed to have been built around 1630 by Sir Wilfrid Lawson, and though not open to the public, is of considerable architectural interest.

Hesket Newmarket Agricultural Show, an agricultural show with Cumberland and Westmorland wrestling, horses, ponies, hounds and terriers, is held in early September.

HETHERSGILL [Carlisle]

NY4767: 5 miles (8km) NW of Brampton

The small village of Hethersgill is scattered about a crossroads, surrounded by farmland. Its **church of St Mary** is a

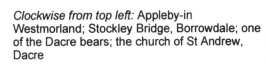

Clockwise from top left: Appleby-in Westmorland; Stockley Bridge, Borrowdale; one of the Dacre bears; the church of St Andrew, Dacre

Above:
Wasdale,
symbol of
Lakeland.

Right:
Sadgill,
Longsleddale.

Below:
Ullswater at
Gowbarrow.

Above:
Cat Bells and
Derwentwater.

Left:
Packhorse
bridge,
Watendlath.

Below:
Haweswater
and part of the
Coast to Coast
Walk.

Above: St John's church, Newton Arlosh.

Right: Brougham Castle.

Below: The main street, Brampton

rock-faced structure built in 1876 as a chapel-of-ease to Kirklinton. It was not until 1984 that the church was finally granted a licence to perform weddings.

Watchmaker and inventor **George Graham** (1673-1751) is thought to have been born in Hethersgill. He worked with Thomas Tompion, and subsequently took over his business. Graham became a Fellow of the Royal Society and invented astronomical instruments for Halley and the French Academy. Both Graham and Tompion are buried in Westminster Abbey.

HEVERSHAM [South Lakeland]
SD4983: 2 miles (3km) S of Levens

The village of Heversham stands a mile or so north of Milnthorpe, and is thought to have been named after an Anglian chief, Haefar. 'Ham' is an Anglian suffix meaning a village of farmstead.

The **church of St Peter** is the oldest church in the former county of Westmorland, and dates from the 8th century. Major restoration work was carried about by Paley and Austin in 1869-70, notably the west tower, built in Early English style.

Heversham Hall is built around a 14th-century pele tower, and until the 16th century it was in use by St Mary's Abbey in York as a base from which to farm lands the abbey owned hereabouts.

Ephraim Chambers (c1680-1740), publisher in 1728 of the *Universal Dictionary of Arts and Sciences*, was educated at Heversham Grammar School, which was founded in 1613.

HIGH HESKET [Eden]
NY4744: 8 miles (13km) SE of Carlisle

High Hesket is little more than one long main street, but is no less pleasant for that. It is strung out along the A6, which itself follows the course of a Roman road, between Penrith and Carlisle.

The **church of St Mary** probably dates from the 17th century. Tradition suggests that a chapel was first built on this spot in the early 16th century, at a time when the plague was wreaking havoc with the population. The mayor of Carlisle would not allow those who had died of the plague to be buried within the city walls, and agreed that if they were buried at a place, then called Walling Stone, a chapel would be consecrated there.

HINCASTER [South Lakeland]
SD5084: 5 miles (8km) S of Kendal

This tiny hamlet on the road to Kendal had a gunpowder mill until the 1920s from which gunpowder was transported on the **Lancaster Canal**. The canal was opened in 1797 between Preston and Tewitfield, and an extension to Kendal added by 1819, followed by a further stretch to Glasson Dock. Near Hincaster the canal goes through a tunnel, and here the barges were 'clogged' through by the men lying on their backs on top of the barges and 'walking' along the roof of the tunnel.

HILTON [Eden]
NY7320: 3 miles (5km) E of Appleby-in-Westmorland

Hilton is a modest-sized, quiet village at the foot of Hilton Fell and adjoining Hilton Beck in the north Pennines. Virtually the whole of nearby Hilton Fell, and adjoining fells, is used as part of the Warcop Artillery Training Area.

One of the village's sons, **Christopher Bainbridge** (c1464-1514), became Archbishop of York (1508) and a cardinal (1511), as well as Provost of Queen's College, Oxford. In 1509, during the first year of his reign, Henry VIII sent Bainbridge as an ambassador to the Pope, and he was later given command of the Pope's forces against France.

HOLKER [South Lakeland]

SD3676: 3 miles (5km) SW of Grange-over-Sands

Holker is a small village strung out along the road to Flookburgh overlooking the Cartmel Sands.

The site of the **Holker Hall**, to the north-west, belonged to Cartmel Priory until the Dissolution of the Monasteries, when it was bought by the Preston family, who were already substantial local land-owners. The hall was built in the early 17th century, though the architectural interest in the hall today is almost entirely Victorian. Later in the 17th century, the hall transferred by marriage to the Lowther family, and in 1756 became Cavendish property, and has remained so ever since.

There is evidence of building of more than one period in both the hall and its estate buildings. The Victorian element is a replacement, following a fire in 1871 in the west wing, and is regarded as one of the finest in what was Lancashire by those renowned architects, Paley and Austin.

The hall is in a most beautiful setting, backed by the low Furness Fells, its parkland providing a haven for fallow and red deer, as well as a collection of rare trees and unusual plants.

Within the grounds of Holker Hall is the **Lakeland Motor Museum**, containing over 150 cars, motor-cycles, tractors, cycles and engines. The museum also houses the Campbell Legend Bluebird Exhibition, featuring the exploits of Sir Malcolm and Donald Campbell.

HOLME [South Lakeland]

SD5278: 2 miles (2km) SE of Milnthorpe

Holme is a long, straggling village adjoining the Lancaster Canal, at the southern edge of Cumbria. When the canal was in operation and coal barges plied its course, there was a wharf at Holme. At the southern end of the village is the **church of the Holy Trinity**, an early Victorian creation, restored in 1902, each occasion being marked by a lack of imagination. Further south lies Holme Mills, which for many years provided the main source of employment for villagers, operating both a corn mill and a flax mill, which made matting and carpets. The mills closed in 1975, and have been converted to industrial units.

HOLME ST CUTHBERT [Allerdale]

NY1047: 3 miles (5km) NE of Allonby

Occupying land formerly attached to Holme Cultram Abbey, the village of Holme St Cuthbert is in an area of farmland not far from the coast. Its **church of St Cuthbert** was built in 1845 as a chapel-of-ease, much as had been done in times past when the abbey built a number of small chapels-of-ease in the parish.

HOLMROOK [Copeland[]

SD0799: 3 miles (5km) SE of Seascale

The **church of St Paul**, in the tiny village of Holmrook on the River Irt, contains a 9th-century cross of the Irish style, and memorials to the Lutwidges, the family of **Lewis Carroll** (Charles Lutwidge Dodgson (1832-98)).

HOUGHTON [Carlisle]

NY4159: 2½ miles (4km) N of Carlisle

The village of Houghton is essentially a dormitory suburb of Carlisle, sandwiched between the M6 and the road to Longtown.

The **church of St John the Evangelist**, built in cream-coloured stone in 1840, is unusual in having its altar at the west end of the church, rather than the east.

HOWGILL [Eden]

SD6395: 2½ miles (4km) N of Sedbergh

Backed by a range of fine fells that take its name, the village of Howgill lies along the course of a Roman road running north from Sedbergh to a fort at Low Borrowbridge in the Lune Gorge. Howgill is exclusively a farming community, the last mill closing before the end of the 19th century.

The village is rather widespread along winding, narrow lanes, but focuses on its church, dedicated to the **Holy Trinity**, and built in 1838.

HUNSONBY [Eden]

NY5835: 1 mile (2km) E of Salkeld

Hunsonby is a pleasant, small village in the Eden Valley, alongside Robberby Water, a bright stream that flows from the northern Pennines. Many of the houses are of the familiar red sandstone of the area, and are between 200 and 400 years old. The village chapel, also of sandstone, is less ancient, and was preceded by a small chapel, last used as a cow shed.

HUTTON ROOF
[South Lakeland]

SD5778: 2½ miles (4km) W of Kirkby Lonsdale

The secluded village of Hutton Roof is mainly known for the extensive plateau of limestone pavement nearby, a Site of Special Scientific Interest.

The small but beautiful **church of St John** is another of Paley and Austin's architectural undertakings; not among their finest, but a skilled effort nonetheless. The church stands at the northern end of the village. Surprisingly, perhaps, the church is made of local sandstone, not the ubiquitous limestone, since sandstone is also found nearby and was quarried for some years.

IREBY [Allerdale]

NY2338: 9 miles (14km) N of Keswick

Tucked away behind Binsey and the Uldale Fells of northern Lakeland the small, former market village of Ireby lies on the edge of (but just outside) the Lake District National Park. It was granted a market charter in 1237, and flourished for a time, mainly at the expense of Cockermouth.

The **church of St James**, a creation of 1845-6, was built to replace an old church, late Norman, about half a mile (1km) to the north-west. This is by far the oldest building, and only the chancel now survives.

IRELETH [Barrow-in-Furness]

SD2277: 5 miles (8km) N of Barrow-in-Furness

One of two almost contiguous villages, the other is Askam, with fine views across the Duddon Sands to Millom; Ireleth is by far the more ancient of the two villages. A packhorse turnpike used to the run through the village. Apart from a few new houses, little has changed in Ireleth. The name of the village means 'the hill slope of the Irish'.

The **church of St Mary** was built in

1865 on the site of an Episcopal chapel that dated from 1612. The site is elevated, and as a result commands a fine view across the Duddon estuary.

A mile (2km) to the north of Ireleth, is the small hamlet of Paradise, and just beyond this a track leads to Marsh Grange. This late 17th-century, five-bay house was the birthplace of **Margaret Askew**, who, at 17 years of age, married Judge Fell of Swarthmoor, and, after his death, married George Fox, founder of the Quaker movement.

IRTHINGTON [Carlisle]

NY4961: 2 miles (3km) W of Brampton

Irthington is small village straddling the Roman Stanegate, and adjoining the River Irthing, across which it looks to the town of Brampton. Stanegate ran from Corbridge to Carlisle, and a number of Roman remains have been found around the village. Very little remains, however, of the old castle, where King John is said to have stayed in 1201, just a low mound covered with daffodils.

The **church of St Kentigern** was restored between 1849 and 1853, though a good portion of the chancel is Norman. No doubt many of the stones used in building the church came from Hadrian's Wall, which has throughout its length, proven to be a ready supply of prepared building material.

IRTON WITH SANTON [Copeland]

NY1000: 3½ miles (6km) E of Seascale

Irton with Santon is less of a village, more a gathering of small hamlets, including Santon, Hall Santon and Santon Bridge, sandwiched between the River Irt and the River Mite. Coleridge came here in 1802,

and observed 'green Hazel Trees, with Hay-fields & Hay-makers...beyond them the River with a beautiful single Stone arch thrown over it, & shadowed by Trees.'

The **church of St Paul** was built in 1856-7 on the site of a much older church, and contains in its churchyard an outstanding example of a pre-Norman, sculptured sandstone cross, thought to be at least 1000 years old. The **Irton Cross** bears intricate decoration and knotwork of that time, and clearly displays Celtic influence.

The church itself is rather unattractive externally, but its interior is quite the opposite, with a painted iron screen in the tower arch and Victorian banners on the walls, as well as some interesting narrative windows. These include four panels by Sir Edward Burne-Jones, among which is the Tiburtine Sibyl.

ISEL [Allerdale]

NY1533: 3 miles (5km) NE of Cockermouth

Perched close to the wooded banks of the River Derwent, the tiny hamlet of Isel is renowned for its **church of St Michael**, built in 1130. The setting is typical of the times when much of Lakeland was densely wooded, and travellers resorted to the rivers and woodland tracks to move about. Places of worship were often set up where such routes crossed, and St Michael's is clearly one such place.

During the restoration of the church in the 18th century and later, carved stones that clearly pre-date the church were found. One bears a swastika and another a triskele, a three-armed symbol used by early Christians.

The church has a large number of windows, unusual for its size, and varying from the familiar narrow Norman slits to the large west window, installed in 1878. There would once have been a tower, a prerequisite of churches and large buildings constructed close to the Scottish border, but the tower of St Michael's has been replaced with a small belfry. One of the 15th-century chancel windows has three Mass-dials carved in its stonework.

The oldest part of nearby **Isel Hall** is a pele tower, a splendid building with a fine view to the south. Other parts of the building date from the 16th century. To the south-west stands **Hewthwaite Hall**, a three-bay fronted house dating from Elizabethan times, though, as with Isel Hall, there is evidence that parts date from the reign of Henry VIII.

IVEGILL [Eden]

NY4143: 8 miles (13km) S of Carlisle

Ivegill is a small village in a deep cleft formed by the River Ive, from which the village takes its name. An old packhorse bridge suggests that a settlement has been here since at least the 15th century.

The lovely **Christ Church** was built in 1868 to replace a chapel-of-ease that had served the villagers since 1338. It was paid for by the first incumbent, the Reverend A.E. Hulton.

KEEKLE [Copeland]

NY0016: 2 miles (3km) SE of Whitehaven

Stretched along the road between Whitehaven and Cleator Moor, the village of Keekle is little more than a row of terraced houses, all more than 150 years old. A disused railway nearby, which required a seven-arch viaduct, used to carry coal from Cleator Moor to Workington. The viaduct was built in 1877.

KELD [Eden]

NY5514: 1 mile (2km) SW of Shap

The tiny farming community of Keld sits at the edge of the Lake District National Park, and adjoining the River Lowther as its passes Shap.

Keld Chapel, now in the care of the National Trust, is a small pre-Reformation chapel, still occasionally used for services.

KENDAL [South Lakeland]

SD5191: 19 miles (31km) N of Lancaster

Kendal, the largest town in the defunct county of Westmorland, was formerly an important woollen textile centre, an industry that was founded by John Kemp, a Flemish weaver, in 1331. The town is always bustling, and it remains an important Cumbrian settlement. It is largely built from grey limestone, the local rock.

When she visited it on her tour in 1698, Celia Fiennes wrote: 'Kendall is a town built all of stone, one very broad streete in which is the Market Crosse, its a goode tradeing town mostly famed for the cottons; Kendal Cotton is used for blankets and the Scotts use them for their plodds and there is much made here and also linsiwoolseys and a great deale of leather tann'd here and all sorts of commodityes twice a weeke is the market furnished with all sorts of things.'

The main artery is Highgate – part of a devilish one-way system – from which flows a series of wynds or courtyards, now less obvious than of old, but linking Highgate with the River Kent. It has been suggested that these many named and numbered yards and alleyways were part of the town's defensive system, and characteristic of settlements that were constantly under threat from raiders, but many of them were built long after the Scottish raids ended, and may, therefore, reflect no more than the pattern of development that had evolved by the 18th century, when most of them were built.

The town stands on the banks of the River Kent, crossed by six bridges, and has been a place of strategic importance since the Romans built a fort, of which little is now visible, to the south of the town. The fort was called Alauna, and seems to have been occupied from AD80 to the 4th century, and would have been built to command the roads to Lancaster, Ambleside, Low Borrow Bridge in the Lune Valley, and Brougham.

The town is also famous for its Kendal bowmen, skilled archers clad in **Kendal Green** cloth who fought against the Scots at the Battle of Flodden Field (1513). Not only were the bowmen renowned, but the Kendal Green, too, for Falstaff speaks of 'three misbegotten knaves in Kendal green' in Shakespeare's *Henry IV*.

But it wasn't only Kendal Green for which the town was renowned. Joseph Budworth, on his *Fortnight's Ramble to the Lakes*, describes how 'men and women, were knitting stockings as they drove their peat-carts into the town'. While in the 19th century, Kendal Black Drop was a popular mixture of opium and spices, and in the 20th century, pipe smokers were able to get the very strong Black Kendal Twist, much favoured by Arthur Ransome.

Now occupied by Jacqui's Attic is **Sandes Hospital** where Thomas Sandes (1606-81), cloth merchant and former mayor of Kendal founded a school and eight almshouses for poor widows. The gatehouse, once the master's house had single-storey wings and housed the school and a library in the chamber over the gateway. The houses were rebuilt in 1852 by Kendal architect Miles Thompson. In 1886 the school merged with Kendal Grammar School, which was succeeded in 1980 by Kirkbie Kendal School. Just inside the archway is a 'Poore Box' the proceeds from which still go towards the almshouses beyond.

The **Shakespeare Theatre** was Kendal's first purpose-built theatre, designed by local architect John Richardson, and opened in the centre of town in 1829. The nationally famous actor Edmund Kean played here in 1832, but general poverty in the town and opposition from Quakers, Presbyterians and Temperance groups forced its closure after five years. It continued in use as a ballroom for many years, and was converted to a church in 1994.

Stramongate School was founded by the Society of Friends in 1698, occupied premises in Stromingate from 1792 to 1932, and has connections with two famous scientists: John Dalton (1766-1844), English chemist born at Eaglesfield, near Cockermouth, the son of a Quaker weaver, became the founder of the atomic theory and taught at the school, then kept by a cousin, from 1781 to 1793. Sir Arthur Stanley Eddington (1882-1944), the English astronomer and pioneer of stellar structure, and considered by many to be the greatest of modern English astronomers, was born at Stramongate.

Kendal Castle, a roughly circular earthwork surrounded by a ditch, stands on a hill just outside the town, and probably dates from the 12th century. Additional features date from the 13th and 14th centuries, when it was the home of the barons of Kendal and their centre of administration and defence.

In the 16th century, the castle was owned by Sir Thomas Parr, father of **Katherine Parr** (1512-48), the last wife of Henry VIII, who was born in the castle in the 16th century. Her Book of Devotions is housed in the town hall in Stricklandgate.

By the late 16th century, the castle was in an advanced state of decay, and has remained so ever since. Even so, most of the castle wall survives along with one of its towers. The manor hall was by far the most important building in the castle, and parts of this also remain. Because several footpaths run through the grounds, the castle is open at all times.

Above Gillingate and All Hallows Lane stands the motte and bailey of **Castle Howe**, since 1788 crowned by a limestone obelisk to 'The Glorious Revolution of 1688'. It failed, however, to impress Joseph Budworth who said it was, 'too small...both for the subject, and the noble rise it stands upon...it looked like a tall chimney; one could imagine, from its scantiness, there had been a want of money.'

Along the main road through Kendal stand the offices of the *Westmorland Gazette*, the oldest still publishing newspaper, in Cumbria. In 1818-9, it was edited by Thomas de Quincey, and published work by Wordsworth and Coleridge; in more recent times, it used to publish the works of Alfred Wainwright and the poems of Margaret Cropper.

The **Abbot Hall Museum of Lakeland Life and Industry** displays traditional rural trades of the region, and shows how the Cumbrian people worked, lived and entertained themselves over the last 300 years. **Abbot Hall Gallery** is an imposing Georgian house in Kirkland, built in 1759 at a cost of £8000, that also houses an art gallery with a highly-acclaimed contemporary exhibition programme, as well as a permanent exhibition.

In Station Road is **Kendal Museum of Natural History and Archaeology**, one of the oldest museums in the country, charting development from prehistoric times to the 20th century. Opened in 1981, the Lake District Natural History Gallery provides glimpses of many Lakeland habitats in the form of a miniature natural trail that begins 520 million years ago. The World Wildlife Gallery houses a unique collection of rare and extinct animals, while the Wainwright Gallery charts the emergence of Cumbrian Man from prehistoric times.

Each year, on Spring Bank Holiday Monday, Kendal commemorates the granting of its market charter by Richard I in 1189. A **Medieval Market** is held in May when everyone dresses in medieval costume. The first Medieval Market was held in 1989 to celebrate the 800th anniversary of the charter.

Part of the proceedings centre on the legend of **Dickie Doodle**, which tells how he, a page of King Richard, was sent north to deliver the charter to the people of Kendal. Arriving in the town, Dickie first called at an inn, the Cock and Dolphin, where he drank excessively, made a medieval nuisance of himself, and was put in the stocks to cool off. The next day he was chased across the river to the east bank, where he was saved from his pursuers because of local rivalry between the two communities, east and west. Dickie received a warm welcome on the east bank, and its people, too, sought a charter from the king to claim their own independence. Not only did the king agree – he had quite a soft spot for Dickie Doodle, less so his eye for the ladies, which had got him into trouble in the first place – but he also suggested that this part of the town should be called Doodleshire, with Dickie as its first mayor.

There have been a number of markets and fairs in Kendal over the years. Castle Howe used to be the site of a 'beast fair', or cattle market; a wool and cheese fair was held in June, July and August; there was a horse market on New Road; a fish market in Finkle Street; a corn market, and a hiring fair at which servants could be hired for work in houses and on farms. Today, outdoor markets are held on Wednesday and Saturday, and here you still find 'Butter Ladies' selling their wares on Saturday mornings, much as they would have done down the centuries. The indoor market is open six days a week.

The **church of the Holy and Undivided Trinity** is Cumbria's largest parish church, and dates from the 13th century, though it is essentially a Victorian creation, having been significantly altered during restorations that took place between 1850 and 1852. It was built on the site of an earlier church, and has five aisles, two each side of the nave and chancel, and a fine western tower with a peal of 10 bells.

There are a number of other churches in Kendal, including the **church of St Thomas**, at the northern end of Stricklandgate, which was built in 1837. The Inghamite chapel at Beast Banks dates from 1844, but is late Georgian in style rather than early Victorian. Almost opposite, the Methodist church is built in Italianate style, and dates from 1882, while St John's Presbyterian church in Sandes Avenue is even later, 1895-7. Much earlier is the Unitarian chapel in Market Street, which pre-dates all of them, having been built in 1721, a simple building with plain features. Equally simple in design is the Friends' Meeting House in Stramongate, built in 1816.

Some 2½ miles (4km) S of Kendal stands **Sizergh Castle**, the ancestral home of the Strickland family for 750 years. The land on which the castle stands was granted in the 12th century by Henry

II to Gervase Deincourt, in which family it remained until 1239. It then passed by marriage into the Strickland family, where it has been ever since.

The building consists of a pele tower dating from the 14th century; a Great Hall, extended in Elizabethan times, and remodelled in the 17th century; a central block and two Elizabethan wings. Most of the many outbuildings date from the 16th century. There is nothing remaining of the very earliest buildings on the site.

When Thomas Gray toured Lakeland in 1769 he visited Sizergh, and provided a fascinating glimpse of life at the time. 'This seat of the Stricklands, an old catholic family, is an ancient hall-house, with a very large tower embattled...I soon came to the river; it works its way in a narrow and deep rocky channel overhung with trees. The calmness and brightness of the evening, the roar of the waters, and the thumping of huge hammers at an iron-forge not far distant, made it a singular walk: but as to the falls (for there are two) they are not four feet high. I went on, down to the forge, and saw the demons at work by the light of their own fires: the iron is brought in pigs to Milthrop by sea from Scotland, &c. and is here beat into bars and plates.'

The Stricklands long supported the Crown in fighting against the Scots, and for his support, Walter Strickland was made a Knight of the Bath in 1306. A year later he was granted a charter of free warren, which conveyed the exclusive right to kill game on his land, something normally reserved to the king. The actual charter is on display in the castle.

The castle also contains a fine collection of oak furniture and paintings, and is surrounded by attractive gardens. The castle and its grounds are now in the care of National Trust, and are open to the public from April to October.

Author **Alfred Wainwright** was born in Blackburn, Lancashire, but lived in Kendal from 1941 until his death in 1991. He eventually became the town's borough treasurer, but is renowned for the many books he composed in his unique style about both the Lakeland he loved and other parts of Britain, especially Scotland and Wales. The tourist information office in Kendal Town Hall used to be Wainwright's office from 1947 to 1967.

KENTMERE [South Lakeland]

NY4504: 4 miles (6km) N of Staveley

The vale of Kentmere contains the source of the Kent, a river that gave its name to Kendal. At the head of the dale, the village of Kentmere gathers around its church.

There used to be a lake, or 'mere', just to the south of the church, where now there is nothing more than a swelling in the river, but the lake was only a shallow affair, and was drained in about 1840 to provide land for agriculture. Before then the vicar of Kirkby Thore, near Appleby-in-Westmorland, a renowned traveller, always with notebook in hand, had observed that the lake was about half a mile long and had a boat. It was apparently good for two kinds of trout, and hosted a large number of wild swans and duck.

In 1955, dredging along the river to gather diatomite for a processing plant at nearby Waterfoot uncovered what were believed to be two 10th-century, wooden, canoe-like boats, the best of which was later presented to the National Maritime Museum. These finds give a clear indication that the valley was inhabited from early times, and may well have been when the Romans were here, building their great highway across High Street.

The grey limestone **church of St Oswald** has roof beams that date from the 16th century, though most of the building is from 1866, with further alterations carried out in the 1950s.

Kentmere Hall, to the west of the village, is the oldest remaining structure, built around a 14th-century tunnel-vaulted pele tower. The adjoining farmhouse is a later addition, either 15th or 16th century. Neither is open to the public.

The hall used to be the home of a giant, **Hugh Herd**, the so-called Cork Lad of Kentmere, son of a nun from Furness who was cast out following the Dissolution. The giant was, not surprisingly, a champion wrestler, and served Edward VI during the time of the Border Troubles. The hall was also the home of **Richard Gilpin**, who has the notorious distinction of having killed the last wild boar in England, and of **Bernard Gilpin** (1517-83), a church reformer known as 'The Apostle of the North'.

Traditional **sheepdog trials** are held in the village at the end of August, and include fell racing and sheep shows.

KENTS BANK
[South Lakeland]

SD3975: 2 miles (3km) SW of Grange-over-Sands

Kents Bank is a mainly residential village on the edge of the Kent Estuary, providing for the holiday trade, but also serving as a starting and finishing point for guided crossings of Morecambe Bay, conducted by the Queen's Guide, naturalist **Cedric Robinson**, who lives in the village. The post of guide is a royal appointment, made by the Duchy of Lancaster, and in 1985, Cedric led a carriage procession, that included the Duke of Edinburgh, across the sands.

From the *Lonsdale Magazine* of February 1821, comes a vivid, perhaps slightly concocted, account of one crossing: 'There could not be fewer than forty carts, gigs, horses, chaises, etc. with men, women, children, dogs, and I can hardly tell what beside, all in the river at once...The waves dashing through the wheels – the horses up to the breast in water – the vehicles, some driving one way, some another, in all imaginable confusion – the carriers swearing – the drivers cracking their whips – the women and children screaming – and the apparent impossibility of any of them ever escaping'.

On a slightly sardonic note, Lancashire humorist Edwin Waugh wrote in *Rambles in the Lake Country* of a man who asked a guide if any of his colleagues were ever lost on the sands. He replied 'I never knew any lost...there's one or two drowned now and then; but they're generally found somewhere i'th bed when th'tide goes out.'

KESWICK [Allerdale]

NY2623: 16 miles (26km) W of Penrith

Keswick is the largest town in the Lake District National Park, and developed largely from its importance as a mining centre during Elizabethan times, when German miners were brought in to exploit the lead and copper deposits in the surrounding fells. But for most people, Keswick is a place superbly situated at the head of a splendid lake and beneath the gaze of one of Lakeland's finest mountains, Skiddaw. It is an enormously popular place, at the northern end of arguably Lakeland's most beautiful valley, Borrowdale.

Leland, writing in 1540, said, 'Where as the water of the Darguent [Derwent] risith is a lytle poore market town cawled Keswike, and it is a mile fro D. Hereberts isle that Bede speketh of.'

In spite of its early beginnings, the 'lytle poore market town' of old is largely a Victorian town, built after the

Derwentwater from Cat Bells

coming of the railway – the Cocker-mouth, Keswick and Penrith Railway – that must have been sheer delight to travel. The railway, alas, is no more, though its trackbed around Keswick is used by walkers.

It has been said that towns and villages built from local stone blend into the land-scape, they belong. So it is with Keswick's tortuous streets of beautiful buildings. The Moot Hall was built in 1813 on the site of an earlier building, and was, until fairly recent times, used as the town hall. The word 'moot' means 'to ar-gue or discuss', so the Moot Hall was a place of discussion. It still is, in a sense; it now houses the information centre. The town's oldest building is the church of St Kentigern at Crosthwaite (see Great Crosthwaite).

It is generally accepted that the Lakes in general and Keswick in particular were 'opened up' to the outside world by the first poets and travellers to venture into the region – Gray, Coleridge, Keats, Southey, Scott, Tennyson, Ruskin and Stevenson. To them, and those who fol-lowed in their footsteps must go the credit (or blame) for bringing this re-markable town to the notice of others.

Thomas Gray (1716-71) explored the "turbulent chaos of mountain behind mountain, rolled in confusion" that awaited him in Borrowdale the day after his arrival in Keswick, at the beginning of October in 1769. Samuel Taylor Coleridge (1772-1834) came to live in Greta Hall in 1800, and the hall later be-came the home of his brother-in-law Robert Southey (1774-1843). The writ-ings of these men inspired others to fol-low them, establishing a literary tradition that continues to this day, though Keswick can boast only one indigenous writer of note. Eliza Lynn, an emanci-pated careerist who, nevertheless, ar-gued passionately that the role of the woman was that of domestic anchor, was born at Crosthwaite vicarage in 1822. When she died in 1898, her ashes were

Castlerigg Stone Circle

buried in Crosthwaite churchyard, at the foot of her father's grave.

Keswick is, geologically, very much a threshold. To the north the mountains are composed of Skiddaw slate, the oldest rocks in the Lake District. To the south, as you pass down Borrowdale, you enter the heart of Lakeland, and that is made of much harder stuff, the Borrowdale Volcanic Series of rocks.

On the fells to the south-east of the town, rocks feature in the famous **Castlerigg Stone Circle**, believed to date from about 3000BC, and so pre-dating the great circles at Stonehenge and elsewhere. It is commonly regarded as the most superb stone circle of the many to be found in the county, the most exciting, the most mysterious. Enthusiasts of stone circles consider Castlerigg, spectacularly set among the mountains of Lakeland, to be among the earliest stone circles in Europe. John Keats, however, was not impressed, describing the stones as a 'dismal cirque of Druid stones upon a forlorn moor'.

As well as copper and lead, graphite was also mined in Borrowdale, where it was first discovered, and this brought about the establishment of a pencil factory. **Cumberland Pencil Museum**, found at the Southey Works, Greta Bridge, illustrates the pencil story from the discovery of graphite to present-day methods of pencil manufacture.

Each year Keswick holds a **Bible Convention**, now more than 120 years old, which attracts Christian people from around the world.

Keswick's **agricultural show**, which includes the **Cumbrian Champion Sheepdog Trials**, is held at the end of August on the showground at Crossings Field.

The **Keswick Museum and Art Gallery** in Fitz Park is the only purpose-built Victorian museum, and has a local history collection ranging from Roman times to the original manuscript of *Goldilocks and the Three Bears*.

On the shores of Derwentwater to the south of Keswick, between Calf Close Bay and Broomhill Point, stands a rather unusual rock. Called **'The Hundred Year Stone'** it is, in fact, a modern sculpting by Devon-based Peter Randall Page, commissioned by the National Trust (North West), and completed in 1995, to mark the centenary year of the National Trust in the Lake District.

KINGS MEABURN [Eden]

NY6221: 4 miles (6km) W of Appleby-in-Westmorland

Kings Meaburn is a long, linear, farming hamlet, part of the parish of Morland, and strung out along each side of a road parallel to the River Lyvennet. Most of the houses, many of which date from the 17th century, are built of local stone.

The name 'King's Meaburn' is of interesting derivation. The early manor of Meaburn also included Mauld's Meaburn to the south, which was held by Roger de Morville. Following his death the manor was divided between his son and daughter, Hugh and Maud. Hugh was involved in the murder of Thomas à Becket, and for this the king recovered his part of the manor, which then became known by its present name.

KIRKANDREWS-UPON-ESK [Carlisle]

NY3871: 2 miles (3km) NE of Longtown

Kirkandrews is little more than a fine church and a medieval tower, but they are both outstanding buildings.

The **church of St Andrew**, which is

Pele Tower, Kirkandrew

the estate church for Netherby Hall on the other side of the River Esk, was built in 1776 in red sandstone and is of an unusual rectangular design. The west tower houses a large clock, and this in turn is topped by an open rotunda of columns and a stone cap.

Not far away stands **Kirkandrews Tower**, built in the 16th century with defence clearly in mind. Both buildings are only a short distance away from Scotsdyke, a defensive line at the western end of the Anglo-Scottish border.

KIRKBAMPTON [Allerdale]
NY3056: 5 miles (8km) W of Carlisle

Kirkbampton is a lovely farming village almost linked to nearby Thurstonfield by new houses. It is set in farmland on the outer edges of Carlisle, with good views of the hills of southern Scotland beyond the Solway Firth. The village is a designated conservation area, and contains a number of Grade I and Grade II listed buildings.

The parish **church of St Peter** is a

Grade I building, and an interesting Norman church, renowned for its sculptured tympanum. The east window is thought to be by Morris, Burne-Jones and Co.

One of the incumbents of the church in Kirkbampton, **Thomas Story**, is said before his own death in 1739 to have officiated at the burial of every man, woman and child living in the parish when he assumed responsibility for it in 1679.

KIRKBRIDE [Allerdale]
NY2356: 5 miles (8km) N of Wigton

Lying close by the course of the former Maryport to Carlisle railway line, the pleasant village of Kirkbride has quite a history of traditional sports such as Cumberland wrestling, hound trailing and even cockfighting. Many of the buildings are probably composed of stone taken from Hadrian's Wall or from nearby forts. The **church of St Bride** to the north of the village pre-dates 1189 occupies the site of a large Roman settlement, and was certainly built using material from the wall.

KIRKBY LONSDALE [Eden]

SD6178: 14 miles (23km) NE of Lancaster

Built on high ground overlooking the River Lune, Kirkby Lonsdale is a typical Westmorland market town, and a very ancient settlement, having witnessed (and no doubt suffered) the attentions of Romans, Normans and Danes. It appears in the Domesday Book as 'Cherchebi', which simply means 'the village with the church'. It is an old market town, having been granted its charter in 1227, and has a school dating from the time of Elizabeth I (1558-1603). There are numerous splendid stone buildings which spread out from the market square. Market day these days is Thursday, and a wide mix of traders sell everything from fruit and vegetables to antiques and curtains.

The landscape around Kirkby Lonsdale inspired both the artist J.M.W. Turner (1775-1851), who painted the valley as viewed from near the churchyard, and the poet John Ruskin (1819-1900), who described the landscape as 'one of the loveliest scenes in England – therefore in the world'. How extensively Ruskin had travelled the world in order to make such a comparison is unclear, but he did go on to write: 'I do not know in all my country, still less in France or Italy, a place more naturally divine or a more precious possession of a true "holy land".'

The town is one of grey-stone houses, and a pleasure to wander through. Off Market Square is Jingling Lane, which is said to 'jingle' if anyone should walk heavily along it; this phenomenon is ascribed to the echo effect from an old tunnel believed to be beneath the surface. The market cross and the octagonal monument in Market Square are especially interesting structures, as is the elegant octagonal gazebo in the church grounds, which was built in the 18th or early 19th century to provide a sheltered point from which to view the Lune valley.

The **church of St Mary**, which provides part of the name for the town, lies hidden behind Market Street, and is reached through iron gates. It dates from Norman times, and is noted for the diamond patterns on some of its columns on the north side of the nave. Pevsner describes the Norman doorway at the foot of the tower as, 'sumptuous...of two orders of shafts with reeded capitals and additional inner mouldings'. He also considers that the interior is 'the most powerful Early Norman display in Westmorland (or Cumberland)'. All medieval periods seem to be represented in the church, from a pulpit that dates from the early 17th century to Jacobean stalls.

The church, which is like a miniature cathedral, was extensively restored in the 1880s, when evidence of burning was uncovered in the tower, probably dating from 1314 when the church was set on fire by the Scots following the Battle of Bannockburn.

The **church of St Joseph** (RC) is in Back Lane and was for over a hundred years a Congregational church, before becoming a Catholic place of worship in the early 1960s.

Two of the town's inns are of particular importance: the **Sun Hotel**, with three pillars at the front, dates from the 17th century; while the **Royal Hotel**, which was the Rose and Crown until 1840, is now named in honour of the widow of William IV, dowager Queen Adelaide, who convalesced here while touring the north in that year. The occasion, by all accounts, was a jubilant one, with flags flying and bands playing. It is said that the red carpet put down for the queen to walk on was, at her request, cut up to make petticoats for the poor women of the town.

The town has two bridges spanning the Lune at a particularly hazardous ford. One was built as recently as 1932, but the other is the **Devil's Bridge**, and dates from the 12th century, though legend claims that it was built by Satan, who claimed the soul of the first living thing to cross it – in the event it was an old dog. Local historians have traced records that itemise repairs to the bridge in 1368. Its construction was originally funded by St Mary's of York and Fountains Abbey, both of which had a keen interest in building an easier crossing of the Lune for their flocks of sheep.

Each September, the town holds a **Victorian Fair**, when everything and everyone goes back 150 years in time: townspeople and traders alike dress in Victorian costume and create an atmosphere that is a magical experience. In August, the **Lunesdale Agricultural Show** is held in the town.

KIRKBY STEPHEN [Eden]

NY7708: 9 miles (14km) SE of Appleby-in-Westmorland

First impressions of Kirkby Stephen suggest that it is larger than it really is, but this overgrown village lacks any real depth, and its eastern boundary in particular is sharply defined by the River Eden. In the opposite direction, low fell pastures begin to rise only a short distance from the town.

The town was built for defence against Border raiders, and has narrow, high-walled passages and spacious squares into which cattle could be driven in times of trouble.

This is an old market town, with a charter since the 14th century, and though ly-ing on a once important route to Carlisle, down the centuries its prominence has been overshadowed by its neighbour, Brough, which had a massive castle that dominated the strategic junction of the Carlisle road and that from Scotch Corner, formerly the main road from London to Scotland. Fortunately for Kirkby Stephen, with the coming of the railways the importance of Brough waned, and Kirkby Stephen began to take precedence. Its Luke Fair replaced Brough Hill Fair as a mecca for cattle and sheep sales.

Work began on the Darlington to north Lancashire railway line in 1857, and the line closed in 1962. The popular Settle - Carlisle line, however, still calls at the station, 1½ miles (2½km) west of the town.

The **Market Square** is surrounded by a ring of cobblestones which demarcate the area used until 1820 for bull baiting, a sport which ended in Kirkby Stephen after a disaster which followed when a bull broke free. The square is also flanked by a number of buildings of especial importance, notably the cloisters, built between the church and the square in 1810, to provide shelter for churchgoers and market people. The money to build the cloisters came from a bequest from John Waller, a naval purser, who was born in the town. The cloisters were also used for a butter market.

The **church of St Stephen**, known locally as the Cathedral of the Dales, bears traces of Saxon and Norman handiwork, and Dalesfolk have worshipped on this site since Saxon times. In the former county of Westmorland the church was second in size only to Kendal, and boasts a long, stately nave and 13th-century arcades. Until the early part of the 20th century, a curfew bell was still rung each evening from the 16th-century church tower.

The church contains the **Loki Stone**, named after a Norse God. The stone dates from the 8th century, and depicts a bound devil; it is one of only two such stones in Europe.

On the southern edge of the town is the site of **Croglam Castle**, a prehistoric oval enclosure with a ditch and external bank. Also on the outskirts of the town, notably at Wharton Hall, are excellent examples of strip lynchets and strip farming.

Wharton Hall, south of the town, was the original home of the Wharton family. The oldest part of the house is the hall, which dates from the 15th century.

KIRKBY THORE [Eden]

NY6325: 4 miles (6km) NW of Appleby-in-Westmorland

The magnificent view across the Eden Valley that Kirkby Thore commands would have appealed to the Romans, who sited their camp, Bravoniacum, here. This was a cavalry fort, guarding the Stainmore Gap, but the stones of the fort have long since been commandeered for more recent buildings, and much of the fort lies under the village.

The red sandstone **church of St Michael** has Norman origins, and additions from the late 13th century. Its bell, believed to have come from Shap Abbey, is said to be the largest in the county.

KIRKCAMBECK [Carlisle]

NY5368: 5 miles (8km) N of Brampton

Kirkcambeck is a small, straggling and isolated village on Cam Beck, in the borderlands north of Brampton. Here the small **church of St Kentigern** was built

in 1885 on the site of an 11th-century church. The original church, like so many in this troubled region, was destroyed by Scottish raiders during the 13th century; only an arched doorway remains of the earlier church.

KIRKLAND [Copeland]

NY0718: 3½ miles (6km) NE of Cleator Moor

Kirkland is a small, isolated village set in the undulating farmlands at the entrance to Ennerdale.

The **church of St Lawrence** is medieval, probably 13th or 14th century, though much restoration was carried out in 1880.

KIRKLAND [Eden]

NY6432: 8 miles (13km) NNW of Appleby-in-Westmorland

Isolated Kirkland is a small, widespread village at the foot of Cross Fell, the highest summit of the Pennines.

The **church of St Lawrence the Martyr** is an attractive and interesting church of some antiquity.

Just outside the village are the **Hanging Walls of Mark Anthony**, three low, artificial cultivation terraces, of no great interest, and without explanation of the name.

KIRKLINTON [Carlisle]

NY4367: 8 miles (13km) NE of Carlisle

Kirklinton is almost a ghost town, being little more than a church set in splendid isolation in farmland adjoining the River Lyne.

The **church of St Cuthbert** was originally dedicated in 1374, and the present church built in 1845 on the site of a former church, the arch of which is retained in the west end of the present building. In the time following the Civil War, the area became a centre for Quakers.

The village's proximity to a major crossing point of the River Esk meant that it was a popular thoroughfare in the days when packhorse trains and cattle drovers were a common feature.

KIRKOSWALD [Eden]

NY5541: 7 miles (11km) N of Penrith

Neat and picturesque Kirkoswald is a market town in the Eden valley, its main street forming a compact line of red sandstone buildings. The river is crossed here by a fine bridge, to Lazonby on the opposite bank.

From the south, the approaches to the village, which was granted a market charter in the 13th century, are dominated by the ruins of an 11th-century castle, later devastated by Border raiders. It is surrounded by a deep moat and embankment, but only the tower remains.

The **church of St Oswald** was built in 1897, on the site of a wooden structure dating from 1747. The bell tower, on a hill near the river, is set apart from the church, which lies in a hollow. Legend has it that when, in the 7th century, St Aidan noticed pagans worshipping at a well in the hollow, he decided to build a Christian church on top of it; the well is under the nave, but there is an outflow in the west wall. The early church would have been a wooden one, and it was replaced with a stone building in 1130. Scottish raiders burned down the village in the 14th century, but some or all of the church seems to have been spared, and alterations and additions were made to it in the 15th and 16th centuries.

In 1523, Thomas Lord Dacre founded a college of six priests, but this was dissolved twenty-four years later, after which the college was sold to the Featherstonhaugh family. The beautiful entrance to the college dates from 1696, and it is known that a pele tower stood here in the 13th century.

Less than 2 miles (3km) north of the village stands the **Nunnery**, built in 1715. It has a fine front of nine bays, while the back of building is the core of a Benedictine nunnery which is believed to have existed here around 1200.

Kirkoswald Castle was built in 1200 by Ralph Engayne, but is now a complete ruin; only a tower and a spiral staircase survives from destruction, probably at the time of the Civil War.

LAMPLUGH [Copeland]

NY0920: 6½ miles (10km) SSW of Cockermouth

Lamplugh is a very scattered village in an area that was once densely covered with trees. Its church, dedicated to St Michael, stands on the site of a former chapel, and was restored in 1768, and then significantly modified by the lord of the manor, James Lamplugh Raper, in Victorian times.

Iron was mined nearby, at Kelton and Knockmurton. The former, when it was opened, was the third deepest mine in England.

LANERCOST [Carlisle]

NY5563: 2½ miles (4km) NE of Brampton

In a splendid setting overlooking the River Irthing, the tiny community of Lanercost is renowned for its priory, and the magnificent Early English architecture to be found in this church.

Lanercost Priory was founded about

1166 by Robert de Vallibus (de Vaux) for Augustinian canons. The priory was first consecrated in 1169, though building continued for a further fifty years, and then rebuilding following raids by Scots in 1296, 1297 and 1346. The priory stands beautifully situated on the River Irthing, and is now in the care of English Heritage.

The nave of the priory is now the parish church, dedicated to **St Mary Magdelene**, with the rest of the priory, which probably never held more than fifteen canons, standing in ruins. It was extensively cannabalised at the Dissolution of the Monasteries to help with the building of the nearby manor house. Much earlier, the builders of the priory did the same to Hadrian's Wall, little more than a few hundred yards distant. The monks, for their part in the Pilgrimage of Grace, were executed, and the buildings granted to Sir Thomas Dacre in 1559.

The west front has a splendid doorway, above which a 13th-century statue of St Mary Magdelene rests in a niche. The interior is equally pleasurable, with interest ranging from a Saxon cross-shaft to windows by William Morris and Sir Edward Burne-Jones.

LANGWATHBY [Eden]

NY5733: 4 miles (6km) NE of Penrith

'Wath' is an old term for a ford, and before the bridge was built, the ford at Langwathby was the longest across the River Eden, linking East Fellside and Penrith. The history of the village has always been closely associated with that of Penrith. Henry I held the manor, and it remained in royal ownership until Henry III granted it to Alexander, King of Scotland, in 1237. After the defection of John Balliol, the manor reverted to the English Crown, and in due course it became the

possession of the Duke of Gloucester, and later still of the Duke of Devonshire.

For centuries the village economy was based on agriculture, mainly a large number of small farms, though only a few of these survive.

The **church of St Peter** is from 1718, with later additions, though it is believed to stand on the site of a previous place of worship dedicated to the Blessed Virgin Mary.

LAZONBY [Eden]

NY5439: 6 miles (10km) NNE of Penrith

Lazonby is built on a hill above the River Eden, and grew in importance with the coming of the railway in 1876. The village was, and still is, surrounded by farmland, and a few of the houses and farms date from the 17th century. Many of the buildings are built in the familiar red sandstone excavated from quarries on Lazonby Fell, some of which went to make the steps for Liverpool's Anglican Cathedral.

The first lords of the manor were the Stuteville family, from whom it passed to the Morvilles, the Multons and the Dacres, by whom they were forfeited to the Crown. In 1716, the manor was sold to the Musgraves of Edenhall.

Burial mounds and a **Bronze Age fort** have been found nearby, while at nearby Plumpton Wall the Romans had a fort (see Plumpton).

On a hill on the east side of the village street is the **church of St Nicholas**, built by Anthony Salvin in 1863, but on the site of a much earlier church originally granted to Lanercost Priory by Sir Hugh de Morville.

LEES HILL [Carlisle]

NY5568: 4½ miles (7km) NE of Brampton

Lees Hill is a small, elongated hamlet

strung out along a quiet lane in the borderlands north of Hadrian's Wall. Its school, as well as serving the surrounding area, also doubles up and serves as a church.

LEVENS [South Lakeland]

SD4886: 4 miles (6km) S of Kendal

The village of Levens is graced by **Levens Hall**, a magnificent Elizabethan house built on to a 13th-century pele tower. It is by far the largest Elizabethan house in the former counties of Cumberland and Westmorland, yet it has managed to keep an intimate scale. The hall was held by the de Redman family from c1225 until 1578, and it was during the reign of Elizabeth that James Bellingham rebuilt the hall as a sumptuous home, giving the house most of what today makes it memorable. It was later extended in the 17th century by Colonel James Graham (originally Grahme), lord of the manor.

The hall has attached to it one of the oldest deer parks in Cumbria, which contained some unusually dark fallow deer. Local legend has it that whenever a white fawn is born to the herd, the occasion foretells some change in the fortunes of the House of Levens. Four cases of this happening are known: the first when Lord Templetown came to Levens after the Crimean War; the second after General Upton's death in 1883; the third after the wedding of Captain and Mrs Bagot in 1885, and finally, in 1896, when Mrs Bagot gave birth to a male heir.

The other side of the superstition details how when a white fawn was born, the then lord ordered it to be shot. Within a few months great misfortune fell upon the family; in quick succession the Hall twice changed hands, while the stewards, servants and gardeners all lost their employment, all, as the gamekeeper firmly

believed, because of the shooting of the white deer.

The gardens and landscape that surround Levens Hall have changed little since they were created in 1690 by Beaumont, a gardener to the aristocracy and in much demand. Even so, he elected to spend the last forty years of his life working on Levens Hall.

The **church of St John the Evangelist** is late Georgian, and dates from 1828.

LINDAL-IN-FURNESS [Barrow-in-Furness]

SD2475: 4 miles (6km) NE of Barrow-in-Furness

A large and ancient village around a beautiful green fringed by sycamore and horse chestnut, Lindal lies along the road between Ulverston and Dalton-in-Furness. It is a very early settlement, being recorded as a grange of Furness Abbey in 1220.

The **church of St Peter**, looking out across the village green, and built on the site of an iron construction that lasted only a few years, is not especially old, but some of the village's properties date back to the 17th century. Iron was mined throughout this area during the 19th and 20th centuries, and Lindal did not escape, being criss-crossed with a maze of railway tracks, and pockmarked with countless open cast pits.

LINDALE IN CARTMEL [South Lakeland]

SD4180: 2 miles (3km) N of Grange-over-Sands

Lindale is a small village just south of Newton Fell and the Newby Bridge to Kendal road, and close by the River Winster.

The **church of St Paul** dates from the time of William IV (1828), with Victorian additions, and lies in a peaceful hollow.

Just outside the village, on the Grange road, is a cast-iron obelisk that commemorates **John Wilkinson** (1728-1808), who developed an iron industry here in the 18th century (see also Clifton). John and his father, Isaac, were both great ironmasters, and the family seat was at Castle Head, near the village, though he worked mainly in Coalbrookdale in Shropshire and in Denbighshire. He made arrangements before his death that when he died he should be buried in an iron coffin in the garden at Castle Head, but subsequent owners of the property had him transferred to the churchyard.

LINSTOCK [Carlisle]

NY4358: 2 miles (3km) NE of Carlisle

The tiny village of Linstock lies on a sharp bend in the River Eden, and close by the course of Hadrian's Wall.

Linstock Castle is built around a pele tower, and during the 12th and 13th centuries was the residence of the bishops of Carlisle, and later served as a front-line defence against Border raiders. It was altered structurally in the late 18th century, and then modernised after the Church Commissioners sold it in 1863.

LITTLE ASBY [Eden]

NY6909: 2 miles (3km) W of Crosby Garrett

- *see Great Asby*

LITTLE BLENCOW [Eden]

NY4532: 4½ miles (7km) NW of Penrith

- *see Blencow*

LITTLE BROUGHTON [Allerdale]

NY0731: 3 miles (5km) W of Cockermouth

The northerly part of the village known as Broughton, formed by Great and Little Broughton combined. Many of the former villagers were weavers, although pipe-making was a more unusual occupation here.

- *see also Great Broughton*

LITTLE CLIFTON [Allerdale]

NY0528: 3 miles (5km) E of Workington

Little Clifton, like its slightly larger neighbour Great Clifton, is a small, scattered former mining village with much modern housing, and adjoins the River Marron near its confluence with the River Derwent. Neither village has much to commend it, although Little Clifton has the **church of St Luke**, built in 1858, but with a Norman south doorway, suggesting that is was built on the site of a former chapel.

LITTLE SALKELD [Eden]

NY5636: 5 miles (8km) NE of Penrith

The two villages, Great and Little Salkeld, face each other across the River Eden, and the 'little' can only be approached from the 'great' by bridges at Lazonby, to the north, and Langwathby, to the south.

There is little of note about the village itself, but about 1 mile (2km) north-east of the village stands a remarkable stone circle known as **Long Meg and her Daughters** [NY570372]. This is the sixth largest of all stone circles, measuring some 360ft by 305ft (109m x 93m), and its internal area is greatly exceeded only by the outer ring at Avebury in Wilt-

Long Meg and her daughters

shire. Other circles – Stanton Drew (Somerset), Brodgar (Orkney) and Newgrange (Co. Meath, Ireland) – do exceed that at Long Meg, but only nominally. Long Meg, the tallest of the stones, stands about 10ft (3m) high, and bears a number of cup and ring symbols.

A little nearer to Glassonby is another circle, **Little Meg** [NY576374]. This is a ruined, small kerb circle, also known as the Maughanby circle, and is about 20ft (6m) in diameter.

LITTLE STRICKLAND [Eden]
NY5619: 7 miles (11km) SE of Penrith

Little Strickland is a small farming village adjoining the River Leith in the low land at the eastern fringe of the Lake District. Its most significant building is the **church of St Mary**, built during the reign of George III.

LITTLE URSWICK [South Lakeland]
SD2673: 3 miles (5km) SW of Ulverston

- *see Urswick*

LONG MARTON [Eden]
NY6624: 3 miles (5km) N of Appleby-in-Westmorland

Long Marton is a pleasant village in the shadow of the North Pennines that satisfactorily combines old and new housing. Frequently the name of the village appears in old records simply as Merton, not acquiring the appendage 'Long' until sometime in the 16th century.

Marton was first owned by the Veteripont family, who lived here during the time of Henry III. Later it passed to the Cliffords, and by the 15th century into the ownership of Sir John de Holland. A century later it was in the hands of Henry VIII, one can only assume by forfeit, possibly because the then owners, the Gray family, had taken part in the Pilgrimage of Grace – but this is not certain.

The village's most interesting building is the delightful, red sandstone **church of St Margaret and St James**, dating from the 11th and 12th centuries, though it was extensively, but tastefully, restored by Cory in 1880. There is evidence that the church, which lies well to the south of the village, stands on the site of a much earlier place of worship; stones have been found bearing Druidic symbols.

The tympanum carvings over the south and west doors are particularly fascinating, and bear representative imagery of

Romanesque churches – a dragon and winged ox in a boat, dragons and mermen.

Long Marton Viaduct, a five-arched construction that carries the Settle - Carlisle railway line, spans Trout Beck.

LONGTOWN [Carlisle]

NY3868: 8 miles (13km) N of Carlisle

The red sandstone village of Longtown grew up along the stagecoach route to Edinburgh, at a crossing point of the River Esk. It developed even further when the Carlisle to Edinburgh railway came this way, and enabled people to expand their home-weaving businesses by working for the mills in Carlisle. By the middle of the 19th century, Longtown was prosperous, although farming was always a principal part of the local economy.

The village has long claimed a connection with King Arthur, possibly based on an entry in the parish register – the parish is called Arthuret – which states that there was a battle fought here in the 6th century, in which the king was involved. According to one Arthurian expert, Arthuret is the last resting place of the king. Another battle took place at nearby Carwhinley in AD573, and is said to have involved Merlin. It proved a decisive victory for the Celtic Christians, putting Aidain on the throne of the Western Highlands, and making Rhydderch of Carlisle the king of Strathclyde, with Kentigern as his bishop.

Arthuret church is dedicated to **St Michael,** and stands half a mile (1km) south of Longtown. Rebuilding was started in 1609 with money collected throughout the country, with the consent of James I. In the churchyard is the gravestone of **Archibald 'Archy' Armstrong** (d.1672), Scottish court jester to James VI and I,

and Charles I. He gained a considerable reputation in Eskdale as a sheep stealer, before moving to London where he gained social distinction and acquired much wealth and influence. He was expelled from Court in 1637 for insolence to Archbishop Laud, and four years later withdrew to Arthuret.

LORTON [Allerdale]

NY1525: 4 miles (6km) SE of Cockermouth

Two small villages, High and Low Lorton, combine to create Lorton, an attractive community of traditional Lakeland character, with many houses between 150 and 300 years old. The valley in which the two villages lie is fashioned by the River Cocker, and is known as the Vale of Lorton. Lorton was described by John Wesley, who preached here between 1752 and 1761, as 'a little village lying in a fruitful valley, surrounded by high mountains'.

George Fox, the founder of the Quaker faith, preached in High Lorton, under an ancient yew tree; among those in the large crowd who heard him were soldiers of Cromwell. The yew tree is over 1000 years old, and is immortalised by Wordsworth in *Yew Trees.* John Wesley (1703-91), the founder of Methodism, also preached here.

Mary Robinson, the Beauty of Buttermere, married her impostor husband at Lorton church at the beginning of October, 1802 (see Buttermere).

The **church of St Cuthbert** is early 19th century, with a tower and short chancel, and a stained glass window by Mayer of Munich in Germany.

Lorton Hall is built around a pele tower dating from the 15th century, while the rest of the hall dates from 1663, with later additions. Charles II stayed here in 1653, when he was out rallying support for his cause, and one of his favourite trees, the beech, was planted by the lady of the manor, at the time of the restoration, and still survives.

LOW BORROWBRIDGE [Eden]

NY6101: 2 miles (3km) S of Tebay

Low Borrowbridge is a small farming community near the confluence of the River Lune and Borrow Beck, where, in addition to the river, the M6, the A685 and the West Coast Railway Line, force their way through the gorge. The village stands at the site of a **Roman fort**. Only a level area remains of the fort, and little is known about its internal layout.

LOW ROW [Carlisle]

NY5863: 4 miles (6km) ENE of Brampton

The small village of Low Row lies to the south of the River Irthing and the Roman wall, surrounded by farms. It was formerly a group of small hamlets (High Row, Middle Row and Low Row), which have grown with an influx of commuters.

The **church of St Cuthbert** is outside the village, and built in 1866 on the site of an older church.

LOWESWATER [Allerdale]

NY1420: 6 miles (10km) S of Cockermouth

Loweswater is a scattered hamlet at the northern edge of and overlooking Crummock Water, but with its own lake, also called **Loweswater**, a short distance away, and owned by the National Trust.

Records maintained by the priory at St Bees mention that a place of worship has existed at Loweswater since the early 12th century, but precisely where is not known, though it may well have been on the site of the present church of St Bartholomew, which was built in 1827 and restored in 1884. Neither its late Georgian pedigree, nor the fact that it cannot with certainty be linked with something much older, does anything to detract from the splendour of its setting against the backdrop of the Loweswater Fells.

Including **sheepdog trials**, hound trailing and shows of cattle, horses and ponies, the **Loweswater and Brackenthwaite Agricultural Society Annual Show** is held in September.

LOWCA [Copeland]

NX9821: 4 miles (6km) S of Workington

A coastal, former mining village on Providence Bay, Lowca stands at the point where the River Keekle meets the sea.

In 1915 a German U-Boat surfaced offshore and opened fire on Lowca, endowing the village with the distinction of being the first land target ever to be attacked by a submarine.

LOWICK [South Lakeland]

SD2885: 2½ miles (4km) S of the southernmost tip of Coniston Water

Lowick, a riverside village above the River Crake, set in farmland at the southern end of Coniston Water, forms with its neighbours Lowick Bridge and Lowick Green an attractive corner of Lakeland. The **church of St Luke** built in local rubble in 1885 on the site of a chapel that had existed since 1577, is in a superb setting, and enhances the landscape of farms, cottages, fells and high mountains.

The village holds an **agricultural**

show each September, which includes traditional Lakeland sports like fell running, hound trailing, and Cumberland wrestling, as well as the conventional showing of cattle and sheep.

LOWTHER [Eden]

NY5223: 4 miles (6km) S of Penrith

The village of Lowther has been the home of the Lowther family since 1283, and the family are still the largest private landowners in the Lake District. Although the family claims its origin is among the Danish invaders of the 9th century, the first appearance in records of the family name was during the reign of Henry II (1154-1189), when they acted as witnesses to a legal document, but the main line of the family begins during the time of Edward I (1272-1307). From then on the family played an increasingly important role in the history of Westmorland and Cumberland. Throughout the history of these two counties, the name of Lowther recurs frequently, as knights, or High Sheriff, and even as a member of the royal household, but it was not until 1689 that a Lowther was raised to the peerage.

During the 18th and 19th centuries they dominated the two counties of Cumberland and Westmorland, and managed them in a feudal manner. At the hands of the Lowthers, Cumberland prospered from the early 18th century, when Sir James and his father (Sir John) were instrumental in bringing the Industrial Revolution to northern England, and Cumberland in particular, many years before it reached other north-west counties, like Lancashire. The used their wealth to expand into mining and shipping, and were key figures in developing the then tiny, coastal hamlet of Whitehaven.

On balance, however, in spite of their influence and the economic good they did, the Lowthers were neither generous nor popular, being regarded as provincial monarchs.

Lowther Castle was the former home of the Lowther family, and was built between 1806 and 1811 on the site of Lowther Hall, where Mary, Queen of Scots spent a night on the way to her execution, and which was burned down in 1720. When the 1st Earl of Lonsdale (1736-1802) decided to have the castle built he chose a promising architect, Robert Smirke (1781-1867), to do the job. That his work was impressive is testified by the fact that Smirke went on to design Covent Garden Theatre and, his best-known building, the British Museum. By the 1930s, however, the grandeur was too much for the Lowthers, and they abandoned Lowther Castle for Askham Hall across the River Lowther. Much of the castle was demolished in 1957, and only the shell now remains.

The village today is a gathering of houses and cottages around two squares with greens in the middle. Lowther Park, where once Lowther deer roamed freely, is now a wildlife park where the emphasis is on British and European species.

The **church of St Michael** stands to the north of the castle, and dates from the 12th century, though it was largely rebuilt by Sir John Lowther in the 1680s. In the porch is a Viking tombstone with a carving depicting the souls of warriors arriving in Valhalla. The church today is mostly a rebuilding from 1856, but it still incorporates many of the features of the earlier church.

When Sir John began work on rebuilding the church he demolished the village and built a new one, Lowther New Town. Much of this, too, was later pulled down because it spoiled the view from the castle, and so another village, Lowther Village, was started in 1806.

Perhaps the most renowned of the Lowthers, however, was the fifth Earl, Hugh Cecil (1857-1944), who early in life indulged his passion for sport, and horses in particular, becoming an accomplished horseman at the age of nine.

As a young man, Hugh toured Switzerland as part of a circus, spent a year in the Arctic during which time he confirmed the presence of gold in the Klondike, and became an expert on hunting. He was a lover of horse racing, though his only notable success was when *Royal Lancer* won the St Leger in 1922, and he became well known in boxing circles, presenting the celebrated Lonsdale Belts. He was a great yachtsman, too, and won 17 prizes in 22 races in Kaiser Wilhelm's cutter *Meteor*.

Hugh Lowther was dubbed the 'Yellow Earl', after his liking for yellow livery on his cars, horse boxes and coachmen. The Lonsdale yellow was adopted by the Automobile Association when Lonsdale became its President in 1907.

LUPTON [South Lakeland]

SD5581: 3½ miles (5km) E of Milnthorpe

A small hamlet of a few scattered houses, farms and a pub along the road linking Kendal and Kirkby Lonsdale, Lupton has passed through a number of ownerships including that of the Earl of Lonsdale. It lies above Lupton Beck, sandwiched between the low fells of Scout Hill to the north and the extensive limestone plateau of Farleton Fell.

The **church of All Saints** is neo-Norman, built in 1867, and the font is said to have come from Kirkby Lonsdale church.

MANSERGH [South Lakeland]

SD6082: 3 miles (5km) N of Kirkby Lonsdale

Mansergh is a small, isolated village set in rolling countryside above the River Lune. Its **church of St Peter** is a Paley and Austin building of 1880, built in Late Perpendicular style.

MARTINDALE [Eden]

NY4319: 3 miles (5km) NE of Patterdale

Reached by a long and winding road from the village of Pooley Bridge, the scattered hamlet of Martindale lies in one of Lakeland's most sequestered spots, surrounded by craggy fells and with a fine view across Ullswater to the distant heights of the eastern fells.

The **church of St Peter** was built in 1880-2 to replace the original church of St Martin, which stands a short distance away, and which was built in 1663. It is recorded that on the day St Peter's Church was consecrated, a terrific storm blew the roof off St Martin's. The damage was repaired, but thereafter the church served only as a mortuary chapel, and was used for burials.

MARYPORT [Allerdale]

NY0336: 6 miles (10km) NE of Workington

Maryport is a small industrial town with a harbour, at the mouth of the River Ellen, and was a sizeable shipbuilding centre up to the end of the 19th century. It used to be a small village, known as Ellenfoot for obvious reasons, but was renamed (after his wife, and not Mary, Queen of Scots as some authorities suggest) when the lord of the manor, Humphrey Senhouse, began to extend the town in 1749, in much the same way that Sir John Lowther had done at White-haven.

The wealth and prosperity of the town was founded on coal and iron mining, and by 1777 there were three shipyards here and a port with up to 80 vessels. In 1846, the town was linked by rail to Carlisle, and this further enhanced its development and growth. The 19th century saw the greatest period of activity in the town, which had been built to a grid pattern by the Senhouse family, but the depression of the 1930s severely affected Maryport, and it never recovered. The harbour was closed in 1961, and, though it is now being dispelled, an air of dereliction hung over the town for many years.

The **Maryport Maritime Museum** in Senhouse Street houses a wealth of objects, pictures, models and paintings that illustrate Maryport's maritime and painting tradition. There are also displays about Fletcher Christian, and Thomas Ismay, the owner of the Titanic.

The **Maryport Steamship Museum** at Elizabeth Dock provides an insight into life aboard a 1950s steam tug.

At The Battery, Sea Brows, is the **Senhouse Roman Museum** covering the Roman occupation of north-west Cumbria. Displays are based around a large collection of Roman military altar stones recovered from the nearby Roman fort.

The location of Maryport has always been significant since the Romans used it as a supply port, and built a fort here which they called Alauna. It was an important defensive position, too, against raids from the barbarians north of Hadrian's Wall. The fort, on high ground to the north of the town, was still occupied in the 5th century, immediately prior to the Roman withdrawal from Britain.

The red sandstsone **church of St Mary** is Victorian, originally of 1847, and re-built in 1890-2. Only the tower remains of the earlier structure.

At **Castle Hill**, at the southern end of town, lie the remains of a pre-Norman motte and bailey castle, though there is little to see.

MATTERDALE END [Eden]

NY3923: 1 mile (2km) N of Dockray

A scattering of farms below the twin peaks of Great Mell Fell and Little Mell Fell comprise Matterdale End. At one time the community was part of the parish of Greystoke, but that church was regarded as being too far distant for the people of Matterdale, and so they petitioned for the building of their own church.

Without dedication, the church at Matterdale is a low structure with a tower of slate that was added in 1848, at the time that the thatched roof was replaced. A huge beam in the church bears the date 1573, which may signify the date it was completed or the date from which it was licensed for services; it was not consecrated, however, until 1580.

MAULDS MEABURN [Eden]

NY6216: 1 mile (2km) N of Crosby Ravensworth

The manor of Meaburn is divided into two separate villages, King's Meaburn and Mauld's Meaburn. It was one of the properties of Hugh de Morville who took a leading part in the murder of Thomas à Becket, for which, it is thought, he forfeited his lands, though some authorities suggest there may have been other difficulties that contributed to his plight. As a result, the northern part of the manor reverted to the Crown, but the remainder was granted to Sir Hugh's sister, Maud, and became Mauld's Meaburn.

Meaburn Hall was built in 1610, and was the home of the 1st Earl of Lonsdale, who embalmed the body of his mistress and placed it in a coffin with a glass lid, which he then kept in a cupboard.

The village was the birthplace of **Lancelot Addison** (1632-1703), the father of Joseph Addison (1672-1719), the English essayist and politician, and creator of Sir Roger de Coverley.

MEALSGATE [Allerdale]

NY2042: 14 miles (22km) SW of Carlisle

Mealsgate is a scattered village along the course of a Roman road, north of the River Ellen, and closely associated with the adjoining village of Fletchertown.

The **church of All Hallows** is known as Old All Hallows to distinguish it from New All Hallows at nearby Fletchertown. It was originally built in 1587, and restored by George Moore in 1862.

Philanthropist **George Moore** (1806-76), a wealthy London merchant, was born in Mealsgate, and buried there.

MELMERBY [Eden]

NY6137: 8 miles (12km) NE of Penrith

The attractive village of Melmerby, set against the backdrop of the northern Pennines, is comprised of low, red sandstone buildings, typical of the area, strung out around and overlooking the village green.

The village church, dedicated to **St John the Baptist**, is on the edge of the village and is largely Victorian, but has two late medieval windows in the north wall. Nearby is **Melmerby Hall**, the manor house, dating mainly from the 17th century, and with a number of its outbuildings converted into a village bakery.

MIDDLETON [Eden]

SD6286: 5 miles (8km) N of Kirkby Lonsdale

Middleton is a widespread village caught between the River Lune and Middleton Fell. It is built along the course of a Roman road, and a Roman milestone stands on a hill overlooking the river.

The **church of the Holy Ghost** has had two predecessors, and was built in 1878. It has some interesting and attractive stained glass.

Middleton Hall, once the manor house, now a farm, was for centuries the home of the Middleton family. It stands less than a mile (1km) north of the village, and is passed closely by the line of a dismantled railway. It dates from the 14th and 15th centuries, and is a fine example of domestic architecture of that period.

MILBURN [Eden]

NY6529: 6 miles (10km) N of Appleby

Milburn is a classic example of a medieval fortified village, its sandstone buildings forming a defensive rectangle around the village green, and facing in towards it. The village is especially interesting for this reason, and has scarcely changed from the form it had in the 12th century. The arrangement of houses and streets is a typical Cumberland pattern, and a reminder of the days when bands of reivers roamed the Marches either side of the Anglo-Scottish border, killing and burning, and sheep and cattle rustling. The narrow entrances to the green at each of its four corners were easily sealed in times of danger.

Behind the village, Daniel Defoe's 'wall of brass', the Pennines, rise to their greatest height at Cross Fell four miles distant. These wild summits are now quite bleak and bare, but there is evidence that they were once tree-covered almost to the summits.

Howgill Castle, a former manor house, was originally built in the 14th century, though much of it dates from the 18th century. The **church of St Cuthbert** dates in part from the 11th century, but was extensively renovated in 1894.

MILLOM [Copeland]

SD1780: 5 miles (8km) SW of Broughton-in-Furness

Surrounded by sea and mountains the largely industrial village of Millom was built to work a rich haematite seam discovered at Hodbarrow in 1868, and which continued working until the 1960s. This juxtaposition of sparkling Irish seascape on the one hand, and a rich legacy of an only recently demised iron mining industry on the other, creates something of an odd sensation on first encounter, though this is fast disappearing as the town and its people fan the flames of a new prosperity founded on its fascinating past.

This is nowhere better exemplified than in the town's **Folk Museum**. The museum is also a true 'local' museum, and deals with the development and decline of the iron mining and steel making industries in the Millom area over the last 150 years. Displays include a reconstruction from the Hodbarrow Iron Ore Mine, and a miner's cottage kitchen.

The red sandstone **church of the Holy Trinity** is a late Norman building, and contains the Huddlestone Tomb (see Egremont Castle). It has elements from the 12th-14th centuries, though most of the restoration is Victorian. Architects Paley and Austin were commissioned to build a second church of the Holy Trinity between 1874 and 1877, as a sign of the town's industrial prosperity.

Less than a mile to the north of Millom lie the ruins of **Millom Castle**, the family seat of the Huddlestones. It was John Huddlestone who administered the last sacrament to Charles II, and the prosperity of the family had always been linked with the loyalist cause. The family chapel is a late Norman church, built in red sandstone, and has several beautiful 14th-century windows, including a rare fish window, in the west wall.

Millom Castle, now a farmhouse, was originally made of wood, but was strengthened against Scottish raids, notably after the Scottish victory at Bannockburn on 24 June 1314. The castle received further aggressive attention during the Wars of the Roses, while during the Civil War, being in Royalist ownership, it attracted the attentions of the Parliamentarian forces.

Number **14 St George's Terrace**, Millom was the birthplace of Norman Cornthwaite Nicholson (1914-1987), the best-known Cumbrian poet of modern times. The Folk Museum has an exhibition dedicated to Nicholson, who became one of the leading poets and dramatists of his generation. He wrote extensively about the Lake District, and his two main works of this genre *Cumberland and Westmorland* and *Portrait of the Lakes* have long been regarded as standard reading for anyone with even a fundamental interest in the region. He received the Queen's Medal for Poetry, and the OBE.

About 2 miles (3km) west-north-west of Millom are the **Lacra stone circles**, overlooking the sea to the west. Specialists in stone circles enthuse greatly about the Lacra circles, which are Bronze Age, and typical of the majority of stone circles. Although geographically close to other circles, at Brat's Hill, on Burn Moor, near Boot, and at Swinside, the Lacra circles are about 1000 years later [SD150814].

MILNTHORPE
[South Lakeland]

SD4981: 7 miles (11km) S of Kendal

Colonised by the Celts, the Romans and Norsemen, the village of Milnthorpe, owes its ancient name, Mylna porp, which means 'the village around the mill', to the Norse-Irish who arrived here more than 1000 years ago. It is an ancient settlement, now with newer development imposed upon it. Earthworks around Dallam Tower, a manor house dating from 1720-2, on the edge of the village, are thought to date from the Iron Age.

Until 1896, Milnthorpe was part of the larger 'township' of Heversham-with-Milnthorpe, and did not have its own place of worship until the consecration of the **church of St Thomas** in 1837. The ecclesiastical parish only became free of its connection with Heversham in 1924; much of Milnthorpe's history is, therefore, inextricably linked with Heversham.

The Milnthorpe Mill belonged to the manor of Heversham, which had, in turn, been granted by Ivo de Taillebois to St Mary's Abbey at York in 1094. In 1460, the Archbishop of York, William Booth, retained most of the revenue from Heversham church, but allowed the vicar a stipend of £20 from the earnings of the 'Mill of Milnthorpe anciently belonging to the said church'.

Milnthorpe was originally a seaport, until the River Bela silted up. The road through the village brought prosperity, notably during the 18th century, when much of the village as it appears today was fashioned. Numerous coaching inns catered for travellers, and for a thriving local industry that flourished along the River Bela. Its market tradition goes back to 1280, and the village's location was ideal for the purpose, situated at the junction of the road leading from the port to the High Road at Crooklands, and the less important north-south route.

As well as its busy Friday market, Milnthorpe also holds an annual fair, a reminder of the days when 'fairs' were occasions when wealthy merchants would meet and exchange goods. The tradition of fairs in this sense dates from the 13th and 14th centuries, and is often associated with the wool trade. Markets, by comparison, were primarily intended to serve the needs of the local people.

Now largely spared the heavy trails of Lake District-bound traffic that once jammed the village crossroads, this ancient village of limestone buildings arranged in nooks and crannies and along narrow lanes, combines both the intimacy of modest scale with a real sense of spaciousness. It is a lively, thriving and socially mixed community with a range of small industries and commercial activity, notably around the market square. The centre of the village has been designated a conservation area.

Dallam Tower, to the west of the village, stands in a deer park. It was built in 1720 around the remains of a pele tower.

Harmony Hall is Milnthorpe's finest house, and thought to have been built in the early 19th century by Captain Joseph Fayrer, a naval commander, who prospered at the end of the 18th century. The house was for a time used as a hotel, following which it was bought by a local publisher.

MILTON [Carlisle]

NY5560: 1½ miles ESE of Brampton

Milton is a small farming community adjoining the Newcastle to Carlisle railway. The first stationmaster at Milton was the person who invented the system of small cardboard railway tickets that were only superseded with the arrival of computer-generated tickets.

MONKHILL [Carlisle]

NY3458: 4 miles (6km) NW of Carlisle

For all its apparent peacefulness today, the small hamlet of Monkhill, on the course of the Roman Vallum, stands near what was a popular crossing point of the River Eden. The crossing would have been used both by invading Scots, and their later descendants, who came this way droving cattle, for here the Eden was at its narrowest.

MOOR ROW [Copeland]

NY0014: 3 miles (5km) SE of Whitehaven

The small, mainly residential village of Moor Row on the coastal plain between Cleator and Whitehaven grew following the discovery of iron ore in the 19th century, which persuaded many Cornish tin miners to come to the region in search of prosperity; the terraced houses that still remain are a legacy from this time.

MORESBY [Copeland]

NX9921: 2 miles (3km) NE of Whitehaven

As with many of the small villages on the coastal plain of Cumbria, Moresby is a coal mining community, and its prosperity has developed since the opening of the first mines in the 19th century.

The site of a large **Roman fort** (Gabrosentum) stands near the church and a steep slope running down to the sea. The Roman settlement was later built on when Moresby Hall was erected. Mary, Queen of Scots is said to have stayed at Moresby Hall on her way to imprisonment at Carlisle. Other mansions followed, all palatial residences for the big names in the coal mining industry, which almost equalled that of nearby Whitehaven in its turnover.

The **church of St Bridget** was built in 1822-3 to commemorate the Irish saint who visited Cumberland in the 6th century. It stands on the site of the Roman fort, and succeeds a number of other churches on the same site.

MORLAND [Eden]

NY5922: 6 miles (10km) NW of Appleby-in-Westmorland

Morland is a most attractive village in the Eden valley, comprising low houses on either side of Morland Beck, a modest stream that once powered small mills.

The **church of St Lawrence** is fortunate in having the only Anglo-Saxon tower in the former counties of Westmorland and Cumberland, although the top storey is a 17th-century addition. It is thought that the tower was built in the late 11th century by King Rufus, following his capture of Carlisle from the Scots.

The church contains some interesting items: ladders in the tower are hewn from a single tree trunk, there is a palimpsest of an early 16th-century brass with a small figure of a knight, and a particularly attractive, 13th-century coffin lid.

MUNGRISDALE [Eden]

NY3630: 8 miles (13km) NE of Keswick

This tiny community lies at the eastern edge of the northern fells of Lakeland, where suddenly the fells give way to much lower, flatter ground.

The lovely **church of St Kentigern** was built in 1756 and has a triple-decker pulpit and box pews.

Immediately behind the village rises **Souter Fell**, in walking terms nothing special, but it is a mountain to fuel the imagination, for it is said to be haunted. Harriet Martineau (1802-76), the English writer who eventually made her home in Ambleside, describes in *A Complete Guide to the English Lakes* how, 'This Souter, or Soutra Fell, is the mountain on which ghosts appeared in myriads, at intervals during ten years of the last century – presenting precisely the same appearance to twenty-six chosen witnesses, and to all the inhabitants of all the cottages within view of the mountain; and for a space of two hours and a half at one time – the spectral show being then closed by darkness.'

The story starts on Midsummer Eve in 1735, when a farm servant saw the whole of the eastern side of the mountain covered with marching troops coming from the northern end and disappearing on the summit. Predictably, when he told his story 'he was insulted on all hands'. Two years later, also on Midsummer Eve, the farmer himself saw men on the summit, apparently following their horses, but when he looked again a few minutes later, they were mounted and followed by 'an interminable array of troops, five abreast, marching from the eminence [at the northern end] and over the cleft'. Now it was the farmer's turn to be insulted. So, on Midsummer Eve of 1745, the year of the Jacobite rebellion, the farmer expressly invited twenty-six people to witness the occurrence. This time carriages were interspersed with the troops; and everybody knew that no carriages ever had been, or could be, on the summit of Souter Fell. 'The multitude was beyond

imagination; for the troops filled a space of half-a-mile, and marched quickly until night hid them, – still marching. There was nothing vaporous or indistinct about the appearance of these spectres. So real did they seem that some of the people went up, the next morning, to look for the hoof-marks of the horses; and awful it was to them to find not one foot-print on heather or grass.' Everything the witnesses saw was attested by them before a magistrate, when it also came out that two other people had seen the same thing in 1743.

By way of explanation, the editor of the *Lonsdale Magazine* reported that it was discovered that on Midsummer Eve of 1745, the Scottish rebels were exercising on the western coast of Scotland, and their movements, it was claimed, had been reflected by some transparent vapour. Of course, that may have explained the 1745 appearances, but what of earlier years?

Less than 2 miles (3 km) north of the village stands **Carrock Fell**, uninspiring as Lakeland fells go, but its summit conceals a fort that is something of an archaeological enigma. It pre-dates Roman times, and may well have been a stronghold of the Brigantes. If this is the case, it was certainly one of the largest forts of the time, measuring 245m by 110m, and its size and, therefore, importance is almost certainly to have brought it to the attentions of the Romans. They, it has been suggested, were responsible for casting down large parts of the fort's outer defences in order to render it useless without major rebuilding.

MURTON [Eden]

NY7221: 3 miles (5km) E of
Appleby-in-Westmorland

The small community of Murton is a typical north Pennine limestone village, lying at the foot of Murton Fell and approached along narrow lanes. Murton Fell forms part of the Warcop Military Training Area.

The **church of St John the Baptist** is Victorian and used to be lit by oil lamp; it houses a triple-decker pulpit.

NATEBY [Eden]

NY7706: 1 mile (2km) S of Kirkby Stephen

A small farming village around a village green, along the River Eden and on the edge of the wild uplands of Nine Standards Rigg, Nateby is regarded as the gateway to Swaledale and the moors of Mallerstang Edge. Many cottages here are built from bokram, a stone native to the Kirkby Stephen area.

NATLAND [South Lakeland]

SD5289: 2 miles (3km) S of Kendal

Natland is a sizeable, lovely village of old stone houses built around its green, and closely associated with nearby Oxenholme. The village is dominated by a small hill of Silurian rock, the Helm.

The impressive-looking **church of St Mark** was built during the reign of Edward VII by Austin and Paley on the site of one built in 1825. Natland was the chapelry of Kendal, and so there would have been a chapel on the site of the present church in the past.

NEAR SAWREY
[South Lakeland]

SD3695: 2½ miles (4km) SW of Bowness-on-Windermere

The two small villages of Far Sawrey and Near Sawrey lie amid a rolling, wooded landscape between the lake of Windermere and Esthwaite Water. Far Sawrey is surrounded by trees, along a lane that runs down to the Windermere ferry.

The Victorian **church of St Peter** (1866-72) is set on a grassy hillock along a wooded lane that continues to Newby Bridge, and which provides many glimpses of Windermere and the low, rolling fells beyond.

Graythwaite Hall is an Elizabethan house, reconstructed in part in 1840 and again almost 50 years later. The gardens are open to the public, and contain some fine topiary work.

The adjacent village of Near Sawrey, however, is renowned for its association with writer **Beatrix Potter** (wife of local solicitor Mr William Heelis). The 17th-century **Hill Top Farm**, now owned by the National Trust, was acquired with royalties from Peter Rabbit, and it was here that she created the world of Jemima Puddle-Duck and Pigling Bland. The house contains her furniture, china and pictures, and features prominently on the Lakeland tourist trail.

NENTHEAD [Eden]

NY7843: 4 miles (6km) SE of Alston

The mining village of Nenthead did not exist before the 1700s; it was built by the Quaker owners of the London Lead Mining Company, who were responsible for exploiting much of the mineral wealth of the northern Pennines. They established in Nenthead the first free library and the first compulsory schooling in the country. Before the arrival of the company, no one paid much heed to the welfare of the miners, many of whom lived in Alston and walked to work each day.

This did not please the benevolent owners of the company, who acquired the majority of the Nent valley mining leases, and in 1753 began construction of Nenthead, and encouraged the miners to develop an interest in farming, as a hedge against lean times. The foresight of the Company, and its caring attitude towards its employees, brought immense prosperity to one of the most remote and inhospitable regions of the country. In 1767, the income from 121 mines amounted to more than £77,000, at a time when the highest paid worker was earning less than £100 per year.

Once a major centre for the northern lead mining industry, Nenthead now houses the **Nenthead Mines Heritage Centre**.

NETHERBY [Carlisle]

NY3971: 2 miles (3km) N of Longtown

Netherby is neither a village nor a hamlet, being essentially the parklands that surround **Netherby Hall**, lived in by the Graham family since the 16th century. The hall, which looks Victorian, is built around a 15th-century tower, though much of the later building is mid-18th century.

The British statesman **Sir James Robert George Graham** (1792-1861), who became First Lord of the Admiralty under Earl Grey in 1830, was born in Netherby. He warmly supported Robert Peel in carrying through the legislation to repeal the Corn Laws, and on Peel's death became leader of the 'Peelites'.

Kirkandrews Suspension Bridge, spanning the River Esk, is a pedestrian bridge dating from 1877, and leads directly to the church and pele tower on the other side of the river.

NEW HUTTON [South Lakeland]

SD5691: 3 miles (5km) E of Kendal

New Hutton is a charming hamlet of houses and farms, many of which date from the 16th and 17th centuries. Until the time of Edward I, New Hutton was always linked with Old Hutton to the south, only achieving its separate identity in 1297.

The **church of St Stephen** was rebuilt during the reign of George IV to replace a chapel built in 1739.

NEWBIGGIN [Eden]

NY6228: 6 miles (10km) NW of Appleby-in-Westmorland

A small village in the shadow of Cross Fell, Newbiggin lies to the east of the main road to Appleby-in-Westmorland; one of numerous Newbiggins in Cumbria.

Containing a small amount of Norman masonry, the **church of St Edmund** was built in 1853-4 on the site of a former church. The east window contains some stained glass that probably dates from the 14th or 15th century.

Newbiggin Hall was rebuilt by the Crackenthorpe family in 1533, though much of the hall today is either Georgian or Victorian.

NEWBIGGIN-ON-LUNE [Eden]

NY7005: 4 miles (6km) SW of Kirkby Stephen

Newbiggin-on-Lune is a small farming village set in limestone country on the northern edge of the Howgills. Nearby St Helen's Well is fed by a spring that is said to be the source of the River Lune, which wanders westwards down the valley before turning south for Lancaster and ultimately the sea at Morecambe. Most writers, however, accept that the source of the Lune is high above Greenside Beck on Green Bell.

Farming, mainly fell sheep, has long been the mainstay of the village economy, but supplemented for many years by knitting, a feature of many Cumbrian villages.

NEWBY [Eden]

NY5921: 6 miles (10km) W of Appleby-in-Westmorland

Newby, in the parish of Morland, is a pleasant, small hamlet close by the River Lyvennet, with some 17th-century properties. It is mainly a farming community with some attractive stone cottages. One of them, Cross House, has a plague stone set into its garden wall. Plague Stones, or Plague Troughs were a common feature on the outskirts of towns at the end of the 16th century, and were places where well-wishers could leave food or money for the infected people.

NEWBY BRIDGE [South Lakeland]

SD3786: 8 miles (13km) NE of Ulverston

The village of Newby Bridge adjoins the River Kent, and earned its name from the five-arched, stone bridge built across the river in 1651 to replace an earlier wooden structure. It caters largely for the passing tourist trade.

NEWLAND [South Lakeland]

SD3079: 1 mile (2km) N of Ulverston

Newland is a small cluster of houses in a cul-de-sac on the outskirts of Ulverston. The hamlet was founded on the iron industry, and held the distinction of having the first blast furnace in the Furness region.

On the Hill of Hoad above the hamlet of Newland stands a memorial built in 1850 to Ulverston-born **Sir John Barrow** (1764-1848); it resembles Eddystone Lighthouse.

NEWTON ARLOSH [Allerdale]

NY1955: 2 miles (3km) SW of Kirkbride

Newton Arlosh is a straggling village south of the Solway, surrounded by peat lands and salt marshes. Its name signifies that is was, indeed, a 'new town', but new is relative here since the village it replaced, Skinburness, was washed away by the sea as long ago as 1301.

The delightful church, dedicated to **St John the Baptist**, was founded in the 14th century by the abbot of Holme Cultram Abbey, and has a tiny doorway, only 2ft 7ins wide; clearly it was constructed with defence against the Scots in mind. It is one of three examples remaining in Cumbria of fortified churches, built during the 14th century, as protection against the predations of Border raiders. Other similar churches exist at Burgh-by-Sands and Great Salkeld. Until the Dissolution of the Monasteries, St John's was the parish church for Abbeytown, but then the abbey church (see Abbeytown) was used, leaving Newton's church to fall into ruin. Fortunately, this delightful building was restored in 1844.

NEWTON REIGNY [Eden]

NY4731: 2½ miles (4km) NW of Penrith

An attractive gathering of old and new properties, the village of Newton Reigny takes its name from the de Reigny family who owned this part of the then Cumberland in the 12th century. Its **church of St John** was built by Ewan Christian in 1876, though the interior is 12th and 13th century.

To the north of the village is Catterlen Hall, an L-shaped building around a small pele tower, and of some interest. The hall dates from 1577, though the pele is certainly earlier, as are other parts of the building.

OLD HUTTON [South Lakeland]

SD5688: 3 miles (5km) SE of Kendal

Until the time of Edward I, Old Hutton was always linked with New Hutton to the north, only achieving its separate identity in 1297. The village is another among many in Cumbria that in former times needed to be self-contained, milling its own corn, tending to the needs of its animals, focusing their efforts internally on the village, as well as finding external markets for their wool.

The church is dedicated to **St John the Baptist**, and was built in 1873, replacing a number of earlier ones. John Wesley is known to have stayed here overnight on his way from Leeds to the Cumberland coast.

Blease Hall lies a short way along the Oxenholme road, and was built around 1600. It has large mullioned and transomed windows, and was built by Roger Bateman, a cloth manufacturer from Kendal.

ORMATHWAITE [Allerdale]

NY2625: 1½ miles (2km) N of Keswick

The small hamlet of Ormathwaite lies tight against the lower slopes of Skiddaw, and is the place where, at Ormathwaite Hall, William Brownrigg (1711-1800) lived. He was a leading scientist of his day, and received among his visitors, Benjamin Franklin (in 1772). Together, by experimenting on Derwentwater, they proved that you could, indeed, calm troubled waters by pouring oil on them, noting, 'The water, which had been in great agitation before, was instantly calmed, upon pouring in only a very small quantity of oil.' The hall was later the home of Joseph Wilkinson, the artist.

ORMSIDE [Eden]

NY7017: 2 miles (4km) SE of Appleby-inWestmorland

Ormside is comprised of two small hamlets, Great and Little Ormside, on gently rising ground above the River Eden.

Ormside Hall dates from the 14th or 15th century, and stands close by the **church of St James**, which has a sturdy fortified tower, stonework of the 11th century, and a 15th-century roof.

ORTON [Eden]

NY6208: 2½ miles (4km) N of Tebay

The lovely village of Orton, surrounded by trees and developed around a village green between two streams, is a popular staging post on the Northern Coast to Coast Walk, prior to the long haul to Kirkby Stephen. Granted a market charter during the reign of Edward I, Orton lies in a beautiful spot at the foot of Orton Scar, and is overlooked by its 13th-century **church of All Saints**, which stands on a knoll by the northerly approach to the village.

Many of Orton's dwellings date from the 17th and 18th centuries: Petty Hall, on the main road through the village, once belonged to the Birkbeck family, and bears the date 1604 on a panel over the doorway. Not far away, Orton Hall was built in 1662, and for many years was the home of the Burn family; it is now holiday flats.

The most famous of Orton's sons was **George Whitehead**, one of the founders of the Society of Friends. Born in Orton in 1636, he fell under the spell of George Fox, and, much to his family's distress, became a Quaker while still a youth. It was not uncommon at the time for Quakers to be baited and beaten by those – Anglicans, Presbyterians and Baptists – who hated them. Yet somehow, Whitehead coped with this trauma, and embarked on a personal crusade, preaching widely, and arguing with preachers and teachers alike. He visited imprisoned Quakers, at first freely, and then as a prisoner himself; he was placed in stocks, and frequently whipped. Undeterred, he continued to hold services on windswept hillsides, petitioned the House of Commons, and spent more and more time in prison.

Nothing, however, could dissuade him from his cause; he even persuaded Charles II to free every captive Quaker, only to see them later thrown back in prison and robbed of their land. From James II he secured immunity from persecution, but it was not until after the Revolution that Parliament passed an act recognising Quakers as citizens. It has been said that if George Fox was the creator of the Society of Friends, Whitehead "was the lawgiver, the Moses of his creed". He appeared before seven sovereigns, gathering concessions that later went into the Quaker Magna Carta of 1696. Whitehead died in 1723, at the age of 86.

OUSBY [Eden]

NY6134: 10 miles (16km) NNW of Appleby-in-Westmorland

Ousby is a small community of houses and farms with little unity, scattered along the base of the northern Pennines, and in the shadow of Cross Fell, the highest of the Pennine heights.

The **church of St Luke** stands isolated from the village, and nearer to Townhead. It is a plain, stone building, and was substantially restored in 1858, though one window may be Early English. The church contains an interesting oak effigy, thought to date from the 14th century, of a knight in armour, with crossed legs resting on his dog.

OUTHGILL [Eden]

NY7801: 4½ miles (7km) S of Kirkby Stephen

A small and scattered farmland hamlet, Outghill lies in a beautiful setting below Mallerstang Edge in the Vale of Eden.

Pendragon Castle is a late Norman pele tower, which was restored by Lady Anne Clifford in 1660, following its destruction by fire in a Border raid in 1541.

The **church of St Mary** is a 17th-century church, partially renovated by Lady Anne Clifford.

OXENHOLME [South Lakeland]

SD5389: 2 miles (3km) SE of Kendal

A large village of mainly modern housing on the main West Coast railway line, that serves the Lake District. The village is closely linked with nearby Nateby, and both are dominated by the Helm, a fine summit of Silurian rock.

PAPCASTLE [Allerdale]

NY1031: 1 mile (2km) NW of Cockermouth

The village of Papcastle is built on the site of the **Roman fort** of Derventio, a garrison that was of some size and located at a major road junction. The fort was of strategic significance, and able to send troops to the defences along the Solway section of Hadrian's Wall. The site of the fort is now buried beneath fields, but there is evidence that a large village (a vicus) occupied land around the fort. Stones for Cockermouth Castle were long ago filched from the Roman fort, which was occupied until the end of the 4th century.

PATTERDALE [Eden]

NY3915: 7 miles (11km) NNE of Ambleside

Buttressed by high fells all around, Patterdale is an elongated village at the southern tip of Ullswater that caters today largely for walkers and day trippers. To the south of the village, the main road winds its way up and across the Kirkstone Pass to Ambleside and Windermere.

The dale that today we call Patterdale is named after St Patrick, one of three famous missionaries (the others were St Ninian and St Kentigern) thought to have travelled in this region on evangelical missions during the early years of the 5th century.

The modern village was described by Baddeley in his *Guide to the English Lake District* as 'one of the most charmingly situated in Britain, and in itself clean and comely'. Many of these remote villages were presided over by one dominant family. In Patterdale it was the Mounseys, who were described as the 'kings of Patterdale', and lived at Patterdale Hall, now rebuilt, but dating from around 1677.

It would be unthinkable to have in Patterdale a church that wasn't dedicated to St Patrick. Small and neat, with a tower and saddleback roof, **St Patrick's** church

was rebuilt in 1853 following storm damage.

Patterdale's annual **Dog Day** at the end of August is a traditional show with sheepdog trials, sheep shearing, hound trailing, shows of foxhounds and terriers, and numerous rural crafts.

PENNINGTON [South Lakeland]

SD2677: 2 miles (3km) SW of Ulverston

A small, spread out village on the outskirts of Ulverston, Pennington consists mainly of farms and small, isolated communites. As with many places in south Lakeland, the iron industry created much employment, and attracted miners from as far away as Cornwall. The industry flourished for over 100 years, but then saw a gradual decline after 1880.

The **church of St Michael and All Angels** was built in 1826 on the site of a former church, and altered a hundred years later. In the south aisle is a re-set Norman tympanum with an inscription in runic characters. It is certainly one of the most fascinating relics of the former manor.

PENRITH [Eden]

NY5130: 18 miles (29km) SE of Carlisle

There is little evidence of the extent to which Penrith and its neighbourhood was occupied during pre-Roman times, but it remains certain that early Bronze Age man would have lived in small communities here, moving about with their sheep and cattle from clearing to clearing: travellers have been passing through ever since.

The Romans built a fort, **Voreda**, about 5 miles (8km) north of the town, roughly midway between their strongholds at Brougham and Carlisle.

During the 9th and 10th centuries, Penrith was the capital of the ancient kingdom of Cumbria. As such it was a semi-independent state, and until 1070 formed part of the kingdom of Scotland and Strathclyde. Paradoxically, it later played a significant part in the defence of the surrounding countryside against Scottish reivers.

The town was granted a charter by Henry III (1216-1272), and soon began to thrive. By the 18th century it was an important market town, being situated on the long-established main north-south route between England and Scotland. In consequence it has had to bear the attentions of numerous invaders: first the Romans, then the Angles, the Saxons and the Danes, as well as the Scots, who found its prosperity too much temptation to resist.

Inevitably, the town developed to serve the needs of travellers, and its economy was based on brewing and a wide range of traders, cattle dealers and shopkeepers.

Penrith, unlike Appleby, was never a county town, and has always played a supporting role to Carlisle. Although the town did have its castle, it was never the formidable stronghold that Carlisle was. Nevertheless, Penrith's importance was not a trifling matter: it was not only a Border town in the sense of the border with Scotland, but it also stood on the border between the former counties of Westmorland and Cumberland. In addition, it was the centre of that part of Cumberland known as the Leath Ward in the **Forest of Inglewood**. In this context a 'ward' corresponds roughly with the 'hundreds' of south and west England, or the former 'ridings' of Yorkshire. Westmorland had four wards – East, West, Kendal and Lonsdale, and Cumberland five – Eskdale, Cumberland, Leath, Allerdale-below-Derwent and Allerdale-above-Derwent.

The English romantic novelist Ann Radcliffe (1764-1823), remembered for her romantic novel *The Mysteries of Udolpho* toured the Lake District in 1794. At that time she noted, Penrith was a much less developed place than today 'consisting chiefly of old houses'. 'Penrith,' she went on, 'despite its many symptoms of antiquity, is not deficient of neatness'. The houses are chiefly white, with door and window cases of the red stone found in the neighbourhood. Some of the smaller have over their doors dates of the latter end of the sixteenth century. [The town spreads] prettily along the skirts of a mountain, with its many roofs of blue slate, among which the church rises near a dark grove.'

Celia Fiennes, who visited Penrith on her great tour of 1698, recorded: 'The stones and slatt about Peroth look'd so red that at my entrance into the town thought its buildings were all of brick, but after found it to be the coullour of the stone which I saw in the Quarrys look very red, their slatt is the same which cover their houses; its a pretty large town a good market for cloth that they spinn in the country, hempe and also woollen; its a great market for all sorts of cattle meate corne etc.'

Today, Penrith is still a great market town. The former livestock market, which replaced the traditional open markets held in Great Dockray, the Market Square and Sandgate, has itself succumbed to a modern counterpart. Great Dockray, however, is still used for a weekly street market (Tuesdays), and was formerly used for the twice yearly hiring fairs that were a feature of (mainly) northern life. The town is very much the focal point of the Eden valley, with a sizeable shopping centre and a good mix of traditional shops and attractive arcades. Yet it retains, as Ann Radcliffe observed, the intricate street pattern typical of Border towns, where the ability to corral cattle (and people) against raiders was of key importance; as a result, Penrith is a delightful mix of open spaces and narrow streets. In the centre of the Market Square stands the monument and clocktower built in 1861 as a tribute to Sir George and Lady Musgrave of Eden Hall, and to commemorate the death of Philip Musgrave at the age of 26.

The railway, the London and North Western, reached as far as Lancaster by 1840, but controversy then surrounded the best route by which to proceed to Scotland. Four years later, a Royal Commission determined the route that was to go through Penrith. It fell to Joseph Locke (1805-60), the English civil engineer, to extend the line under the terms of what was at the time the largest single railway contract ever placed, in the sum of £1.2 million. The building of the line employed almost 10,000 men and 100 horses, at times working non-stop around the clock. The labour force was a mix, commonplace at the time, of English, Irish and Scottish, and, perhaps not surprisingly, disturbances and riots were a frequent occurrence. Nevertheless, the line was completed in December 1846. The Eden Valley line followed in June 1862, and the Cockermouth, Keswick and Penrith line at the beginning of 1865.

High above the town rises tree-covered **Beacon Hill**, its summit topped by Beacon Pike, a monument built in 1719 (restored in 1780) on the spot where beacons have been lit in times of war and emergency. The beacon system was developed during the time of Henry III, and by 1403 it was a statutory requirement. A commission was issued in October 1429 to Richard Neville, Lord Warden of the local March, to set 'Bekyns' up in suitable places to give warning of the approach of the enemy. The last time the Penrith Beacon was fired for this purpose was in 1804, during the Napoleonic Wars, when it was seen by Walter Scott,

Dame Ann Birkett's school, Penrith, attended by William and Dorothy Wordsworth

who was travelling through Cumberland, and who is said then to have hurried home to join his volunteer regiment.

It is the presence of such a prominent landmark close by the town that has given rise to some controversy over the meaning of its name. Down the centuries it has been known variously as Penreth, Penerith, Perith, Perath and Penryth, before reaching its present spelling. Some authorities consider that the name signifies a place under the 'red hill', alluding to the dominance of red sandstone around the neighbouring countryside. Others conjecture that the name is of Celtic origin, meaning 'the ford by the hill', equally plausible since there used to be two fords at nearby Eamont Bridge.

In the centre of town, now part of the Tudor Coffee Room, is **Dame Ann Birkett's school**, attended by William and Dorothy Wordsworth and by Mary Hutchinson, who was to become William's wife. In the Market Square was Cookson's draper's shop, owned by the father of Anne Cookson, later to be the mother of the Wordsworth family, who was born here on 20 January 1745. Anne died in 1778, following a visit to London, and she was buried in Penrith churchyard, though the exact spot is not known.

Penrith Castle was built c1400 by William Strickland (later Bishop of Carlisle and Archbishop of Canterbury), and enlarged in the 1470s by the Duke of Gloucester (later Richard III), when he was Lord Warden of the Western Marches, a post that meant he had the unenviable task of maintaining peace along the border with Scotland.

The castle is unlike other Cumberland castles. A licence to crenellate was given to Strickland in 1397 and 1399, and so he built a large square structure around a central courtyard, reminiscent of Bolton Castle in North Yorkshire. The castle has lain in ruins since 1550.

Originating in Norman times (1133), the sandstone **church of St Andrew**, dates from the 13th and 14th centuries, of which time only the tower remains: most of the church was rebuilt between 1720 and 1722, possibly under the direction of Nicholas Hawksmoor, a pupil and colleague of Sir Christopher Wren.

The church has a three-sided gallery and a brass candelabra suspended from the ceiling which was a gift from the Duke of Cumberland in 1745 as a reward for the town's loyalty during the Jacobite Rising. A plaque in the church commemorates over 2200 people who died of the plague in 1597. The first vicar of Penrith, Sir Walter de Cantelupe, was installed in 1223.

In the churchyard, the **Giant's Grave** comprises two interesting crosses, each about eleven feet high (3.5m), and standing separated by four 10th-century hogsback tombstones made from red sandstone. The grave is said to be that of a legendary giant, Ewan Caesarius, King of all Cumbria, who reigned from 900-937. He was renowned as a slayer of monsters, men and beasts, and the hogsback tombs that stand by his grave are thought to represent wild boar he killed in the nearby Inglewood Forest. More prosaically, the 'grave' is now thought to be a group of Saxon crosses.

The town hall was created in 1905-6 by the modernisation of properties designed by Robert Adam (1728-92), the Scottish architect, and built in 1791 as two houses, one of which housed **Captain John Wordsworth**, cousin of the poet. Wordsworth Street is named after the captain, not the poet.

The town hall incorporates into its facade a facsimile of the town seal. For many years the original brass seal was missing until it was discovered in a ditch at Brampton, near Carlisle, where, presumably, it had been lost by a Scottish reiver retreating from a raid, possibly one of the two occasions when Penrith was laid waste. During the 19th century the seal came into the possession of the Member of Parliament for Carlisle, who gave it to the old local Board of Health.

Robinson's School is a listed building, an Elizabethan structure altered (and inscribed) in 1670. It was used as a school until the early 1970s, and today houses the **Penrith Tourist Information Centre and Museum**, which contains displays of local history, geology and archaeology of the Penrith area, including exhibits of Roman pottery and 'cup and ring' marked stones from Maughanby. The founder of the school was William Robinson, a local man who became a prosperous London merchant, and left an annuity of £55 for the upkeep of the school.

Middlegate used to be known as Long Front. Before the 19th century there was no direct route through this street, the main thoroughfare being along the present Queen Street (then known as Middlegate), over the archway of Fallowfield's Bridge, and across Thacka Beck, before meeting the present main road.

Thacka Beck used to be one of the town's important water supplies, having been diverted from the River Petteril to the north of the town by William Strickland in 1400.

In Castlegate is the **Penrith Steam Museum**, housing a display of steam traction engines, farm machinery, a blacksmith's forge and a Victorian cottage.

Friargate contains a number of interesting buildings. The Mansion House, built in 1750, is one of the grandest houses in Penrith, and now houses the offices of the

district council. Nearby, Abbots Bank, dating from 1820, stands on the site of a 13th-century chapel of the Augustinians, while next door is the Friarage, from 1717, built on the site of the original house of the Grey Friars of the Order of St Augustine.

Hutton Hall, an 18th-century mansion, was built on to an original pele tower, one of many built in this troubled region. They were generally three or four storey stone towers surrounded by a palisade, and in later years by a stone wall which enclosed a yard.

PENRUDDOCK [Eden]

NY4227: 5½ miles (9km) WSW of Penrith

Penruddock is a small village of old and new houses along the boundary of the Lake District National Park; it is one of a number of old Celtic settlements in the area, adjacent Motherby is another.

All Saints church is a roughcast structure, built in 1902, with windows in the Late Perpendicular style.

PLUMBLAND [Allerdale]

NY1539: 5½ miles (9km) NNE of Cockermouth

An active farming village, though essentially just one long main street, beyond the northern fells of the Lake District, Plumbland is in a part of the Lake District that has been inhabited since Neolithic times. On the gently falling slopes beyond the northern fells, the village looks out to the hills of southern Scotland, and being off the tourist route retains much of its traditional village atmosphere.

Lime was quarried locally for agricultural use, and taken to kilns a short distance away, where, after treatment, is was distributed further afield by rail.

The **church of St Cuthbert** is Victorian, but it stands on the site of a Norman church of 1130. There may well have been a Saxon place of worship here, too, perhaps as early as the 8th century; certainly two Viking hogsback tombs from the 10th century have been dated.

Plumbland is another Cumbrian village where the stream was said to have run red when Charles I was beheaded (see also Bothel).

PLUMPTON [Eden]

NY4936: 4 miles (6km) N of Penrith

Plumpton used to be part of Lazonby parish, and is a scattered village on the River Petteril. It is particularly renowned for the Roman fort of **Voreda** which lies to the north of the village. The fort was occupied from the time of Hadrian until the 4th century.

Today, Plumpton is its own parish, its **church of St John the Evangelist** having been built in 1907, to replace a chapel-of-ease.

In medieval times Plumpton was a 'hay', a special hunting ground, set apart for the keeping of deer, and often enclosed, as was Plumpton Park during the time of Henry III.

PONSONBY [Copeland]

NY0505: 1½ miles (2km) NW of Gosforth

- see Calder Bridge

POOLEY BRIDGE [Eden]

NY4724: At the NE end of Ullswater

Spread out along its two main streets, both lined with charming, old, stone houses and cottages, Pooley Bridge spans the River Eamont, which used to be the boundary between Cumberland and Westmorland. Before the bridge was built in the 16th century, the village was simply called Pooley, a corruption of the 'pool by the hill'. The hill in this case is Dunmallet, which bears a small, but undistinguished Iron Age fort.

Today, Pooley Bridge, with its splendid views down the length of Ullswater, caters for tourists, though it has been a busy place in its own right in past times. That the village held a regular market can be seen from the widening of the village streets to accommodate the one-time market square, where, among other things, there used to be a fish market. There is no doubt, however, that Pooley Bridge was always overshadowed by Penrith, and by the middle of the 19th century the only evidence of trading at Pooley Bridge was its sheep and cattle fair.

In the centre of the village, the **church of St Paul** is purely Victorian, built in 1868, and with few distinguishing features. Before it was built the nearest church was St Michael's at Barton.

Eusemere, near the bridge and just to the south-east of the village, was the home of Catherine Clarkson, the wife of Thomas Clarkson (1760-1846) the anti-slavery campaigner. Mrs Clarkson, referred to as such throughout her journals, was a close friend of Dorothy Wordsworth, and both Clarksons and Wordsworths spent much time together and in correspondence.

PORT CARLISLE [Allerdale]

NY2461: 10 miles (16km) NW of Carlisle

This coastal hamlet on the Solway Firth was once known as Fisher's Cross, and lies at the western end of the Carlisle Canal. The canal, originally financed by businessmen, was begun in 1819 and opened in 1823. In travel terms, it meant that passengers and goods from Carlisle could reach places down the Irish Sea coast, like Liverpool. in one day, instead of a much longer overland route. Within a matter of years, however, the canal was running into financial difficulties, and was closed, finally being drained in 1853; some of its course was used for the Maryport to Carlisle railway, which has now also gone.

PORTINSCALE [Allerdale]

NY2523: 1 mile (2km) W of Keswick

A pleasant village at the northern end of Derwentwater, Portinscale both caters for tourists and maintains its agricultural traditions. There is evidence of prehistoric settlement here. In 1901 an ancient stonesmith's place of work was excavated, revealing a collection of axeheads in various stages of completion.

PRESTON PATRICK [South Lakeland]

SD5483: 5 miles (8km) SSE of Kendal

Preston Patrick is a mainly farming village that comprises the hamlets of Gatebeck, Goose Green, Nook and Millness, and was mentioned in the Domesday Book as in the manor of Torfin.

The **church of St Patrick** has suffered something of an identity crisis. When it was built and later rebuilt in 1852 it was known as St Gregory's, but by the time the chancel was rebuilt in 1892 it appears to have been renamed St Patrick's. It is, nevertheless, a large and pleasant church, standing on a small hillock overlooking the M6 and undulating fields. Its tower

carries a large cross that is illuminated at night. It was in the old chapel here that George Fox came preaching the perfectibility of all men through inward personal experiences, the doctrine of the Quaker faith.

RAMPSIDE [Barrow-in-Furness]

SD2366: 3 miles (5km) SE of Barrow-in-Furness

Rampside is an ancient and pleasant village at the mainland end of the causeway to Roa Island. The village is so called because the promontory on which it is built was considered to have the form of a ram's head. Most of the village is modern residential development, though there were a number of 17th-century houses here for many years, including Rampside Hall.

The village's church stands half a mile (1km) to the north, beside the Barrow road, and is dedicated to **St Michael**. Built in 1840, it is a replacement for a chapel of 1621 in which George Fox came to preach.

RAUGHTON HEAD [Carlisle]

NY3745: 6 miles (10km) S of Carlisle

Pronounced 'Raftonhead', Raughton Head is a very small village of little more than a few whitewashed farms on a wedge of ground between the River Caldew and Roe Beck. A short distance away across the Caldew is the red sandstone **Rose Castle**, a magnificent building that has been the residence of the bishops of Carlisle since the 13th century, though the present building is thought to be 19th century. The original medieval castle was damaged by fire in

1646, following which one of the bishops pulled down two of the ranges.

The large-towered **church of All Saints** was restored in 1761 and 1881, and before 1936 had no dedication.

RAVENGLASS [Copeland]

SD0896: 4 miles (6km) SE of Seascale

Once a centre for pearl-fishing and smuggling brandy and tobacco, and formerly a Roman supply base (Glannaventa), the village of Ravenglass is today renowned for the narrow-gauge Ravenglass and Eskdale Railway, though it is still popular with sailors and anglers. In 1208, King John granted the Lord of Egremont the right to hold a market here, and an annual fair, although the market trade was terminally affected by the coming of the railways.

The village lies on an estuary where three rivers – the Esk, the Irt and the Mite – meet, and enjoys a sheltered position that in the past made it an important harbour. The name derives from 'Yr afon glas', meaning the grey river.

Of the fort built here by the Romans, nothing now remains. The ivy-clad ruins of the Bath House, known locally as Walls Castle, however, are a prominent feature in the town, and remarkable for being among the tallest and best preserved of Roman constructions in the country.

Muncaster Castle, set in beautiful gardens to the east of Ravenglass, has been the home of the Pennington family since the 1200s (some authorities say 1325 – the date of the pele tower around which it is built), though the present structure is the product of extensive alterations in 1783 and 1862-6.

The castle, which is open to the public, is now the home of the Gordon Duff Pen-

nington family, and houses a wide variety of classical furniture, some fine tapestries, and paintings by renowned artists such as Joshua Reynolds and Gainsborough. One of its greatest treasures is the **'Luck of Muncaster'**, an enamelled glass bowl given to a 15th-century member of the family, Sir John Pennington, by Henry VI, who took shelter in the castle after a battle. Legend has it that the king was found wandering by a local shepherd and taken to Muncaster. On his departure the king left behind his drinking bowl in gratitude, and tradition decrees that so long as the bowl remains intact, the Pennington family will prosper. Needless to say, the real bowl is locked safely away, and only a replica is on display.

Muncaster Corn Mill, a mile up the River Mite, stands on a site that has been occupied by a mill since at least 1455. The present building dates from the early 18th century, and electricity was generated by the mill until 1958, using a waterwheel. Regular working at the mill ended in 1961, but the mill was restored to working order in 1976-7. A large waterwheel turns in the mill race, and traditional stoneground flours are once more produced. The mill operates regularly throughout the summer.

Between Ravenglass and Boot in Eskdale runs the **Ravenglass and Eskdale Miniature Railway**, on a track that is only 15 inches (38cms) wide. The original line was much wider, and was opened in 1875 to transport iron ore from the Nab Gill mines at Boot, about 8 miles (13km) higher up the valley. It started carrying passengers a year later, but has experienced a chequered history. In 1877, the Railway Company became bankrupt, but, because of the pressing need still to carry iron ore, the line continued to operate under the official receiver. Over a period of time, however, the demand for iron reduced, as did the remaining supplies of ore in the mines, and the line once again encountered financial difficulties. The line was closed in 1913, but was re-opened as a narrow gauge railway in 1915 by Mr Bassett-Lowke, a model-maker. The smaller trains took up the carrying of goods and passengers, aided by the opening of granite quarries and a developing tourist trade. But tourism proved insufficient to sustain the service after the granite quarries closed in 1953.

In 1960, the line was bought at auction by a group of enthusiasts, and is now run by a new company as one of the county's major tourist attractions.

The **Ravenglass Railway Museum** contains old rolling stock, reconstructions and models telling the story of the railway.

The coastline around Ravenglass provides habitats for a wide range of coast-favouring flora and fauna; the dunes and beach are both nature reserves, as are the Eskmeals Dunes on the opposite side of the estuary.

Each year the village stages the **Muncaster Country Fair and Sheepdog Trials**, which also feature Cumberland and Westmorland wrestling, gun dog displays, falconry, and rural crafts.

RAVENSTONEDALE [Eden]

NY7204: 4 miles (6km) SW of Kirkby Stephen

Tucked away along the northern flank of the Howgills, the village of Ravenstonedale is comprised mostly of attractive, limestone-built cottages. The name derives from a custom, still observed as late as the 18th century, of paying a bounty of two pence for every raven's head.

The **church of St Oswald**, a fine Georgian church, is scheduled as one of the historic churches of England, and has a history that indicates a very early settlement in the dale. The tower dates from 1738, and the rest from 1744. Inside, the church has tiered box pews opposing each other across a central aisle, and overlooked by a triple-decker pulpit. The east window displays a memorial to the last woman burnt at the stake at Tyburn in 1685, apparently for performing an act of kindness in the cause of her Protestant faith!

The ruins of a small monastery, thought to be of the Gilbertine Cell from Watton, have been excavated in the churchyard, and it is certain from documentary evidence that the church and manor existed in the 13th century.

Monks of the order of Sempringham brought with them Rights of Sanctuary, later to be abolished by James I. A Refuge Bell used to hang in the tower, and its tolling would signify a fair trial, and even escape from arrest, by the Court of the Dale for any fugitive who managed to ring it, a ploy that was still taken advantage of into the 17th century. Even after the Rights of Sanctuary were abolished, the court continued to legislate on local issues. Those awaiting trial, presumably those who had not managed to ring the bell, were imprisoned in a vault on the north side of the church.

In 1738 the ruinous tower was rebuilt at a cost of £264 3s. 5¾d, and by 1744 the entire church was rebuilt, its 13th-century south porch reconstructed stone by stone. Rebuilding of the tower was evidently thirsty work for a detail in the parish accounts notes that on July 18th, 1738, when the foundation of the steeple was laid, the sum of two shillings was spent at each of the four alehouses.

RENWICK [Eden]

NY5943: 3 miles (5km) NE of Kirkoswald

Renwick is an attractive farming village along the foot of the high northern Pennine summits, adjoining Raven Beck. The name is a contraction of Ravenswick, meaning 'a place near the banks of Raven Beck'. Most of the properties in the village date from the 18th and 19th centuries.

The **church of All Saints** is built on the site of a church which was probably founded by Celtic missionaries around AD600. The present church was built in 1845 on the site of a former church rebuilt in 1733.

There is a story prevalent in Renwick, that when the old church was being rebuilt in 1733 an enormous bat flew out and frightened the villagers. One man, however, remained, and slew the bat, and was rewarded by the grant of his estate in perpetuity. Ever since the natives of Renwick have been known as Renwick Bats.

ROCKCLIFFE [Carlisle]

NY3661: 4 miles (6km) NW of Carlisle

Rockcliffe is a scattered community on a wide neck of land where both the River Esk and the River Eden flow into the Solway Firth; and was once an important port, shipbuilding centre, and crossing point for the River Eden. Little remains of these maritime connections, and today the village is quiet and rather secluded, quite a contrast to days when it had a feverish smuggling trade, conveying salt and whisky from Scotland on a rather grand scale.

The village's **church of St Mary** is Victorian, and very attractive, but it is the 1000-year-old **Norse cross** in the churchyard that is the outstanding feature.

Overlooking the ford there used to be a large castle, a defence against Border raids, which was originally built in the 16th century, but no trace of it now exists.

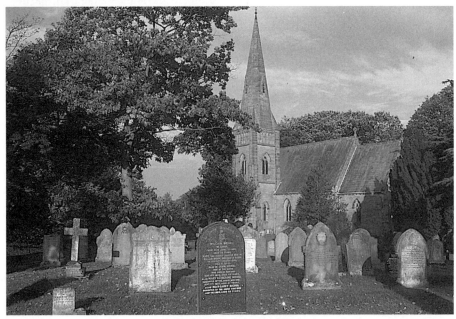

St Mary's Church, Rockcliffe

ROSLEY [Allerdale]

NY3245: 8 miles (13km) SW of Carlisle

Rosley is a tiny village of old houses and farms beyond the northern fells of Lakeland. The name means 'a place where horses were kept', and indicates that an ancient horse fair used to be held here.

The **church of the Holy Trinity** is about 1 mile (2km) north of the village and built in 1840, but has little of interest.

ROSTHWAITE [Allerdale]

NY2614: 5 miles (8km) S of Keswick

An attractive village of grey-stone and white cottages, farms and hotels at the southern end of Borrowdale, sitting between two rivers – the Derwent and Stonethwaite Beck. Nearby **Johnny Wood** (National Trust), is a typical and fine oak wood with ferns and liverworts in profusion, such that it is listed as a Site of Special Scientific Interest.

Each year in September, Rosthwaite hosts the **Borrowdale Shepherds' Meet and Show**, which features sheepdog trials, fell racing, Cumberland and Westmorland wrestling, hound trailing, and a range of rural crafts and displays.

ROTTINGTON [Copeland]

NX9613: 1 mile (2km) NW of St Bees

Rottington is a small farming hamlet on the nose of high coastal ground between Whitehaven and St Bees. Legend has it that a Viking giant, Rottin, is buried here, but before his death, he and his allies had carried off several of the nuns from the abbey.

RUSLAND [South Lakeland]

SD3488: 2½ miles (4km) NW of Newby Bridge

Rusland is both a valley, probably little changed over hundreds of years, and a small community of cottages and ancient farms. It lies in a tranquil corner of Furness between Windermere and Coniston Water, mainly surrounded by woodland and moss. The valley river is known as Rusland Pool, a name that more than suggests there may have been a lake here in the past. Up-valley is Force Beck, Force Mills and Force Forge, the latter a profitable business run by the Rawlinsons of Rusland Hall.

In the woodland around the village, along the minor road to Haverthwaite, are the renowned **Rusland Beeches.** These splendid trees may originally have formed part of a massive hedge, but in the 1990s became a cause for concern because of their age and condition. A furore broke out when the national park authority announced plans to fell the trees, but in the end some remained, others received surgery, while a few had to be removed and replaced with new trees. In a similar context, **Rusland Moss** is a Site of Special Scientific Interest as an area of undamaged moss, and has a number of native pine trees that were used by foresters in the 18th century for seed.

Georgian **Rusland Hall** has had several owners, and was largely restored in 1845. The **church of St Paul** was first built in 1745, and substantially rebuilt in 1868.

The ashes of **Arthur Ransome** (1884-1967), journalist and author of *Swallows and Amazons*, lie buried in St Paul's churchyard.

RYDAL [South Lakeland]

NY3606: 1 mile (2km) NW of Ambleside

There is little to the scattered grey-stone village of Rydal, strung out along the main road running north from Ambleside. The nearby lake, **Rydal Water,** was a favourite spot of the Wordsworths, who would often have picnics on the island. It lies sandwiched between the beetling slopes of Nab Scar and those of Loughrigg Fell, and would frequently freeze over, providing the Wordsworth household with another opportunity for enjoyment – skating.

Rydal Mount was home to William Wordsworth and his family from 1813 to his death in 1850. He was at the peak of his fame at this time, though his best work had all been accomplished, mostly at Dove Cottage. Socially, the house was a significant step up for Wordsworth, and put him on calling terms with the local gentry. Rydal Mount is open to the public during summer months, and receives many visitors, much as it did (though on a lesser scale) when Wordsworth lived there. Originally, the house was a farmhouse called Keens. It was enlarged in the 18th century, and renamed in 1803; Wordsworth rented it from Lady Diana le Fleming of Rydal Hall.

Not far away is **Nab Cottage**, a fine farmhouse dated 1702, and also with poetic associations. **Thomas de Quincey** (1785-1859) followed the Wordsworths into Dove Cottage, but spent much time at Nab Cottage courting Margaret (Peggy) Simpson, whom he later married. The Wordsworths did not approve the of the match, and Dorothy, when Peggy had a child, had this to say: 'At the up-rouzing of the Bats and Owls he regularly went thither – and the consequence was that Peggy Simpson, the eldest daughter of the house presented him with a son...'

De Quincey, alas, inherited considerable debts, and was forced to sell Nab Cottage in 1833 to William Richardson and his wife, and their lodger, Hartley Coleridge.

So it was that **Hartley Coleridge**

(1796-1849), eldest son of Samuel Taylor Coleridge, spent his last 11 years at Nab Cottage. He was another noted writer, less high profile (in more ways than one, for he was of small stature) than the mainstream 'Lake Poets', and gravely addicted to drink, often disappearing into the fells on drinking sprees. Nevertheless, he was a popular man among the local farmers and shepherds, possessing a childlike manner and an irrepressible sense of fun. Wordsworth came to regard him as an adopted son.

The **church of St Mary** was built during the reign of George IV, of simple construction, with a tower, nave and chancel. Wordsworth helped to choose the site for the church, but appears not to have been too impressed with the finished product. It was built for the benefit of local people by Lady le Fleming in what had been her orchard, and was formerly known as Rydal Chapel.

The young John Ruskin attended Rydal Chapel in 1830, while on a tour with his parents, and observed: 'We were lucky in procuring a seat very near that of Mr Wordsworth.' He was not impressed, however. 'We were rather disappointed in this gentleman's appearance especially as he appeared asleep the greatest part of the time He seemed about 60. This gentleman possesses a long face and a large nose with a moderate assortment of grey hairs and 2 small eyes grey not filled with fury wrapt inspired with a mouth of moderate dimensions that is quite large enough to let in a sufficient quantity of beef or mutton & to let out a sufficient quantity of poetry.'

Behind the church is **Dora's Field**, bought by Wordsworth in 1826, when there was the prospect of them being turned out of Rydal Mount. He did so with the intention of deterring Lady le Fleming from giving the Mount to her aunt, by threatening to build a house on the field. He later gave the field to his daughter.

The poet's grandson, Gordon Wordsworth, gave the field to the National Trust in 1935.

Nearby **Rydal Hall** has an early Victorian front, concealing a 17th century house. It stands below Rydal Mount, and on the opposite side of the lane. Here the local landowners, the le Flemings, formerly of Coniston Hall, used to live. Just below, in Rydal Park, is the scene of the annual **Rydal Sheepdog Trials**, held each August.

ST BEES [Copeland]

NX9711: 4 miles (6km) S of Whitehaven

St Bees is a small seaside town on the western edge of Cumbria, raised to fame from peaceful anonymity when the late Alfred Wainwright devised a coast to coast walk linking St Bees with Robin Hood's Bay on the Yorkshire Coast. There are outstanding views over the sandy bay and a shingle beach that during the 18th century would have seen its share of the smuggling activity along this coastline.

The village lies in a valley, that of Pow Beck, a direct link with the industrial development of Whitehaven to the north. Coming to the village from the south, it is always with surprise that it springs into view, spread haphazardly, like a Scottish crofting settlement, against the backdrop of St Bees Head, and seeming to fit harmoniously into the landscape.

North of the village, the two red sandstone cliffs of St Bees Head are a nature reserve, and the only real cliffs on the north-west coast of Cumbria; predictably they support a diverse range of flora and fauna. The head is topped by a lighthouse.

The village is said to owe its name to Bega, a 7th-century saint cast ashore at Fleswick Bay. The earliest records about St Bega come from the *Life and Miracles of St Bega the Virgin*, a manuscript now in the British Museum, and dating from the 12th century.

Tradition has it that on the day that Bega, the daughter of an Irish king, was supposed to be married to a Norse prince, she fled the court, and was transported by an angel to the Cumbrian coast. Here, recovered from her journey, she asked the local lord for land on which to build a nunnery. He replied dismissively that she could have as much land as was covered the next day by snow. He probably thought, it being midsummer at the time, that he had seen the last of the woman. But miracles happen, and the next day it snowed. The lord, true to his word, gave her the land and she went on to found a small nunnery that in time grew to become the powerful Priory of St Bees.

Bega, however, was not to rest, for she was forced to flee once more from her rejected prince, and sought refuge with a king of Northumbria. While in Northumbria, Bega helped to found the Abbey of Whitby, and did much good work among poor people there.

That Bega existed at all is occasionally called into doubt by those claiming she was a mythical character, although her bracelet, or arm-ring, on which oaths were taken, is mentioned in no less than six charters recorded in the early 13th century.

Of the St Bees priory, only the church remains, which dates from around 1120. The nunnery was destroyed by Danes in the 10th century, but it was later rebuilt by William de Meschines. The priory was ransacked by the Scots in 1314, following their victory at Bannockburn, but it managed to survive another 200 years until its dissolution in 1538.

The **church of St Mary and St Bega** is an exquisite place, and has a fine Norman doorway, arch and windows. The **Beowulf Stone**, thought to pre-date the Conquest, depicts St George killing a dragon, and can be found on a lintel.

St Bees School, built in red sandstone, centres on a courtyard opposite the chancel of the church. The school was founded by royal charter in 1583 by **Archbishop Edmund Grindal** (1519-83), the son of a local farmer who became Bishop of London in 1559, Archbishop of York in 1570, and Archbishop of Canterbury in 1575, during the reign of Elizabeth I. First intended as a grammar school for local boys only, a tradition it maintained until 1879, the school later opened its doors to others. The school's fortunes changed when it was discovered that a rich vein of coal ran beneath the land that formed part of the school's endowment. In spite of bitter wrangling in the courts, the Lowthers, who wanted the coal, in the end had to pay for extracting it.

Much of the school building, however, is later than the 16th century, including work by the noted architects Paley and Austin of Lancaster, who built the Headmaster's House, and the laboratories and library to the north of the chapel in 1907-10. **Fletcher Christian**, ringleader of the mutiny on the *Bounty* in 1789, was educated at St Bees School (see also Cockermouth).

In 1981, archaeologists unearthed one of the best preserved medieval bodies in England, a lord of the 14th century; part of his remains are displayed in Whitehaven Museum.

SANTON BRIDGE [Copeland]

NY1101: 8½ miles (14km) Se of Egremont

The tiny village of Santon Bridge is little more than a small cluster of houses on both sides of the bridge crossing the River Irt, yet it is one of the best-known places in the Lake District, and attracts worldwide attention. Why? Because here, each year is held the **Biggest Liar in the World** competition, started in 1974, in memory of Will Ritson, a former licensee of the Wasdale Head Hotel, who always kept his customers enthralled with stories of the folk heritage of this delightful area. Will, regarded as a sincere and genuine man, once claimed that the turnips in Wasdale were so big that after the local people had quarried into them for their Sunday lunch they could be used as sheds for sheep. The official entry form for the competition these days adds that today 'things are quite different; the turnips are bigger and some local people actually live in them'.

SATTERTHWAITE [South Lakeland]

SD3392: 5 milees (8km) SW of Bowness-on-Windermere

As its name suggests, Satterthwaite is a small and attractive village in a clearing in a forest, here the Grizedale Forest. The whole of this area between Windermere and Coniston Water was formerly in the county of Lancashire.

The village **church** is without dedication. It was built in 1835 and restored 53 years later, but stands on the site of a chapel built in 1577.

SCALEBY [Carlisle]

NY4463: 6 miles (10km) NE of Carlisle

The village of Scaleby is a sprawling cluster of houses set in farmland on the outskirts of Carlisle.

Scaleby Castle is an ancient castle with the lower courses of masonry dating from the early 14th century. Licence to crenellate was granted in 1307, and the tower added probably in the 15th century. The castle, now lived in by Lord Henley, was besieged during the Civil War.

The **church of All Saints** is Early English in style, and may date from the early 13th century; restoration was carried out in 1861.

SCALES [South Lakeland]

SD2772: 4 miles (6km) S of Ulverston

Scales is a small, mainly residential hamlet, closely linked with the coastal hamlet of Baycliff. Many of the houses are modern. Farming has been the main industry around Scales for centuries, indeed the name of the village means 'a cattle shed', and probably refers to the fact that the original Norse settlers used the place to corral their cattle.

SCOTBY [Carlisle]

NY4455: 3 miles (5km) E of Carlisle

A straggling village of modern housing occupied by commuters into Carlisle, Scotby is a 13th-century development founded by Scots, as the name suggests. The village developed into one of the earliest Quaker settlements in Cumberland, and a Friend's Meeting House was built in 1718. Now largely a commuter village, Scotby once boasted a renowned tannery, and was also a lively farming community.

The **church of All Saints** was built on top of a small hillock at the northern end of the village green by Salvin, in 1854.

SEASCALE [Copeland]

NY0301: 12 miles (19km) S of Whitehaven

Once a Victorian seaside resort, signifi-cantly enhanced by the introduction of the Furness Railway in the 1850s, Seascale is now mainly a residential area housing many of the workers at **Sellafield Nuclear Power Plant**. A fire and contamination of the seashore effectively put an end to Seascale's popularity as a holiday destination, but the BNFL station itself has a high-profile visitor centre, as a result of which the village once more features in tourist itineraries. There are actually three plants here: Windscale, which opened in 1951, produced plutonium for atomic bombs; Calder Hall, opened in 1956, is a nuclear power station, while Sellafield deals with spent radioactive materials. In 1957, Windscale experienced Britain's worst-ever nuclear accident when the reactor overheated, and a meltdown was only narrowly averted.

Less than half a mile (1km) to the north, lies the **Grey Croft stone circle**, composed mainly of stones of volcanic lava. Upon excavation, a central cairn within the ring was found to contain bone fragments, flint flakes and an Early Bronze Age pulley-ring.

SEATHWAITE [Allerdale]

NY2312: 7½ miles (12km) S of Keswick

This small farming community at the southern end of Borrowdale claims to be **Britain's wettest inhabited spot**, with an average rainfall of 140in (325cm). The Meteorological Office derives statistics of 'warmest, coldest, driest or wettest' over a 30-year period. At the time of writing the period is 1961-90. Figures for this period do show that Seathwaite is the wettest inhabited spot in Britain, but that the true wettest place is nearby at Styhead Tarn, which has an average annual rainfall of 172in (439cm) – see also Whitehaven: John Fletcher Miller.

SEATOLLER [Allerdale]

NY2413: 6 miles (10km) S of Keswick

Seatoller is an attractive grouping of cottages and farms at the eastern foot of the Honister Pass, where the descending road enters Borrowdale. Once no more than a farm, Seatoller has developed latterly along with the interests of walkers, but formerly with the growth of the plumbago mines on the fells to the north-west. Plumbago, or 'wad', is otherwise known as black lead, and was used as a medicine, a dye, and for pencils. It was lead from these mines that enabled the development of the pencil industry in Keswick. Although lead for pencils is now imported, during the 18th century it was such a valuable commodity that an armed guard had to be based at Seathwaite to protect supplies, and once faced an armed robbery.

SEATON [Allerdale]

NY0130: 2 miles (3km) NE of Workington

A large, mainly residential village, mostly of modern houses, and a suburb of Workington, Seaton is the largest village in Cumbria. Like many of the villages along the Cumbrian coast, Seaton was once a mining and farming community. A market charter was granted in the 13th century, which combined with it the right to hold a three-day fair. Occasional fairs are still held, but the market has long since ended.

The village **church of St Paul** is a large Gothic church built in local stone by George Watson of Keswick in 1883 at a cost of £2213 13s 4d.

SEBERGHAM [Allerdale]

NY3641: 9 miles (15km) SSW of Carlisle

A large, scattered village, mainly of farms, along the River Caldew, and on the edge of the northern fells of Lakeland, Sebergham grew mainly during the 13th and 14th centuries. At that time the waters of the River Caldew powered mills, six in all, along its course. The village lies below the modest height of Warnell Fell, and is accessible only by steep roads in and out. Most of the properties in the village today date from the 17th century, and lend a pleasant atmosphere to the place.

The **church of St Mary**, built during the reign of George IV, stands on the site of a chapel built in the 12th century.

SEDBERGH [Eden]

SD6592: 9 miles (14km) E of Kendal

Sedbergh is a small, stone-built town at the southern edge of the Howgills, and only became part of Cumbria in 1974, even though it remains in the Yorkshire Dales National Park, and clearly has many 'Dales' affinities. The town was formerly in the West Riding of Yorkshire, and is largely one long main street.

It is an ancient market town with a charter dating from 1251, and is mentioned in the Domesday Book as among the many manors held by Earl Tostig of Northumbria. Today the fame of the town rests on the laurels of its school. **Sedbergh School** is set in parkland on the edge of the town. It was founded in 1525, and has grown steadily to earn a national reputation. Among its memorable pupils was Will Carling, former captain of the England rugby team. The old building of the school, built in 1716, is now the library, to the south-east of the church.

In spite of its administrative connections with Cumbria, Sedbergh remains one of the largest towns in the Yorkshire

Dales National Park, and is the main western gateway to the Dales.

The Turnpike Acts of 1761 brought improvements to the Askrigg-Kendal and Lancaster-Kirkby Stephen roads, both of which pass through Sedbergh, and these improvements made the town more accessible as a staging post for commercial routes across the Pennines. There followed a time of industrial growth as the domestic knitting trade was augmented by a cotton industry based on mills at Birks, Howgill and Millthrop. As a result, Sedbergh grew at the expense of Dent, further up the valley, which hitherto had been the more important township.

Above the town rise the rounded hills of the **Howgills**, a popular place with walkers and lovers of wide, open spaces.

The attractive **church of St Andrew** is a typical West Riding structure with a tower, a long nave with aisles, a chancel of the same height, and chancel chapels. Parts of the church are Norman, notably the north doorway, while other parts of the building date from the 13th century. Various religions have flourished in this area for centuries. The village also has a United Reformed church and a Methodist church, as well as the Friends' Meeting House at Brigflatts, nearby (see also Brigflatts).

Each week an outdoor market is held on Joss Lane car park, selling everything from fruit and vegetables to household goods and fish.

SEDGWICK [South Lakeland]

SD5186: 3 miles (5km) S of Kendal

Situated on the east bank of the River Kent, the village of Sedgwick prospered under the Wakefield family, who ran a gunpowder mill in the village, and built many of the cottages and houses. The course of the old Lancaster to Kendal Canal used to run through the village, and this enabled the easier transportation of gunpowder. The Wakefields were also responsible for commissioning Paley and Austin to design their Gothic mansion, **Sedgwick House**, which they completed in 1869. The celebrated singer Mary Wakefield spent much of her childhood at Sedgwick House, giving her first public performance in 1873. She went on to a spectacular career in music and inspired the Mary Wakefield Festival, which was held annually until 1906, when it became and remains biennial; it is held in Kendal.

SELSIDE [South Lakeland]

SD5399: 4½ miles (7km) N of Kendal

A small fellside hamlet of scattered houses and farms, Selside stands near a crossing point of the River Sprint, among the fells north of Kendal. Most of the buildings in the village are old, and related to the farming industry that has prevailed here for centuries. The village used to be known as Selside-with-Whitwell, and was a chapelry of Kendal.

On the edge of the village stands the **church of St Thomas**, built just after Queen Victoria came to the throne, and to which a tower was added in 1894. The tower is quite distinctive, and unlike any other in the area, being very broad and forming part of the nave inside the church. The church stands on the site of an 18th-century chapel, on land granted by the Thornburghs on condition that the chapel in Selside Hall could be used by anyone to celebrate Catholic Mass, something of a risky and unusual condition.

The church looks down on **Selside Hall**, an Elizabethan farmhouse that developed from a 14th-century pele tower, and is one of the finest old houses in the area. It was built by the family that took its name, de Selside, but by the time of Edward I, the estate had been granted to a Norman family, the Thornburghs. They were also granted lands by the abbot of Shap in what was undoubtedly a shrewd manoeuvre to keep in favour with the family, who were connected by marriage to many of the important local families. In the end, the Thornburghs, for refusing to attend Church of England services at a time when it was compulsory, incurred enormous recusancy fines, and had to sell all their estates to pay them. The last of the family to reside at Selside Hall was Mary, and by then little more than the hall remained in the family's ownership, and that went when Mary married Ralph Riddell of Northumberland in 1774.

SHAP [Eden]

NY5614: 9 miles (14km) S of Penrith

The village of Shap, two long, parallel lines of grey-stone houses and shops, has little of interest, though many of the houses date from the 18th century.

The main trunk road, the A6, runs through the village, and in winter this is often snow-bound and impassable. Ironically, when the motorway came to the rescue, it spelt disaster for the prosperous shops, hotels, cafés and garages on which the economy of the village had been based.

The **market hall**, now a library, with its curious windows and round-headed arches dates from a few years after the village was granted a market charter in 1687.

The area around Shap was extensively settled in Neolithic times, and a stone circle near the village centre used to be approached down an avenue of stones, but this largely disappeared when the railway came through.

The **church of St Michael** has some 12th-century elements, though its tower dates from the reign of George IV, while the chancel is Victorian (1898-9).

Now managed by English Heritage, **Shap Abbey** is about half a mile (1km) west of the village. The abbey was but one of many monastic houses established during the 12th century. It belonged to an order founded by the German saint Norbert, and owes its foundation to a Norman baron, Thomas, son of Gospatric, who held lands in Westmorland. Towards the end of his life, Thomas made arrangements for the establishment of an abbey on his lands at Preston-in-Kendal, but in 1201 he changed his mind and instead granted the present site of the abbey, along with leave to quarry stone and to fell timber on his land. The place where the abbey was founded was then known as 'hepp', meaning 'a heap', probably referring to the stone circle near the village. Time gradually changed the name from 'hepp', to 'hiap', to 'shap'.

The new abbey was dedicated to Mary Magdelene, though very little is known about it. The order was of Premonstratensian monks, who sought to combine a life of prayer with parish work as priests. Some monks wore white habits, and were as a result known as 'White Canons'.

As with many other abbeys, the end of Shap came with the Dissolution of the Monasteries, a trifle later in the case of Shap, for it wasn't until 14 January 1540 that the last abbot surrendered the abbey and its possessions to the Crown. His co-operation was compensated with the grant of a pension of £40 per year, a sizeable sum in the 16th century.

The abbey lands were then sold to Sir Thomas Wharton of Carlisle, but in

Former market hall, Shap

1729, after the Jacobite Duke of Wharton's forfeiture of his lands, they were acquired by Richard Lowther of Mauld's Meaburn. They remained with this family until just after the Second World War, when they were placed in the hands of the Ministry of Works (later the Department of the Environment) for preservation as an ancient monument.

SILECROFT [Copeland]

SD1381: 3 miles (5km) NW of Millom

Silecroft is an attractive coastal village at the foot of Black Combe and the Whicham Valley, though there is little about the village that is of interest. Its beach is popular with holiday-makers.

From nearby Whicham, an excellent walk leads up onto Black Combe, the southernmost of the sizeable Lakeland fells, composed of the same rocks, Skiddaw Slates, as the eponymous fell to the north of Keswick, many miles distant.

SILLOTH [Allerdale]

NY1153: 10 miles (16km) NW of Wigton

Silloth is an airy seaside resort with wide, cobbled streets, spacious greens, and a stony beach. It springs from the 19th century when it was chosen as the new port for Carlisle, but, as with other towns and villages along this stretch of coastline, its supporting role for the capital city declined dramatically when the railway was built. Nevertheless, it is still a popular place, and affords excellent views both seaward and across the Solway to the mountains of southern Scotland.

Built in 1870-1, **Christ Church** is described by Pevsner as "an ambitious church", and is largely brick-faced, yellow and red inside.

SIZERGH [South Lakeland]

SD4987: 3 miles (5km) S of Kendal

- see Kendal

SKELTON [Eden]

NY4335: 5½ miles (9km) NW of Penrith

Skelton, in the rolling pastures of Greystoke, is a village made larger by modern development, and set on a crossroads beside its village green.

The village **church of St Michael and All Angels** was built when the former 18th-century church was taken down in 1879, though a church has existed on the site since the 13th century.

Each year, in August, the **Skelton Horticultural and Agricultural Show** is held near Skelton, at Hutton-in-the-Forest.

SKELWITH BRIDGE [South Lakeland]

NY3403: 2 miles (3km) W of Ambleside

Skelwith Bridge stands at an ancient crossing point of the River Brathay, near which today's main road forks to enter Greater Langdale or to turn for Coniston. Just upstream of the village, which boasts a small slate manufacturing business at Kirkstone Galleries, the river forms a number of attractive cascades, **Skelwith Force**.

The village of Skelwith Bridge was the home of **Doris and Muriel Howe**, novelists who wrote both under their own names and under the joint pseudonym 'Newlyn Nash'. They wrote more than seventy romantic and mystery novels, many set in Lakeland.

SKINBURNESS [Allerdale]

NY1256: 2 miles (3km) NE of Silloth

A popular and quiet holiday resort that today belies its history as the principal village in this area of Cumbria. Overlooking the Solway Firth it regularly used to hold fairs and markets, and Edward I landed his stores for his army here in advance of his campaign to deal with William Wallace.

The bleak area around Skinburness has the unique tang of the Solway, a wild sense of remoteness and loneliness, and some of the worst of its storms. In the winter of 1304, one storm succeeded in largely destroying the entire village.

SKIRWITH [Eden]

NY6132: 8 miles (13km) NNW of Appleby-in-Westmorland

Skirwith is a most attractive village on both sides of Skirwith Beck and in the shadow of Cross Fell. The village long ago belonged to Adam fitz Swein, and later passed into the Fleming family, whose descendant took the innovative step of enfranchising his tenants. The old manor house, Skirwith Hall, was demolished in the 18th century, but **Skirwith Abbey** still stands, built on land once held by the Knights Templar.

The **church of St John the Evangelist** is an attractive church built in 1856, and stands on the south side of the beck.

SMARDALE [Eden]

NY7308: 2 miles (3km) W of Kirkby Stephen

The small farming community of Smardale is set along quiet lanes on the outskirts of Kirkby Stephen, and at the northern edge of Smardale Fell, one of the oldest inhabited parts of Cumbria, with many of the adjacent fellsides having been occupied since prehistoric times. **Smardale Hall** is a 13th-century fortified building, now a farmhouse, and is more Scottish than English in design, having round towers.

To the south of the village, on Smardale Fell, are two large earthworks marked as **Pillow Mounds** on maps. Legend has it that these are giants' graves, but they are almost certainly the remains of conygers, or rabbit warrens, constructed during medieval times to encourage the breeding of rabbits for the table.

The Settle - Carlisle railway line passes through Smardale and crosses the course of an old mineral railway; both have splendid viaducts.

SOULBY [Eden]

NY7411: 2½ miles (4km) NW of Kirkby Stephen

The small but spacious village of Soulby is divided by Scandal Beck, and still held a Manor Court as recently as 1915. Farming has long been the principal employment, and for many years it was carried out in traditional manorial manner, with a large arable 'infield', and an 'outfield', usually as pasture.

The manor has been held by the Musgrave family since the 15th century, though there are no houses of great antiquity.

The **church of St Luke** was built by Sir Philip Musgrave in 1662-3, following the Restoration, and extensively restored in 1874.

SPARK BRIDGE [South Lakeland]

SD3084: 4 miles (6km) N of Ulverston

An attractive, scattered village surrounded by farmland and woodland. The relaxed air of the village today conceals a busy industrial past that evolved from the bobbin-making industry, which it combined with the production of wrought iron work. The bobbin mill, which still functioned into the 1980s, was built on the site of a forge used for smelting iron ore, which was then taken away by ship from Greenodd a mile or so to the south.

STAINTON [Eden]

NY4828: 2½ miles (4km) SW of Penrith

A large and growing village, Stainton, on the outskirts of Penrith, is built around a triangular green on the site of a Roman settlement. The housing is mostly modern, though some properties date from the 18th century.

STAINTON [South Lakeland]

SD5285: 4 miles (6km) S of Kendal

Buried among the folds of low fells south of Kendal, Stainton is small village with much of its original milling character unspoiled. It stands on Saint Sunday's Beck and close by the course of the Lancaster Canal.

On the edge of the village, the **church of St Thomas** was built in 1875 to replace earlier churches and chapels, the earliest founded in 1190.

STAINTON WITH ADGARLEY [South Lakeland]

SD2472: 3 miles (5km) NE of Barrow-in-Furness

A scattered hamlet of old cottages strung out along a minor road between Dalton and Barrow, and surrounded by farmland and old quarries, Stainton with Adgarley is essentially two small villages combined, each with a village green. The manor house, **Stainton Hall**, has mullioned windows and is at least 17th century since parts of it were damaged during the Civil War. A number of the cottages in the village are early 18th century.

Bronze Age burial mounds and earlier settlements have been traced over an extensive area nearby, but the village's entry in the Domesday Book is brief, mentioning only 'Two farms near limestone quarries'.

STAPLETON [Carlisle]

NY5071: 6 miles (10km) N of Brampton

A widespread village of farms and cottages on mossland above the River Lyne, a tributary of the Esk.

The **church of St Mary** is large and built as William IV was succeeding to the throne, on a site where places of worship have existed since the 13th century.

STAVELEY [South Lakeland]

SD4698: 5 miles (8km) NW of Kendal

A large, mainly residential village, now bypassed, of grey slate cottages and houses, and sandwiched between the River Gowan and the River Kent, at the southern end of the valley of Kentmere. The area around Staveley has been inhabited since about 4000BC, at a time when trees grew extensively on the fellsides. The first permanent settlers were Celtic-speaking British farmers, and they were followed in AD90 by the Romans, who had a road to the south of the village linking Kendal and Ambleside.

During the Dark Ages and later medieval times, the village and its neighbours grew, developed, and were plundered in much the same way as many other villages throughout Cumbria. But by the time of the Industrial Revolution, the village was quick to expand as transport improved. So it was that Staveley became the bobbin-turning capital of Westmorland, so much so that by 1851 there were more families working at the manufacture of bobbins than there were engaged in farming.

By the 20th century, the bobbin industry had ended and new manufacturing industries developed – diatomite, motor cycles and photographic paper – and Staveley is still a small industrial village.

Staveley was granted a market charter in the 13th century, and also held a three-day fair each year. In 1338 the lord of the manor, Sir William Thweng, agreed to build a chapel in honour of St Margaret. St Margaret's Church, of which only the tower now remains, was founded in 1388. A plaque on the tower commemorates Staveley men of the F Company, Second V B Border Regiment, who served in the South Africa Campaign 1900-01 under Major John Thompson. In 1864 it was decided to build a new church, and this was dedicated to **St James**. This later church has

St Margaret's church, Stavely

some beautiful stained glass designed by Burne-Jones and made by William Morris's company.

STAVELEY-IN-CARTMEL [South Lakeland]

SD3785: At the foot of Lake Windermere

Staveley-in-Cartmel is little more than a small cluster of houses surrounded by lanes, at the southern tip of Windermere, but it is an old community. Its **church of St Mary** stands on a spot where a church has existed since 1618, though the present church was built much later, and restored in 1896.

SWARTHMOOR [South Lakeland]

SD2777: 1 mile (2km) SW of Ulverston

The village was originally developed to accommodate workers from the nearby Lindal Moor Mines, as the Miners Arms pub in Fox Street testifies. The name, however, clearly indicates that the village was on the edge of Swarth Moor, or Black Moor. It was here, coincidentally, that the young impostor Lambert Simnel (c1477-c1534) and an army of some 8000 German mercenaries captained by Martin Schwarz, camped overnight on their way from Ireland to claim the throne from Henry VII. In the event, they were defeated at Stoke Field in Nottinghamshire, in what was the very last battle of the War of the Roses, on 16 June 1487.

Swarthmoor Hall, however, has a considerable history. It was built about 1586 by George Fell, a local lawyer and landowner, and during the Civil War housed Roundhead soldiers. In 1652, Margaret, the wife of George Fell's son, Judge Thomas Fell, heard George Fox preach, at a time when he was being subjected to considerable harassment and imprisonment for his beliefs. She persuaded the judge to give him protection in Swarthmoor Hall, which became the first settled centre of the Quaker faith. Eleven years after the judge died in 1658, Margaret married George Fox, who in 1687 bought a small property nearby for the sum of £72, and converted it into the Friends' Meeting House.

TALKIN [Carlisle]

NY5457: 3 miles (5km) SE of Brampton

The village of Talkin largely developed during the 18th and 19th centuries, when many of the present houses were built. In those times farming was the principal employment, though coal was also mined, and stone and lime were quarried.

The **church**, which has Norman antecedents, was built in 1842 by one of the Grahams of Edmond Castle; it has no dedication.

Just to the north of the village, the area of and around **Talkin Tarn** has now been designated a country park, and, like much of this wild north Pennine countryside, provides habitats for a wide range of birdlife.

TEBAY [Eden]

NY6104: 10 miles (16km) NE of Kendal

This straggling village of terraced houses grew up when the nearby railway was being developed. Sheep farming was once a major occupation in Tebay, but most employment seems to come via the nearby motorway, especially in the service areas.

The church, built in 1880, and dedicated to **St James**, was paid for by the railway company and its workers. It is an attractive Gothic building in Shap granite.

TEMPLE SOWERBY [Eden]

NY6127: 6 miles (10km) NW of Appleby-in-Westmorland

Temple Sowerby is a pleasant, neat and attractive village of red sandstone Georgian houses around a large green. Among these is **Acorn Bank**, now owned by the National Trust, though the house, which is let to the Sue Ryder Foundation, is not open to the public. This fine sandstone house, mainly from the 18th century, but in part from the 16th, was formerly the home of Dorothy Ratcliffe, a Yorkshire dialect writer.

The manor of Temple Sowerby was held by the Knights Templar and, after their suppression in 1308, by the Knights Hospitaller, until the Dissolution under Henry VIII, when the manor was granted to Thomas Dalston.

The **church of St James** was built in 1754, and enlarged sixteen years later.

THORNTHWAITE [Allerdale]

NY2225: 3 miles (5km) NW of Keswick

Once closely associated with nearby Braithwaite, forming the parish of Thornthwaite-cum-Braithwaite, the village of Thornthwaite gazes out across the expanse of Bassenthwaite Lake to the moulded hills of Longside Edge and the Skiddaw massif beyond.

Originally built in the 18th century, and later rebuilt in the 19th, the **church of St Mary** is the mother church of the parish, and is set in pastoral splendour.

Just to the north of the village, on the craggy slopes of Barf Fell, stands a prominent white 'figure', the **Bishop of Barf**. In reality, this is a natural rock about 6ft (2m) high, which by tradition is kept whitewashed by the landlord of the nearby pub. Lower down, in the fields behind the pub, is the Clerk, another whitewashed rock, lesser in stature.

Thornthwaite Gallery is housed in a converted 18th-century barn, and deals in fine arts.

THRELKELD [Eden]

NY3225: 4 miles (6km) E of Keswick

Though little is known of its early days, the history of the village of Threlkeld goes back over 800 years. The name, derived from the Norse, means 'the well of the thrall' – a thrall being a medieval term for a man bound in service to his lord, though there appears to be no record of who the lord might have been.

At the time of Neolithic Man, the area around Threlkeld (and indeed much of Lakeland) would have been densely wooded at least to a height of around 2000ft, the valley itself probably proving to be an impenetrable swamp. The landscape today is completely man-made; the trees have been cut down for firewood and to make charcoal, and to clear the ground to provide pasture for sheep.

Occupying an area of ground largely cleared of trees, there used to be a previous settlement here, though only a few collapsed walls and buildings remain, and it is not clear why it was abandoned. It is thought to have existed during the Dark Ages, approximately from AD300-900, though it may well have been occupied before Roman times.

By the 13th century (around 1220), the settlement was sufficiently large to justify its own priest, a man by the name of Ranulph, who was witness to a manuscript now in the British Museum, and so known to have existed at that time. The present **church of St Mary**, however, dates from 1777 and stands on the site of a previous (and possibly other) church. A report from 1703 records a custom, no longer observed, that applied to marriages performed in the church. The bishop (Nicholson) who made the report wrote: 'Their Register Book begins at 1573…[and] we must observe one extraordinary custom of the place to be proved by it. Formal Contracts of Marriage are herein recorded; and Sureties entered for the payment of five shillings to the poor by the party that draws back.' Anyone breaking their marriage vows had to face paying what was a considerable sum for those days, for the benefit of the poor.

Far from being rich or ornate, Threlkeld church, nevertheless, is a fascinating place of considerable antiquity. In the churchyard there are some intriguing tombstones, and a monument to 45 foxhunters, among them John Crozier, master of the Threlkeld Hunt, whose hounds are still kennelled here, for 64 years. Unlike many southern hunts, Lakeland hunts are renowned for being carried out on foot, by men who in former days would wear grey coats (D'ye ken John Peel in his coat so grey?) rather than scarlet. To these fox-hunters, the chase was neither sport nor pastime, but an essential job to protect sheep.

The village today lies on a narrow roadway winding its way through attractive old cottages, and is now bypassed by the A66. In days gone by the village streets would have echoed to the sound of packhorse trains, cattle and sheep droves, and the comings and goings of a regular stagecoach service. The Horse and Farrier Inn, which dates from 1688, is a clear reminder of these bygone days, when it would have done brisk business among the frequent travellers.

The village is, of course, dominated by the massive bulk of **Blencathra**, one of Lakeland's most popular summits. Known in the past as Linthwaite Pike, Threlkeld Fell, Blencrater and Blenkarthur, the mountain today occasionally attracts the unimaginative name of Saddleback, for the view it presents to the traveller arriving from the direction of Penrith.

The mountain is immensely popular with walkers and may be ascended by any of almost a dozen routes. One in particular passes **Scales Tarn**, set in a wild sanctum at the eastern edge of the mountain, of which Harriet Martineau (1802-76), who just before her death settled in the Lake District and became a friend of the Wordsworths, wrote: 'The tarn is so situated at the foot of a vast precipice, and so buried among crags, that the sun never reaches it, except through a crevice in early morning.' This account may explain why the tarn long held a reputation for its ability to reflect the stars at noonday, though early travellers, including one who was so overcome by the power of the scenery that he 'wished to lose blood and return', were often disappointed in their anticipation. Sir Walter Scott in *The Bridal of Triermain*, and Hugh Walpole in *A Prayer for my Son*, both used the setting of Scales Tarn to good effect.

High up on the slopes of Blease Fell is the site of one of the earliest English sanatoria built for tubercular patients, and opened in 1904. The money to build it was raised by subscription, and it was almost the first such establishment to be opened in England, being just beaten to that distinction by Meathop in the former county of Westmorland. The Blencathra Sanatorium closed in 1975.

The **Threlkeld Quarry and Mining Museum** houses an extensive collection of original artefacts, plans, maps and other mining and quarrying memorabilia, including a display of minerals and geological specimens. Lead mining in the Lake District has been going on since Roman times, and the history of mining at Threlkeld cannot be isolated from mining in the whole of this region. Miners would often walk considerable distances to work in the Threlkeld mines, though many families elected to stay and live in Threlkeld itself. The work was unpleasant at best, and the pay, even in 1900, only four shillings (20p) a day, for an eight-hour day.

Each year in August, the village holds **sheepdog trials** on Burns Recreation Field, including foxhound and terrier shows, and hound trailing.

THURSBY [Allerdale]

NY3250: 6 miles (10km) SW of Carlisle

Thursby lies on the old Roman road to Carlisle, and takes its name from the Saxon god, Thor. The village church, dedicated to St Andrew, is a large, ashlar-faced structure, built in 1846 on a site that has been occupied by churches since the 7th century. When the church was rebuilt, a 'new' pulpit was brought from Carlisle Cathedral, and that was at least 100 years old. These days Thursby is very much a commuter village.

THURSTONFIELD [Carlisle]

NY3156: 5 miles (8km) W of Carlisle

Almost adjoining neighbouring Kirkbampton, Thurstonfield is a small farming village, with a millpond, Thurstonfield Lough, surrounded by woodland. It was a busy community in the late 19th and early 20th centuries, mainly based on agriculture, and much

social life centred on the millpond, which was a swimming pool in summer and an ice rink in winter; now it's used for fishing. Most of the land and houses, and even the lough, used to be owned by a Quaker family, the Stordys from Moorhouse.

TIRRIL [Eden]

NY5026: 2 miles (3km) S of Penrith

Separated from its near neighbour, Sockbridge, by a small stream, the tiny farming village of Tirril used to be one of the main centres for the Quaker movement during the 18th century, and a meeting house was built here in 1733. It is no longer used as such, but in the adjoining graveyard lies **Charles Gough**, a man whose name will be familiar to anyone who has climbed Helvellyn by Striding Edge. He was killed in a fall from the mountain, and above the spot a memorial has been erected. His faithful dog stayed by the body of its master for three months, and the story found its way into Wordsworth's *Fidelity* and was alluded to more recently in Richard Adams' *The Plague Dogs*.

TORPENHOW [Allerdale]

NY2039: 1 mile (2km) NE of Bothel

Lying along a minor road between Bothel and Ireby, and on the northern slopes of Binsey Fell, the small village of Torpenhow is surrounded largely by farmland, and is easily missed. Yet the **church of St Michael**, a mix of early and late Norman, and 17th-century alterations, is one of the most pleasing and architecturally interesting churches in the county, being among the few unspoilt churches of that period.

Low and wide in profile, and supported by massive buttresses on two sides, the south entrance porch has a fine Norman doorway. Externally, restoration work was carried out in 1913, following a major restoration in 1882.

TORVER [South Lakeland]

SD2894: 2½ miles (4km) SW of Coniston

The moors above Torver have been settled since prehistoric times. W G Collingwood, in *The Lake Counties* writes, 'All these fells must once have been the happy hunting-grounds of primitive races, children of the mist, perhaps surviving long after the outskirts were settled by civilized folk.'

Long involved with the many traditional industries of Lakeland – stone and slate quarrying, iron smelting, charcoal production, bobbin manufacture, farming and milling – Torver, overlooking Coniston Water, developed significantly when the Furness Railway came here in 1859.

Although a 12th-century chapel stood on the site of the present-day **church of St Luke**, burials were not permitted there until 1538; before then the village's dead had to be carried to Ulverston. When Archbishop Cranmer allowed burials to be carried out at Torver, the long, bier-laden treks over mountain passes ended. A new church was built in 1849, and that replaced by St Luke's in 1883-4.

Torver was the home of a renowned Icelandic scholar, **Thomas Ellwood**, rector of Torver chapel, who wrote a small, but rather uninteresting, history of the village, *Leaves from the Annals of a Mountain Parish*.

TROUTBECK [South Lakeland]

NY4002: 3 miles (5km) N of Windermere

An elongated, attractive and relatively old-fashioned village along the long-established, narrow and hilly coach route from Windermere to Penrith, now by-passed by a more modern highway. The main part of the village stands above the modern road, and the buildings, on closer inspection, are gathered together in groups. This arrangement stems from the days when the villagers drew their water from wells, and so their houses were built in this convenient way.

Beatrix Potter used to live in the village, at Troutbeck Park Farm, where she bred Herdwick sheep. The area around Troutbeck Park was once a massive deer estate, hunted by the lords of Kendal. The property, and the sheep, are now owned by the National Trust.

Along the approach road to the village are a number of drinking troughs bearing saints' names, and provided for horses as they tackled the long climb over the Kirkstone Pass to Patterdale and beyond. Many of the houses are 17th century, and some still have spinning galleries and mullioned windows.

The church, **Jesus Chapel** was built in 1736 on the site of a 15th-century chapel, and renovated in the 19th century. It stands below the main village on the modern road over the Kirkstone Pass, and has a delightful east window created in 1873 by English craftsman, poet and socialist William Morris (1834-96), the English painter Sir Edward Burne-Jones (1833-98) and the British historical painter Ford Madox Brown (1821-93).

At one time many of the farms in Troutbeck were owned by 'statesmen', farmers who owned a small area of land from which they struggled to eke an existence. Such a farm is **Townend**, a fine building with whitewashed walls and stone-mullioned windows, originally a yeoman's house, built around 1626. It contains various tools of a yeoman's trade, many of which were accumulated by the Browne family who lived here until 1944. The house, now owned by the National Trust, has a tall, tapering chimney, typical of Lakeland vernacular architecture of that era. The original 17th-century house is divided into two sections: the part where the work of the farm was done, known as the 'down house', and the living quarters, called the 'fire house'.

At the northern end of the village stands the **Mortal Man Inn**, a 17th-century coaching inn, formerly a small cottage called the White House. It gained its present name about the beginning of the 19th century, when a customer, the painter Julius Caesar Ibbetson, who lived in Ambleside and then Troutbeck, painted a new sign for it. On one side he depicted a thin-lipped person, obviously a teetotaller, and on the other someone quite the opposite, both said to be well-known people who lived nearby. From their mouths came in true cartoon fashion 'balloons' containing the couplets:

'Thou mortal man who liv'st by bread,
What is it makes thy nose so red?
Thou silly fool that look'st so pale,
'Tis drinking Sally Birkett's ale!'

From then on the inn was called the Mortal Man; the present sign is a copy of the original.

Troutbeck has the distinction of being the home of one of the earliest Cumbrian poets, **Thomas Hoggart** (c1640-1709), a farmer, known as 'Old Hoggart', and said to be an uncle of the painter William Hogarth.

ULDALE [Allerdale]

NY2536: 7 miles (11km) S of Wigton

Perched above the infant River Ellen, Uldale is an isolated village on the northern edge of the Lake District National Park. Its name means 'Wolf's Dale', a

clear indication of what roamed here in centuries gone by. This formerly self-contained village has always been a sheep farming concern, and remains so.

The village used to have a church, St John's built in 1868, but this became unsafe in the 1950s and was finally demolished in 1963.

ULPHA [South Lakeland]

SD1993: 4 miles (6km) N of Broughton-in-Furness

The name of this small village near River Duddon means 'the enclosure where wolves are trapped', or 'Wolf's Hill', from Old Scandinavian.

The **church of St John** is notable for its simplicity. It is a typical dale chapel, low in profile, with a nave and chancel all in one, with a bellcot at one end. The church was restored in the 19th century, but the 16th- or 17th-century east window remains. Wall paintings, discovered in 1934, include the royal arms of Queen Anne.

St John's Church, always white-rendered, was described by Wordsworth in *Duddon Sonnet XXXI*:

'The Kirk of Ulpha to the pilgrim's eye
Is welcome as a star, that doth present
Its shining forehead through the peaceful rent
Of a black cloud diffused o'er half the sky.'

ULVERSTON [South Lakeland]

SD2878: 8 miles (13km) NE of Barrow-in-Furness

Standing between Morecambe Bay and the Lake District hinterland, the town of Ulverston centres on its market place. For hundreds of years Ulverston was an isolated community, reached by crossing the treacherous sands of Morecambe Bay.

The town's market charter was granted by Edward I in 1280. The market grew considerably, and eventually took over from the markets at Broughton, Cartmel and Hawkshead.

During the early 18th century, the Leven estuary was often filled with ships at anchor from Baycliff to Greenodd. By the 1790s local businessmen joined forces with the directors of the Canal Committee to improve the so-called 'slate road' from Gawthwaite to Ulverston and so link the collieries of Lancashire with the suppliers of Westmorland slate. The canal project which followed was designed to enable coastal and merchant vessels to operate safely, without the need to beach or ground ships. Numerous Ulverston merchants had Liverpool connections, and trade with the developing Furness markets improved considerably. By the 19th century, Ulverston had become a busy commercial port, exporting copper, malted barley, bobbins, linen, hats, gunpowder, cotton, iron, slate and leather. Today, it is a friendly place of cobbled streets and alleyways, and still holds a street market on Thursdays and Saturdays.

The town was eventually linked to the Leven estuary by the **Ulverston Canal**, England's shortest canal, being merely a mile and a third long (2km). It was masterminded by John Rennie, and opened in 1796. It certainly made Ulverston the undisputed principal port of Furness. As elsewhere, however, the coming of the railway, here the Ulverston and Lancaster Railway in 1857, improved communications, but signalled the decline of canals generally, and ultimately, that at Ulverston in particular.

Ulverston, until 1974 in Lancashire, was the birthplace of **Stan Laurel** (1890-1965), the more slender half of the Laurel and Hardy duo. Born Arthur Stanley Jefferson, he spent his first 15 years at number 3 Argyle Street, a small terraced house, the local pub has been renamed in his memory.

The **Laurel and Hardy Museum** in Upper Brook Street displays photographs and relics of the pair, and contains a small film theatre where Laurel and Hardy films are shown all day while the museum is open.

Sir John Barrow (1764-1848), English naval administrator (Secretary of the Admiralty for 40 years) and traveller, founder and vice-president of the Royal Geographical Society in 1830, was also born in the town, in a cottage in the southern part, and was educated at Ulverston School. On Hoad Hill, overlooking the town, there is a monument to Barrow in the form of a 100ft (30m) tall replica of Eddystone Lighthouse, built in 1850. Hoad Hill is the scene each Easter Monday of the traditional Pasche Egg Rolling.

Here, too, was born **William Norman Birkett** (1883-1962), 1st Baron Birkett of Ulverston, a lawyer and politician who was Britain's representative at the Nuremberg War Crimes Trials (1945-6), and who also represented Mrs Wallis Simpson when she filed for divorce prior to marrying Edward VIII. Birkett was a Liberal Member of Parliament in the 1920s, and was raised to the peerage in 1958.

The **church of St Mary**, dating in part from 1111, is the oldest building in Ulverston, though it was restored and rebuilt in Victorian times, and the chancel added in 1903-4. The church is renowned for the splendour of its Norman doorway, and some outstanding 19th-century and early 20th-century stained glass, including one window which used a design by Sir Joshua Reynolds (1723-92), the English portrait painter. The church tower was built during the reign of Elizabeth I (1558-1603), the original steeple having been destroyed in a storm in 1540.

UNDERBARROW
[South Lakeland]

SD4692: 3 miles (5km) W of Kendal

Underbarrow is a widespread village of farms and houses at the head of the Lyth Valley, an area inhabited since ancient times, though most of the village today dates from the 17th century. The village's **church of All Saints** is Victorian, described as having 'a naughty design', and replaces an earlier 18th-century chapel.

UNTHANK [Eden]

NY4536: 5 miles (8km) NW of Penrith

Lying in the rolling pastures of Greystoke, Unthank is a small and scattered farmland hamlet. Its finest building is **Hutton in the Forest**, a house of considerable architectural interest dating from the Middle Ages, and converted from an old medieval pele tower into a dwelling in 1605.

URSWICK [South Lakeland]

SD2674: 6 miles (10km) NE of
Barrow-in-Furness

A small village of two hamlets built around **Urswick Tarn**, in the coastal lands of Furness between Ulverston and Barrow-in-Furness. The tarn is not over large, but local legend has it that it is bottomless. It is a popular habitat for water birds, and swans are reputed to have nested here since the 18th century. Traditionally, those born in Urswick, whether Great or Little Urswick, are known as 'Ossick Coots'.

The tarn is also the source of another legend, which may explain why the church is sited so far from the village. A priest, often condemned as worthless and criticised for doing nothing to remedy the lack of water in the village, ultimately sought his revenge in an unchristian manner by inducing an earthquake that destroyed the village and its inhabitants, replacing them with a tarn. Ridiculous, of course, but why is the church so far away?

The village is a delightful mix of rough-hewn, pale grey-stone cottages and others of pebble-dash; one building near the Derby Arms pub is especially attractive and has an external stone staircase. The village's other pub commemorates **General John Burgoyne** (1722-92), English soldier and dramatist who distinguished himself in the Seven Years' War in the Iberian peninsula (1756-63), but, having been sent to fight in the American War of Independence, was forced to surrender to General Gates at Saratoga in 1777.

The **church of St Mary and St Michael**, built in the 13th century, extended in the 14th, and restored in 1908, is set back from the tarn on a site that has seen Christian worship for over 1000 years. Grooves on the porch pillars are said to have been made by men sharpening their arrows in readiness, apparently, for archery practice, which often followed Sunday service.

The church contains some excellent wood carving, much of which was carried out by the Campden Guild, an organisation of over 100 Cotswold-based craftspeople established by C R Ashbee (1863-1942) between 1888 and 1908, originally as the Guild of Handicraft in London's East End. There are also some fragments of a Saxon cross, and a Viking cross bearing runic inscriptions. The altar painting of the Last Supper is by a local artist, James Cranke Senior (1707-81), who did much to inspire and guide Dalton-born artist George Romney in his early years.

A **rush-bearing** ceremony is held in the church towards the end of September each year, followed by a service at the church. Part of the ceremony, which provides a colourful procession, includes placing flowers on the grave of some forgotten person.

To the west of the village are a number of **burial mounds** and traces of a prehistoric settlement [SD260741]. There are also two non-concentric rings of stones on Birkrigg Common to the east of Great Urswick, which yielded cremated remains on excavation, and are thought to be the site of a Druidic temple. About 1 mile (2km) east-south-east of Little Urswick is a polygonal site containing the foundations of two circular huts, thought to be Iron Age or a native Romano-British settlement.

WABERTHWAITE [Copeland]

SD1093: 2 miles (3km) SE of Ravenglass

There is much evidence around Waberthwaite to prove that prehistoric man roamed these coastal stretches, but little to indicate that he stayed longer than was necessary to hunt prey for a short while before moving on. The Romans had a fort at Ravenglass, and it seems certain that they will have explored the area to the south, fording the River Esk to do so.

Quarrying used to be a main occupation in the village, notably during the 20th century, though this ended after the Sec-

ond World War. The quarry is now a Site of Special Scientific Interest.

Found near the estuary of the River Esk, the isolated 'dales chapel' **church of St John the Evangelist** has fine views of the Lakeland fells. The building is a simple one, crowned by a double bellcot dating from the late 18th century, though the main body of the church is probably Norman. Of earlier date is the Saxon cross-shaft in the churchyard bearing examples of loop knotwork.

WALTON [Carlisle]

NY5264: 2½ miles (4km) N of Brampton

Walton is a small, attractive village with a number of village greens, set in open countryside, with good views to the north-east, such as would have been experienced from the nearby Hadrian's Wall. The village **church of St Mary** was built by Paley in 1869-70.

Castlesteads, a mile (2km) south-west of the village was built by the Johnson family, who still live there, in the 18th century, and is one of the important buildings associated with the village. Likewise, **Roman House**, which is an outstanding example of a cruck-framed cottage.

WARCOP [Eden]

NY7415: 3 miles (5km) W of Brough

The ancient bridge over the River Eden, linking the village of Warcop with the hamlet of Bleatarn, is thought to be the oldest spanning the Eden still in use; it was built in the 16th century.

The name of the village is associated with the nearby military training area, but a far more endearing occasion takes place on St Peter's Day (June 29), known locally as Peter Day, when the children of the village take part in an annual **rush-bearing** ceremony culminating at the village's **church of St Oswald**.

The north wall of the church is Norman, but it is mainly Early English or Perpendicular in period and style, and enlarged in 1855.

WARWICK [Carlisle]

NY4656: 4 miles (6km) E of Carlisle

Warwick is an attractive village of brick-built houses with some modern development, overlooking and on the west bank of the River Eden.

The village's **church of St Leonard** is commonly regarded as the most outstanding Norman village church in the former county of Cumberland.

Warwick Hall, overlooking the Eden, is a neo Georgian, 20th-century building, replacing one built in 1828.

WARWICK BRIDGE [Carlisle]

NY4756: 5 miles (8km) E of Carlisle

Warwick Bridge is pleasant village that combines old and new. It stands across the river from the nearby village of Warwick, and it was here that the Jacobite army gathered in November 1745, and moved to attack Carlisle.

The bridge which gave the village its name has three segmental arches and was built by Dobson of Newcastle in 1837.

There are two churches in the village. The youngest, by four years, is the **church of St Paul**, built in the neo-Norman style in 1845. The Gothic Roman Catholic church, **Our Lady and St Wilfred** was built by Pugin in 1841, and is quite small.

Holme Eden Hall was built in the same year as the bridge, 1837, and is in the style of an early Tudor mansion. It was built

for Peter Dixon, who also paid for the building of St Paul's Church, one of the founders of the cotton mills that thrived in Carlisle.

WASDALE HEAD [Copeland]

NY1808: 5 miles (8km) S of Buttermere

Rather better known as a launchpad for the famous and fabulous cirque of fells that surround it, the tiny hamlet of scattering farms and cottages at Wasdale Head, is reached by a long and winding road. Most visitors to Wasdale arrive in mid-valley, usually from Gosforth, and are greeted by a splendid view of the massive mountains of Yewbarrow, Great Gable and Lingmell, a profile that has found its way into the symbol of the national park.

Perhaps the most stunning spectacle, however, on this approach is the **Wastwater Screes**, a seemingly vertical downfall of all things rocky and perilous, that appears to slip without a pause beneath the waves of the lake. The atmosphere is powerful, impressive, intimidating sometimes, but irresistible and unforgettable. It is indisputably a masterpiece of creation. Coleridge was certainly impressed, writing in 1802, 'It is a marvellous sight/a sheet of water between three & four miles in length, the whole (or very nearly the whole of it's right Bank formed by the Screes...consisting of fine red Streaks running in broad Stripes thro' a stone colour – slanting off from the Perpendicular, as steep as the meal newly ground from the Miller's spout.'

The lake itself is the deepest in England, plunging to more than 260ft (80m), the mountains behind it, the highest, rising to the summit of Scafell Pike 3210ft (978m). It is these two extremes that

Wastwater and the head of Wasdale

combine to make Wasdale Head, a mere dot on the scale of things, one of the most outstanding settings in the county.

The valley boasts one of the most simple and endearing churches in the county. Dedicated to **St Olaf**, but only in 1977, this tiny church looks like a low-lying shed, shrouded by yew trees. The church still had unglazed mullioned windows and a soil floor at the start of the 20th century, and was without its own churchyard. The dead of Wasdale were carried across the fells, on a corpse road that can still be traced, for burial at Boot in Eskdale. In the graveyard now are buried some of the early pioneers of exploration on the surroundings mountains, who died in their cause.

Wasdale was, and still is, isolated, and is all the better for it. Even in the mid-19th century, the schoolmaster was able to enjoy the privilege of 'whittlegate', a tradition that allowed him to board at the different farmhouses in turn.

It used to be said of Wasdale that it had the highest mountain, the deepest lake, the smallest church, and the biggest liar.

The liar was one **Will Ritson**, who was born in 1808 at the Wasdale Head Hotel. He was a friend of Wordsworth and de Quincey, a famed huntsman, wrestler and raconteur, who became the uncrowned king of Wasdale. But for most of the 19th century, he was a one-man tourist attraction, famed for his tall stories, textured with his own dry wit. He was a regular entrant in the competition for the Biggest Liar in the World, and won one competition when, having listened to a range of lies, it came to his turn. To everyone's surprise he asked to be withdrawn from the competition. 'Why?' they asked. 'Because I can't tell a lie,' came the reply. The tradition continues today. Each year in November the **Biggest Liar in the World Competition** is held at Santon Bridge.

The **Wasdale Head Show and Shepherds' Meet** is held in October, and includes shows of sheep and sheepdogs, hound trailing, fell racing, Cumberland and Westmorland wrestling, and other attractions of Cumberland origin and character.

WATENDLATH [Allerdale]

NY2716: 4 miles (6km) S of Keswick

Concealed high above the Borrowdale valley, the ancient hamlet of Watendlath, now entirely owned by the National Trust, was used by Hugh Walpole as his setting in *Judith Paris*, one of his *Rogue Herries* titles; Foldhead Farm is generally agreed to be the model for Rogue Herries Farm. Then, as now, the hamlet is remote and unspoilt, a cluster of white-washed cottages beside a trout-laden tarn that is popular with anglers.

Although it is possible to drive up to Watendlath, there is much more to be gained from walking there along well-signposted pathways that weave through mature woodland of birch and pine. From the hamlet, footpaths radiate onto the adjacent fells to Blea Tarn, Dock Tarn, Ullscarf and across the fellsides into Borrowdale.

WATERMILLOCK [Eden]

NY4422: 6 miles (10km) SW of Penrith

A widely scattered village, mostly at right angles to the main road that runs alongside Ullswater, Watermillock is a farming community turned holiday home centre. It holds a beautiful position, overlooking the upper reaches of Ullswater, and backed by the slopes of Little Mell Fell. Much of the high ground surrounding the village was once deer forest wherein the tenants enjoyed certain privileges, as ministers of religion did in other parts of the county. Here 'green hue' is the privilege of cutting brushwood for winter cattle feed, and 'fern bound' permitted the taking of bracken for bedding, or thatching.

The village **church of All Saints** is large and was built in 1884 in slate and the ubiquitous red sandstone.

WAVERTON [Allerdale]

NY2247: 2 miles (3km) W of Wigton

Adjoining the River Waver, the widespread village community of Waverton lies along the Wigton road and adjoining lanes, surrounded by farmland.

The village church, **Christ Church**, was built in 1863 as a chapel-of-ease to Wigton.

WELTON [Allerdale]

NY3544: 4 miles (6km) S of Dalston

The village of Welton gets its name from the large number of wells of pure spring water that surround it. Farming is the main occupation in the village, which has a small green, and once boasted a number of cobblers, grocers, joiners, and various other trades and businesses that made it fairly self-sufficient.

The village **church of St Peter** was built in 1874 by Cory and Ferguson, those 'rivals' of the other renowned architects of the time, Paley and Austin.

WESTNEWTON [Allerdale]

NY1344: 1½ miles (2km) N of Aspatria

Westnewton is a long and attractive village on the Allonby road. Until the **church of St Matthew** was built in 1857, the villagers had to worship at St Mungo's Church in Bromfield.

Many of the houses and cottages date from the 19th century, though **Yew Tree Farm** is dated 1672. There has been some new building here, and during excavations for the houses the remains of a **Roman fort** were discovered, while at the western end of the village there once stood a castle or large house, now identified only by a slight mound in a field. Very little is known about either of these former buildings.

WESTWARD [Allerdale]

NY2744: 2½ miles (4km) S of Wigton

The widespread village of Westward is a collection of old stone-built farms and houses on raised ground above Wiza Beck, its name indicating that it was once part – a 'ward' – of the Inglewood Forest.

Westward is the birthplace of **Sir William Henry Bragg** (1862-1942), the physicist who, with his son, Sir William Lawrence Bragg (1890-1971), pioneered X-ray crystallography, and in 1815 won the Nobel Prize for Physics for their research on radioactivity.

The **church of St Hilda** replaces an early church on this site, and was completely restored in 1879.

WETHERAL [Carlisle]

NY4654: 4 miles (6km) E of Carlisle

There is an air of quiet prosperity about Wetheral, with its large houses, most built of local stone, grouped around a spacious green. The triangular green is dominated by the ornate, brick-built Eden Bank, constructed in 1834, and a number of 18th-century sandstone houses.

The River Eden flows beside the village, and on the other side of it stands **Corby Castle**, a late Georgian mansion owned by the Howard family since the 17th century. The castle has a 14th-century pele tower built as a defence against cross-Border reivers. Members of the Howard family are buried in the **church of the Holy Trinity**, an early 16th-century building, with an octagonal tower in a commanding position overlooking the river. It is said that the church was formerly dedicated to St Constantine, the only church in England with such a dedication.

Just south of the church is the site of **Wetheral Priory**, a Benedictine priory founded around 1100 by Ranulph de Meschines; only the gatehouse remains of the priory, and this dates from the 15th century.

The former **Friends' Meeting House**, which dates from 1718, is now a cottage.

A short distance south of the village are the man-made **caves** constructed in the river bank. Tradition links them with St Constantine, and they are known to have been in use in the 14th century.

Nearby is a five-arched **viaduct** that used to carry the Newcastle-Carlisle railway. It was constructed by Francis Giles between 1830 and 1834, and stands 100ft (30m) high. It was one of the first railway viaducts in the country.

On the banks of the Eden is a new seat sculpture by Londoner Tim Shutter. It is made from St Bees sandstone, and is one of a unique collection of sculptures, known as **Eden Benchmarks**, along the river from Mallerstang to Rickerby Park in Carlisle. They were commissioned by the East Cumbria Countryside Project. The sculptures, which are meant to double as benches, are already also in place at Mallerstang, Kirkby Stephen, Appleby, Edenhall and Lazonby, with more to come at Rockcliffe, Temple Sowerby and Carlisle.

WHICHAM [Copeland]

SD1382: 3 miles (5km) NW of Millom

At the very southern tip of Black Combe, and at the foot of Whicham Valley, lies the tiny hamlet of Whicham, with a delightful, small, dales chapel with a Norman doorway, dedicated to **St Mary**. The most conventional ascent of Black Combe starts here.

WHITBECK [Copeland]

SD1184: 4 miles (6km) NW of Millom

A small village, now mainly of modern dwellings, Whitbeck lies at the foot of

Black Combe and on the edge of the coastal strip between Maryport and Millom. Its **church of St Mary** is ancient, but extensively restored in 1858 and at the beginning of the 20th century.

WHITEHAVEN [Copeland]

NW9718: 7 miles (11km) S of Workington

Today the largest town in Copeland, Whitehaven during the 18th century was one of Britain's major seaports, and still contains much elegant 18th-century architecture, that has given it the nickname the 'Georgian' town. It is certainly less grimy than other West Cumbrian towns and villages.

Its prosperity grew with the export of coal and import of tobacco and rum, and it was the first post-Renaissance town to be planned in Britain. It was formerly owned and largely developed during the 17th and 18th centuries by the prosperous Lowther family.

Daniel Defoe, on his grand tour through England and Wales, noted that Whitehaven had, 'grown up from a small place to be very considerable by the coal trade, which is encreased so considerably of late, that it is now the most eminent port in England for shipping off coals, except Newcastle...and 'tis frequent in time of war...to have two hundred sail of ships at a time go from this place for Dublin, loaden with coals.' Before this time, Whitehaven was just a village, though it was used, notably during the 12th century, as the port of St Bees Priory.

Whitehaven's story is one inextricably linked with sailors, tobacco merchants, and coal and iron mining. Tobacco was imported from Virginia, coal exported to Ireland, and a brisk slave trade operated with Africa. The first of these, however, ended with the American War of Inde-

pendence (1775-83). Yet in 1780, Whitehaven was the foremost port in the country after London, and well ahead of Liverpool, Glasgow or Newcastle.

A steep flight of steps leads down to the massively walled harbour, which is now a conservation area. Formerly, the steps would be flanked with warehouses and cottages, of which a few still remain.

The harbour has twice been under attack from enemy forces. The first occasion, somewhat bizarre, came at the hands of **John Paul Jones** (1747-92), a Scottish-born American naval officer, who served his apprenticeship as a sailor boy in Whitehaven. At the outbreak of the American War of Independence in 1775, he was commissioned as a senior lieutenant, and in 1778 cruised the British waters in the *Ranger*. He make various attacks along the Solway, and sailed into Whitehaven harbour, where he planned to set fire to several ships. In the event, only three ships were damaged, but the raid caused much public consternation, and within a matter of days enough funds had been raised by public subscription to carry out repairs and improvements to the port's defences.

The second attack came in 1915, when a German U-boat surfaced offshore, and shelled the area, causing damage, but no fatalities.

Part of the old quay dates from 1687, though it was altered in 1792 and 1809, and has a lighthouse dated 1730. The so-called Old New Quay dates from 1741, and was lengthened in 1767. The harbour's West Pier is the youngster of the seafront, and was built between 1824 and 1839 by **Sir John Rennie** (1794-1874), who also built London Bridge to his father's design.

The Anglo-Irish poet and satirist, **Jonathan Swift** (1667-1745), author of

Gulliver's Travels, is said to have visualised Lilliput as he gazed down from the cliffs of Whitehaven on to the tiny figures of locals scouring the sand for sea coal. Although Swift was born in Dublin, he spent the first four years of his life in Whitehaven, in the Bowling Green House on the clifftop, and returned there on occasions as a man. The Bowling Green House later became the Red Flag Inn, and is now a private house.

Along the cliffs is a ruined fan house, originally built in 1747 to drive fresh air into Duke Pit mine; the building remains today as a memorial to 136 miners killed in an underground disaster in the nearby Wellington Pit in 1910. The **Wellington Pit**, the first coal mine to work under the sea, was sunk in 1731 and closed in 1933; its lodge, which was the miners' lamp house, is now a café. Behind it stands the impressive Candlestick Chimney, an air vent to the mine, its odd shape suggested to the architect, apparently over dinner, by Lord Lonsdale (Sir James Lowther) who owned the pit, and who built **Whitehaven Castle** in 1769.

There used to be two parish churches in Whitehaven: one St James's and another dedicated to St Nicholas.

The **church of St Nicholas**, in Lowther Street, was originally built in 1693. The present church, consecrated in 1883, is a large church of red sandstone in a style somewhere between Decorated and Perpendicular. It was almost completely destroyed by fire on 31 August 1971, and an attractive garden now surrounds the ruins and the church tower, all that remains. There is a plaque here to George Washington's grandmother, **Mildred Warner Gale**, who lived in Whitehaven, and died in 1700. She is buried in St Nicholas' Gardens.

The **church of St James**, was built in 1752-3 on a hill at the end of Queen Street. Overlooking the town, it is regarded as having the finest Georgian church interior in the county. The ceilings are believed to have been designed by the Italian artists Artari and Bagutti, the painting over the altar is *The Transfiguration* by Guilio Procaccini (1548-1626).

In West Strand is **The Beacon**, an interesting museum describing the varied past of this Georgian port, which embraces slavery, smuggling, mining and shipbuilding.

It was in Whitehaven that the first serious attempt to measure rainfall was conducted. A young scientist, **John Fletcher Miller**, first installed a rain gauge in his garden at 7 High Street in 1833, when he was 17. Ten years later, he had a network of gauges over the southwest part of the county that produced annual rainfall figures that were ridiculed by professional meteorologists. The belief, prevalent at the time, was that only the tropics could produce rainfall of 100 inches a year. Yet Seathwaite in Borrowdale – still the wettest inhabited place in Britain (see Seathwaite) – managed half as much again (152 inches) in 1845.

WIGGONBY [Allerdale]

NY2952: 7 miles (11km) SW of Carlisle

Wiggonby is a widespread village with several large farms, in low-lying land on the outer fringes of Carlisle. The village had an Endowed School founded by Margaret Hodgson in 1792; one of the conditions of her assigning land and property was that anyone named Hodgson should be educated free of charge.

WIGTON [Allerdale]

NY2548: 11 miles (17km) SW of Carlisle

Wigton is an attractive market town on Solway Plain, with a medieval layout and much Georgian architecture. It is the birthplace of **Robert Smirke** (1752-1845), painter and book illustrator of the old English school, and father of the slightly more illustrious Sir Robert Smirke, the architect. Here, too, was born the renowned Cumberland poet, Ewan Clark.

The **church of St Mary** was rebuilt in 1788, and stands on the site of an earlier church. The red sandstone Roman Catholic **church of St Cuthert** is a substantial building dating from 1837. Of slightly earlier date is a Friends' Meeting House, an ashlar-faced building of some dignity.

In the busy Market Place is a square **fountain** with a pyramid spire, and on its sides are depicted four Acts of Mercy. At the end of the main street is **Wigton Hall**, neo-Tudor in design with Georgian windows.

WINDERMERE [South Lakeland]

SD4198: 7 miles (11km) NW of Kendal

Windermere is a large village/small town less than half a mile (1km) from the lake, the largest in England, of the same name. The village was originally called Birthwaite, but when the Kendal and Windermere Railway opened in 1847, and the station built at Birthwaite, the name was not thought sufficiently inspiring, so the railway company named the station, Windermere. Much confusion between the village and the lake arose at the time, and continues.

Since the coming of the railway, Win-dermere has been developed largely as a tourist resort, and may have lost some of its edge had plans to extend the railway as far as Ambleside not been confounded by landowners and conservationists. Because of Windermere's rapid and fairly recent growth, it contains little of interest, though many of the larger houses, now hotels and guest houses, were built for commuting industrialists who took advantage of the railway line.

Orrest Head, north of Windermere, is an outstanding viewpoint, and popular with walkers as a result. It was the first 'summit' visited by the late Alfred Wainwright on his first visit to Lakeland in 1930, more than twenty years before he began work on his *Pictorial Guides*, that were to inspire and captivate generations of visitors to the Lake District. 'Our way,' he wrote, 'led up a lane amongst lovely trees, passing large houses that seemed to me like castles, with gardens ·fragrant with flowers. I thought how wonderful it must be to live in a house with a garden.'

The **church of St Mary** in Ambleside Road, is Victorian, but has a complicated history in architectural terms. Little remains of the original 1848 chapel, to which an aisle was added four years later, a north aisle in 1857, a nave extension in 1861, a transept in 1871, and a chancel by Paley and Austin in 1881-2. The **church of St John the Evangelist** in Lake Road, by contrast, is much simpler to follow, being built by a local man in 1886 in the 13th century style.

The **lake of Windermere** is the largest in England, being 10½ miles (17km) long and 1 mile (2km) wide at its broadest point. The lake was formed following the last Ice Age, a time when glaciers, flowing away from the central fells, gouged out deep troughs that were to be filled by meltwater. The lake and its surrounds are unquestionably among the most beautiful settings in England; much of the shoreline is well wooded, islands punctuate its middle reaches, in the case of Belle Isle almost cutting it in two, and high ground flanks much of the lake, providing high vantage points from which to survey the heartlands of the region.

The ease with which progress can be made up and down the lake meant that from the earliest times it has served as a highway. The Romans, heading for their fort at the lake head (Galava), brought quarried stone, and later the waterway was used to transport iron ore to a number of smelting furnaces, bloomeries, that developed along the lakeshore, fuelled by the plentiful supply of wood for charcoal.

The lake is renowned for char and deep-water trout, the former, in its potted form, being a considerable delicacy among the wealthy families of the 17th and 18th centuries. One local landowner, Daniel Fleming, considered char to be an instrument of social diplomacy, which he used to sweeten intercourse with politicians and friends.

By the middle of the 19th century, however, as Victorian tourists came to explore the 'Lake Mountains', the utilitarian functions of the lake had given way to pleasure sailing, and so it has remained. But it will take many years to explore the many sequestered retreats that Windermere, the lake, has to offer.

WINSTER [South Lakeland]

SD2460: 3 miles (5km) S of Windermere

Winster is a small, unspoilt village of whitewashed stone cottages at the head of the valley created by the river of the same name. It is a beautiful valley, running parallel with Windermere lake on its lower eastern side.

The River Winster itself, formerly the boundary between Westmorland and Lancashire, flows through the village.

The **church of the Holy Trinity** is Victorian, and though it may have little of merit architecturally, its setting can hardly be bettered.

WINTON [Eden]

NY7810: 1 mile (2km) NE of Kirkby Stephen

An attractive and pleasant hamlet of stone-built houses and cottages built around a triangular green, on the outskirts of Kirkby Stephen.

In the centre of the village is **Winton Manor House**, a three-storey house built in 1726, which used to be a boys' school with a particularly severe regime that denied boys the opportunity to return home until their education was completed.

WITHERSLACK [South Lakeland]

SD4383: 2½ miles (3km) N of Lindale

Boasting a number of attractive old cottages, Witherslack is a peaceful village above the River Winster and below Whitbarrow Scar. Until the mid-19th century, the Earls of Derby held manor courts at the Derby Arms inn.

The **church of St Paul** was built around 1669 under the wills of **John Barwick**, Dean of St Paul's, and his brother, who was a physician to Charles II, both of whom were born in Witherslack.

WORKINGTON [Allerdale]

NX9928: 17 miles (27km) W of Keswick

Standing at the mouth of the River Derwent, Workington has always been overshadowed by the larger Whitehaven to the south. Although both towns developed significantly as industry in the west of Cumberland grew, they each responded in different ways. In Workington there is none of the grid-plan development familiar in Whitehaven, and the whole town seems to have a more relaxed air about it. In 1540, Leland recorded 'a prety creke wher as shyppes cum to, wher as ys a lytle prety fyssher town cawled Wyrkenton'. Whether anyone would regard it as a pretty little town now is another matter, for the industry that made Workington has not been kind to it, aesthetically at least.

The town's prosperity came, like its neighbour's, from shipping and coal, the latter having been mined here since 1650. Deep mining became possible with the invention of the steam engine, which meant that mines were better drained and better ventilated, and by 1740, four mines were being operated, a number that had grown by a further ten by 1790. Where in Whitehaven it was the Lowther family that dominated the exploitation of the Cumberland coalfields, in Workington it was the Curwens. Notably, it was John Christian Curwen, though it might today be said that there was little 'Christian' about his employment of children as young as five to carry lamps for miners, or the taking of seven-year-olds to be bound as apprentices for fourteen years.

Iron smelting grew rapidly as an industry in Workington following the introduction of coke furnaces, the first major ironworks site being built in 1763; can-

nons, apparently, were in popular demand.

Boat building, too, developed along with the town, but again at a lesser pace than in Whitehaven. Workington had a shipyard before 1756, and by 1829, it had two, along with Harrington and Maryport. Significantly, however, Whitehaven by the same time had six.

Before the end of the 19th century, Workington was a county borough, and remained so until 1974. But during the 20th century the economy of the town began to decline.

Workington Hall, now demolished, was built in 1379, and was the home of the Curwen family. In 1568, Mary Stuart stayed here, as a welcome guest of Sir Henry Curwen, when fleeing to England.

Set in a fine Georgian house in Park End Road, the **Helena Thompson Museum** houses a collection of 19th-century costumes and artefacts, as well as displays of local history, including coal mining, shipbuilding and the iron and steel industry.

The **church of St Michael** was built in 1770, on the site of a 16th-century chapel, and was restored, following a fire, in 1887-90. The church contains some Norman elements, but they do not belong to the original church, and are of unknown origin. There are several coffin lids, and a tomb chest bearing the effigies of a knight and a lady, probably from the 15th century, and presumed to be Lord and Lady Curwen.

The **church of St John** in Washington Street dates from the reign of George IV, its great portico an enlarged copy of that by Inigo Jones at Covent Garden in London.

WREAY [Carlisle]

NY4348: 5 miles (8km) SE of Carlisle

The small village of Wreay (pronounced Wree-a) lies beside the River Petteril to the south of Carlisle. It is home to one of the most original buildings in England, the **church of St Mary**. It was conceived by Sara Losh, one of two daughters of John Losh, a local industrialist. Sara was an exceptionally talented woman, who travelled with, and was devoted to her sister, Katherine, who died young in 1835. The church was meant as a memorial to Katherine and a tour of Europe they made together in 1817.

The church was consecrated in 1842, and is an amazing mishmash of ideas and styles. It contains an ornate reading desk in bog oak, flower and fossil silhouettes on apse walls and windows, and seven 'lamps of the spirit', orange and yellow glass spheres set in a wall. The font is described as Byzantino-naturalistic, made in alabaster, and bearing carvings by Sara Losh herself.

Adjoining the church is a mausoleum for Katherine, built of large blocks of stone, accidental in surface and shape, and laid in an irregular way that Henry Lonsdale in 1873 called 'Druidical' or 'Attic-Cyclopean'.

The village still has its self-elected body of Twelve Men, a group once responsible for villagers' welfare, who now meet once a year in the Plough Inn.

WYTHBURN [Allerdale]

NY3214: 3½ miles (6km) N of Grasmere

The original village of Wythburn has long since succumbed to Thirlmere Reservoir, but the name lingers on and denotes the whole area at the southern end of Thirlmere.

Wythburn Chapel, beside the main road, was built in 1640 and restored in 1872.

YANWATH [Eden]

NY5127: 2 miles (3km) S of Penrith

Yanwath is a small village on the River Eamont renowned for its hall. **Yanwath Hall**, a well-preserved, 14th-century manor house, is now a farm, but was formerly a pele tower, to which additions were made in the 15th century.

Thomas Wilkinson (1751-1836), a friend of William Wordsworth, a Quaker, poet, farmer and landscape gardener, used to live in Yanwath at The Grotto. Wilkinson enlarged the house in 1773, and did extensive landscaping, now mostly lost. He was said to have been inspired in this respect by a visit to the gardens of William Shenstone at The Leasowes at Halesowen, then in Worcestershire.

Bibliography

The Anglo-Saxon Chronicles, (Coombe Books, 1995).

Anon. *A Brief History of St Oswald's Church*, Ravenstonedale.

Berry, Geoffrey. *Mardale Revisited* (Westmorland Gazette, 1984).

Bingham, Roger K.,
The Chronicles of Milnthorpe (Cicerone Press, 1987).
Kendal: A Social History (Cicerone Press, 1995).

Blake, Brian. *The Solway Firth* (Robert Hale, 1955-82).

Blatch, Mervyn. *Parish Churches of England* (Blandford Press, 1974).

Bott, George. *Keswick: The Story of a Lake District Town* (Cumbria County Library, 1994).

Burl, Aubrey. *A Guide to the Stone Circles of Britain, Ireland and Brittany* (Yale University Press, 1995).

Carlisle: The Border City (Pitkin Pictorials, 1992).

Carlisle Castle. (English Heritage, 1992-6)

Chambers Biographical Dictionary.

Collingwood, W. G. *The Lake Counties* (J.M. Dent, 1902-38).

The Concise Dictionary of National Biography.

Davies, Hunter,
Wainwright: The Biography (Michael Joseph, 1995).
William Wordsworth: A Biography (Sutton Publishing, 1997).

Defoe, Daniel. *A Tour through England and Wales* (J M Dent, 1928-1959)

Drabble, Margaret (ed.). *The Oxford Companion to English Literature.*

Dykes, Rev L.G.F., and Hardwick, T. *The Priory Church of St Mary and St Michael, Cartmel.*

Findler, Gerald. *Legends of the Lake Counties* (Dalesman Publishing Company, 1967).

Ffinch, Michael,
Portrait of Kendal and the Kent Valley (Robert Hale, 1983)
Portrait of Penrith and the East Fellside (Robert Hale, 1985).

Fitzgerald, Maurice H (ed.). *The Poems of Robert Southey* (Henry Frowde, London, 1909)

Fraser, George MacDonald. *The Steel Bonnets* (Collins Harvill, 1989).

Hall, J. H. Vine. *Threlkeld Cumbria: Glimpses of Village History* (1977).

Jones, Lawrence E and Tricker, Roy. *County Guide to English Churches* (Countryside Books, 1992).

Laing, Lloyd and Jennifer. *Anglo-Saxon England* (Granada, 1982)

Lefebure, Molly. *The Illustrated Lake Poets* (Tiger Books International, 1992).

Lindop, Grevel. *A Literary Guide to the Lake District* (Chatto and Windus, 1993)

Lofthouse, Jessica. *Countrygoers' North* (Robert Hale, 1965).

Marsh, Terry,
50 Classic Walks in the Pennines (Sigma, 1994).
A Northern Coast to Coast Walk (Cicerone, 1993).
The Pennine Mountains (Hodder and Stoughton, 1989).

Martineau, Harriet. *A Complete Guide to the English Lakes*. (John Garnett, Windermere, 1855).

Mason, William. *The Works of Thomas Gray, Esq* (Dove, London, 1827).

Moorman, Mary (ed.). *Journals of Dorothy Wordsworth* (Oxford Paperbacks, 1971).

Morris, Christopher (ed). *The Journeys of Celia Fiennes* (Cresset, London, 1949).

Mitchell, W R. *The John Peel Story* (Dalesman, 1968).

Parker, John. *Cumbria: A Guide to the Lake District and its County* (Bartholomew, 1977).

Pevsner, Nikolaus,
The Buildings of England: North Lancashire (Penguin Books, 1991).
The Buildings of England: Cumberland and Westmorland (Penguin Books, 1992).
The Buildings of England: Yorkshire: West Riding (Penguin Books, 1993).

Rollinson, William. *A History of Cumberland and Westmorland* (Phillimore & Co, 1978).

Scott, Joe (ed.). *A Lakeland Valley through time: A History of Staveley, Kentmere and Ings* (Staveley and District History Society, 1995)

Smith, Kenneth. *Cumbrian Villages* (Robert Hale, 1973).

Spence, Richard T. *Lady Anne Clifford* (Sutton Publishing, 1997)

Taylor, E. Margaret. *William Wordsworth and St Oswald's Church, Grasmere* (Grasmere Church Publications, 3rd ed. 1991).

Waugh, Edwin. *Rambles in the Lake Country* (John Heywood, London)

Wilson, Roger J.A. *A Guide to the Roman Remains in Britain*. (Constable, 1975-1980)

Index

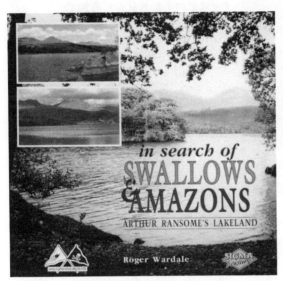

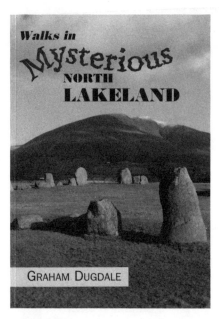

WALKS IN MYSTERIOUS NORTH LAKELAND
&
WALKS IN MYSTERIOUS SOUTH LAKELAND

Two unusual collections of walks which provide unique opportunities to visit places with a strange and mythical history - you can stretch your mind whilst stretching your legs! The walks are suited to both families and individuals alike, and with thirty to choose from in each book, there really is something for everyone.

£6.95 per volume

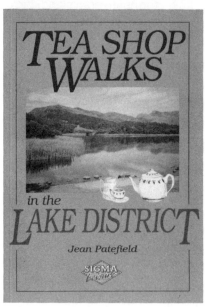

MORE TEA SHOP WALKS IN THE LAKE DISTRICT

Norman and June Buckley have planned more leisurely rambles in this companion volume to the first tea shop book on the region. Crossing both the central regions and the lesser-known fringe areas, their 25 spectacular, circular walks range from 2 to 9 miles. As always, you'll be rewarded by a refreshing break in one of the carefully chosen tea shops along the way.

PLUS: our original *TEA SHOP WALKS IN THE LAKE DISTRICT*

£6.95 per volume